T3-AKD-605

YEMEN
THE UNKNOWN WAR

Howe Library
Shenandoah College
and
Conservatory of Music

Presented by

YEMEN
THE UNKNOWN WAR

DANA ADAMS SCHMIDT

HOLT, RINEHART AND WINSTON
New York   Chicago   San Francisco

Printed in th

To Tania

Contents

++

Eight pages of black and white photographs follow
page 160

Important Dates in the War

‣‣

Coup d'Etat in Sana	26 September 1962
U.S. Recognition of the Republic	19 December 1962
Major Stages of the War:	
Stage 1: Ramadan Offensive	February–March 1963
Stage 2: Royalist Retaliation	January–February 1964
Stage 3: Haradh Offensive	August–September 1964
Stage 4: Royalist Offensive	April-May 1965
First Egyptian Gas Attack at Al Kawma	8 June 1963
Alexandria Summit Conference	5–12 September 1964
Erkwit Cease-Fire	2–8 November 1964
Taif Manifesto	10 August 1965
Jeddah Agreement	24 August 1965
Haradh Conference	23 November – 21 December 1965
Arab-Israeli War	5–12 June 1967
Khartoum Summit Conference	29-31 August 1967
Final British Withdrawal from South Arabia	30 November 1967
Final Egyptian Withdrawal from Yemen	7 December 1967

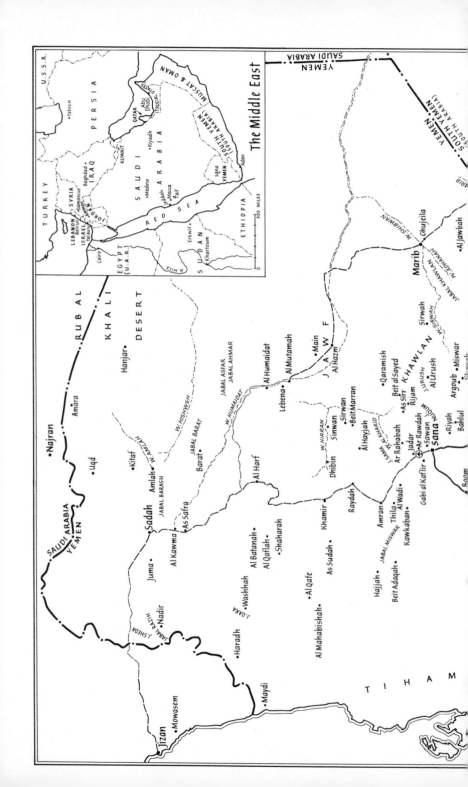

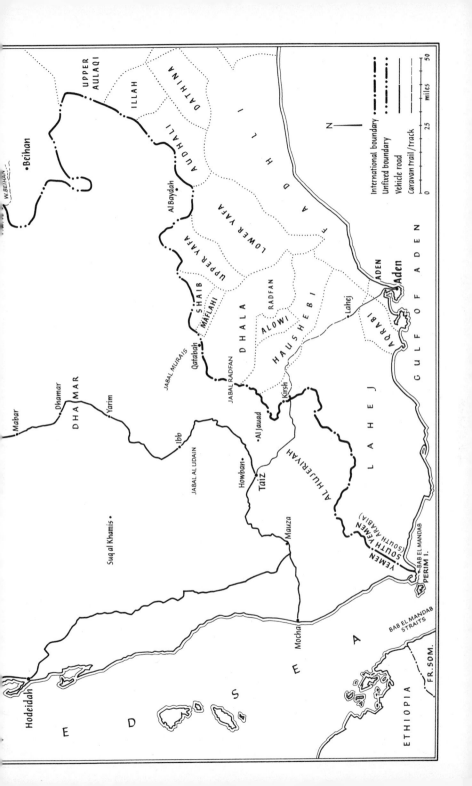

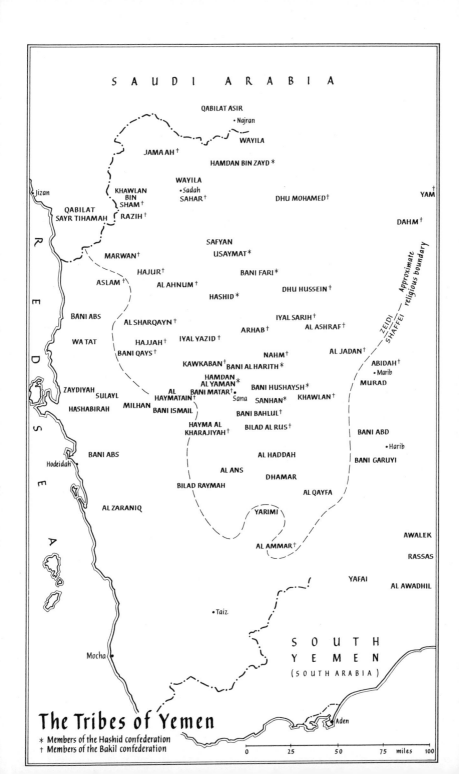

The Tribes of Yemen

* Members of the Hashid confederation
† Members of the Bakil confederation

Introduction

··

THIS is the story of the struggle for Yemen.

The centre of the story is the war between the Yemeni republic and the Yemeni royalists: the republic backed by, and often supplanted by, the Egyptians; the royalists supported by Saudi Arabian arms and gold. The war, which began on 26 September 1962 when Abdullah Sallal's friends revolted against the Imam Mohamed al Badr, is still going on.

Yemen is the only place where the two great competing forces of the Middle East – engaged elsewhere in ideological and political struggle – have been pitted against each other in physical conflict. But the struggle is broader than that. It extends to Aden and South Arabia; it involves the withdrawal of the British from Aden and the withdrawal of the Egyptians from Yemen; it affects the future of the whole region which the Yemenis like to call 'natural Yemen'. The struggle will be influenced by, and will in turn influence, the future roles in this strategic corner of the Arabian peninsula both of the great powers, the United States, Britain and the Soviet Union, and of Egypt and Saudi Arabia.

Yemen's roots are deep. There were Imams in Yemen two hundred years before the Normans invaded Britain; if outside influences are withdrawn then the traditions and aspirations of the Yemeni people will determine the future in this part of the world.

It is hardly possible to examine the present in Yemen in this way without raising questions about the past: one asks what these people were in order to understand what they are, and to divine what they may become. The answers to these questions will show that the quality of Yemen is unique – different from all the rest of the Middle East, geographically, climatically, ethnically and historically. The answers unfold in romantic tales: of the five pre-Islamic kingdoms whose civilizations rivalled those of the Nile valley and

Mesopotamia; of the Jewish and Christian civilizations that preceded the Islamic period; of the Incense Trail, over which frankincense and myrrh were borne from the southern periphery of Arabia to the altars of the ancient world; and of the Zeidi movement out of which came Yemen's Imams. Imam Mohamed al Badr traces his family back to the last of the five kingdoms and to the first of the Imams.

Yemen has waged a successful struggle throughout her existence to maintain her independence against invaders whom she defeated or absorbed – Ethiopians, Persians, Turks, Romans and Egyptians. Four times the Egyptians have returned to Yemen; the fourth time, from its beginning to its ending, is the subject of this book. In this perspective the Yemenis have had no doubts about the outcome.

The story covers a period which opens with the *coup d'état* of 26 September 1962, followed by the arrival of the Egyptians, and draws to its end with the Khartoum agreement of 31 August 1967 under which the Egyptians undertook to withdraw.

Sometimes through my own eyes, during visits to both republicans and royalists, sometimes through the eyes of others, I tell the story of the Imam's flight, the gathering of the princes, and the beginning of royalist resistance and the life in the royalist-held parts of Yemen. I describe the origins of the republic, the attempt to create a viable government, the role of outside powers, including the Soviet Union and the United States, and the struggle between President Sallal and liberal political elements. I recount the long-drawn military struggle, the efforts of the United States and the United Nations to restore peace, and the relationship between the struggling Yemen and events in South Arabia up to the departure of the British from Aden. I follow the stages of negotiation between Saudis and Egyptians, royalists and republicans.

Politically and militarily I describe the whole of this bitter struggle which, almost unknown to the outside world, has devastated the land known in ancient times as Arabia Felix. In the end the people of Yemen are, in the broadest sense, victorious, because the foreigner has been obliged to withdraw from their land. They look ahead to a future that will surely be filled with violent strife but in which the Yemenis will have won the right to settle their affairs among themselves.

A great many people have helped me to gather the information for this book. They include rulers, politicians, diplomats, secret agents, soldiers, tribal chiefs, a fellow journalist. But because there are so many who would not want to be mentioned I will not single out any here. Those who can be mentioned I have named in the text of the book as the story unfolds.

Among the authors on whose works I have drawn I wish to pay a very special tribute to Harold Ingrams, whose books *The Yemen* and *Arabia and the Isles* are classics in this field. I have also made much use of David Holden's splendid book *Farewell to Arabia*. Other sources I would like to acknowledge especially are *In the High Yemen* by Hugh Scott, *Soldiering for Peace* by General Carl von Horn, *Qataban and Sheba* and *Unknown Oman* by Wendell Phillips, and *The Yemen: A Secret Journey* by Hans Helfritz.

PART ONE

••

Royalists and Republicans

I

The Night of the Coup

THE Imam Ahmed, the bulging-eyed tyrant of Yemen, surprised
everyone by dying in his bed and leaving the throne to his amiable
son, Mohamed al Badr.[1] This was 19 September 1962, and the next
day the sheikhs and the ulema, the religious teachers of the realm,
met at Jama al Kabir, the great mosque of Sana, and elected al
Badr, aged thirty-five, as the sixty-sixth Imam of Yemen. As such
he became absolute ruler of four million Yemenis and the religious
chief of nearly half his subjects, who adhere to the Zeidi sect of the
Shiah branch of Islam.

Within a week al Badr was overthrown, his reforms and plans for
reform swept aside by a revolution, partly inspired, partly exploited,
by Nasserite Egyptians. For the Egyptians the revolutionary cause
was a cover for the acquisition of a foothold on the Arabian peninsula whose sands conceal two-thirds of the world's oil reserves.

The revolutionaries bombarded the Imam in his palace and
proclaimed that he was dead. But Imam al Badr escaped to the
mountains and rallied the warrior tribesmen of his Zeidi faith.
Unmindful of the traditional cruelty of imamic rule they preferred
their Imam to foreign rule. The Imam had lost his capital but not
his throne.

While the Imam was escaping three other spheres of activity
were developing. In Sana, Abdullah Sallal was presiding over the
trial and execution of the leaders of the old régime, and attempting
to organize a republic. Meanwhile the Egyptian army was flooding
in.

At Najran, the Saudi Arabian border town at the north-eastern

---

[1] According to Yemeni custom Imams named Mohamed are called 'al Badr',
meaning 'the Moon', much as those named Ahmed are called 'al Shams',
meaning 'the Sun'. In Mohamed's case the name stuck; in the case of Ahmed,
the father, it was rarely used.

end of the Yemeni kingdom, Prince Hassan bin Yahya, al Badr's uncle, was organizing the first resistance to the republicans and Egyptians. He had been proclaimed Imam when al Badr's death under the rubble of his ruined palace had been falsely announced in Sana, but renounced the title as soon as al Badr reappeared. He sent the young princes of the Hamid Eddin family fanning out through the northern and eastern provinces where, with weapons and funds from Saudi Arabia, they organized the tribal forces and were soon engaged in battle with the republicans and Egyptians.

In Aden, by ironical coincidence, the day before the Imam died, the legislature approved the merger of Aden into the South Arabian Federation. Thus began a new phase in the struggle between urban, Nasserite revolutionaries and the sheikhs, sultans and emirs of the Federation.

On 26 September 1962, Imam Mohamed al Badr had called a cabinet meeting at Basha'ir palace in Sana. This palace, relatively modest compared with 'Dar Saad', the 'Palace of Happiness', which had housed earlier Imams in Sana, had been his as Crown Prince, and he had elected to remain there during the week since the death of his father, Ahmed. Al Badr liked this palace on the third floor of which he had furnished comfortable private quarters. He took pleasure in the oriental furnishings of his living room, its Persian carpets, the cushions arranged around the walls, and the low desk at which he could sit cross-legged in the corner. In this room he had done some heavy drinking in the period before his father sent him to Rome for a cure in 1960. From here, during drinking bouts, he would telephone his friends and summon them to the palace. He liked the flowers in his garden, the gold-fish in the little pool, the two white rabbits someone had introduced for the children of the palace staff. The palace was four storeys high, built of stone, with a staircase of irregularly shaped steps, all enormously high, and doorways that were low even for small-statured Yemenis, so that Europeans were forever stumbling and bumping their heads. Al Badr had travelled far in Europe and Asia, but he preferred the Yemeni flavour of Basha'ir palace.

The cabinet meeting, which took place during the evening on the ground floor of the palace, brought together a strange assemblage of future traitors and men destined to be shot. One of the eleven men present was Brigadier-General Abdullah Sallal, the short,

swarthy, blue-jowled chief of staff and principal confidant to the
Imam, who in less than twenty-four hours would be proclaimed
president of a republic. Two of the others, Sheikh Ali Uthman
and Abdurrahman al Iryani, would be ministers in a republican
cabinet; and three would be executed by the republicans within a
few days.

At least four separate plots were afoot in the town of Sana. One
was headed by Lieutenant Ali Abdul al Moghny, who at the very
moment of the Imam's cabinet meeting was waiting in an army
barracks at the edge of the town to set in motion the revolution
that would drive the Imam out of Sana. Another plot, somewhat
longer-term than al Moghny's, had been hatched by Abdullah Sallal.
His plot merged into a third conspiracy which had been fermenting
in the minds of the chiefs of the Hashid tribal confederation ever
since the Imam Ahmed had executed their paramount sheikh and
his son. A fourth plot was being shaped in the minds of some of the
young princes of the realm who wished not to destroy the imamate
but to get rid of Mohamed al Badr as Imam.

The strangest thing of all was that the only men who knew about
all of the plots were the Egyptian chargé d'affaires, Abdul Wahad,
who to a considerable degree controlled them, and the Imam al
Badr himself, who was their target. The Imam had been warned
three times but refused to believe in the danger. He was the victim
of his own weakness of character which ruled out drastic action
against his enemies and gave free rein to his capacity for self-
deception.

The first warning had come from the Imam's minister in London,
Ahmed al Shami, who sent him a telegram on the day his father
died urging him not to go to Sana to attend his father's funeral
because Egyptian officers and some of his own officers were plotting
against him. The Imam did not receive this warning. When his
private secretary, Abdullah al Adhabi, received it he pretended that
he did not understand the code. The Imam went to Sana and was
probably saved by the fact that the gathering of tens of thousands
of tribesmen overawed the plotters. Only later did al Badr learn
what had been in the telegram and how near he had come to being
killed at his father's grave. The private secretary who prevented
him from receiving the warning went on to become a republican
minister of the interior.

The next warning he had received two days before the meeting from Mohamed al Shami, an eighty-eight-year-old dignitary (but not a relative of his minister in London) who for many years had been the Imam's representative during his absences from Sana. The old man had told him he had received reports from the bazaars that army officers were planning to kill the Imam. But al Badr did not take the warning seriously. He thanked the old man and ignored him.

But the most significant warning had come to him only a day before, from Abdul Wahad, the Egyptian chargé d'affaires, who said his information came from the Egyptian intelligence service. Abdul Wahad had warned the Imam against Sallal and fifteen other officers, including Lieutenant Ali Abdul al Moghny, who, he said, were preparing a revolution. That Abdul Wahad should have dared to denounce the two most significant groups of plotters, Sallal and al Moghny's young officers, to the Imam, was character- istic of his absolute self-confidence, of, one might say, the arrogance with which he manipulated his pawns. It was characteristic also of a situation in which almost everyone except poor al Badr was playing a double game. Abdul Wahad knew his pawns so well that he could be as sure of their reactions to given stimuli as Pavlov was of his dogs. His purpose, one may surmise, was threefold: to cover himself and the Egyptians if the *coup* failed; to galvanize the plotters into action now; and to drive al Moghny and Sallal together into a single conspiratorial effort. He achieved these aims perfectly. Sallal got imamic permission to bring in the armoured forces; and al Moghny burst into action after Abdul Wahad had gone to him, straight from his interview with the Imam, and informed him, with a fine show of consternation, that somehow the Imam had discovered the plot: al Moghny must act immediately before he and his officers were arrested. Urging them to action, he said: 'If you can hold the city of Sana, the radio and the airport for three days, the whole of Europe will recognize you.'

Abdul Wahad correctly assumed that the Imam would be in- capable of action; al Badr in fact did nothing but call in his trusted Sallal and tell *him* all about it. He was incapable of believing any such charge against Sallal and gladly allowed himself to be reassured by Sallal's easy, familiar laugh and his denial. This man had for a long time held a special place in his life. On behalf of Sallal, an Iraqi-educated officer who shared his admiration for President Nasser of Egypt, he had quarrelled with his father; he had insisted on the innocence and loyalty of Sallal when the latter stood accused of plotting against the imamate; and after Sallal had served seven years in the dungeons of Hajjah, he had succeeded in getting him released and having him sent to Hodeidah as harbour-master.

Sallal could say quite truthfully that he had no part in the al Moghny plot. However, he almost certainly knew of its existence, although not its timing. According to Ahmed al Shami, the royalist Foreign Minister, after the Imam had called him in Sallal managed to make contact with al Moghny and told him it would be foolish to act now. It would be better, he said, to prepare more carefully and be sure to kill al Badr at the right time.

To the Imam, Sallal said: 'You know my loyalty to you.' As for the other officers, he added, the charges were probably also baseless, but he would watch them, and, to be on the safe side, would disperse them quietly to distant posts so as to eliminate any possibility of trouble. The solution suited al Badr perfectly. Years later, recalling these critical moments, he pathetically justified his weakness: 'My father killed many men; I did not want to be like him; I did not want to start my reign with bloodshed. I thought that if I gave the people what they wanted they would believe in me.'

Long before Abdul Wahad had brought his accusations Sallal had been telling the Imam that the real threat to his rule came from members of his own family, in particular his uncle Hassan, who had been living in exile at the Plaza hotel in New York, as delegate to the United Nations. Now, after the Imam Ahmed's death, Sallal said that Hassan was planning to return and raise the tribes of the north, who were his personal supporters, in a bid for the throne. He had no trouble convincing al Badr, who knew that his father had exiled Hassan to New York because he had encouraged the sheikhs and learned men of the northern mountain tribes to support his long-standing pretensions to the position of Crown Prince. Hassan's pretensions were a challenge to the old Imam, for, although there is no rule of primogeniture among the Arabs, he wanted his son Mohamed to succeed to the throne.[1] Al Badr had not forgotten, either, a message Hassan once sent from

---

[1] By tradition the imamate goes by right to that person who is 'descended from Ali and Fatimah, the daughter of the Prophet; who is wisest in religious questions, and bravest in battle; who is of age, of the male sex, sound in mind and body, of legitimate birth, gifted for government, righteous, generous and pious, and who wins the imamate with the blade of his sword.'

New York stating bluntly that al Badr was 'unfit to be Imam'.

Hassan was not the only prince of royal blood who disapproved strongly of al Badr. In particular there were the Princes Mohamed bin Hussein, a cousin, and Abdullah bin Hassan, a son of the Hassan in New York, who called him 'dissolute, incompetent and gullible'. Mohamed, as a minister in Bonn, and Hassan, as a student in Cairo, had heard a lot about the young Imam's conduct abroad, not to mention the supply of South African brandy kept in the basement of the palace at Taiz. They said he had shown himself disastrously uncritical in becoming an avowed devotee of President Nasser and in involving himself with the Soviet Union and Communist China. They did not think he had it in him to carry out the reforms he talked about. Clearly they thought themselves more suitable candidates for the succession. But the princes had no definite plan of action.

Sallal now exploited al Badr's consternation about Abdul Wahad's accusations by making a move he had long contemplated. He requested that he be allowed to concentrate around Sana the kingdom's small force of armoured cars and tanks so as to be ready to cope with any challenge from Hassan's supporters, and the Imam readily agreed. Sallal's secret purpose, his own deep-laid plot, was to ride into power on a movement organized in Hassan's name (but without Hassan's consent), combining the force of the tribes with that of the armoured units. He conceived his plot as maturing at some indefinite date well in the future. He acted immediately in summoning the armoured force to the capital, but he did not propose an immediate *coup d'état*.

Addressing the cabinet gathered in the reception room of Basha'ir palace the Imam Mohamed al Badr ignored the whole subject of the threat to his own security. Although the threat obviously came from Cairo he even ignored the evidence of Cairo radio, whose fulminations against the reactionary imamate sharply contradicted President Nasser's official telegram of good wishes to the new Imam. The young Imam still believed in President Nasser; he clung to the friendship he believed he had established with the Egyptian during his visits in 1956–57.

He reported to the cabinet about a telegram he had sent that day to President al Kudsi of Syria urging him to come to terms with President Nasser and to 'have faith' in his leadership. Then he spoke long and earnestly about the reforms – vaguely modelled on President Nasser's system – which he had carried out, and about the reforms he planned. He had released all of about 150 hostages, younger sons of sheikhs, for the most part, whom his father, in accordance with ancient custom, had held in the palaces at Taiz and Sana to ensure their fathers' good behaviour. He advocated the formation of a consultative assembly, half of which would be elected. He announced the reform of the systems of tax-gathering and of administration. He said he would develop the economy, exploit mineral resources, construct roads, factories and schools. He would rule by consent because he would give the people justice and progress.

Although overweight, and with a look of dissipation about the eyes, the Imam al Badr was still a handsome man. His appearance contrasted strikingly with that of the members of his cabinet. He was young, with large almond eyes and full sensuous lips; they, all except Sallal, who was aged forty, were old, spare, even gaunt, dried up by age and the chewing of *qat*, the narcotic leaf of Yemen. The Imam was big; they were small, typical in this nation of fine-boned, agile men. The Imam carried a heavy, gold-handled dagger in a jewel-encrusted sheath on his ample stomach. He wore a warm, black, gold-edged cloak and a white silk turban, the long ends of which hung down to his left shoulder, a symbol of his eminence. The others too wore black cloaks, but without gold edging, except for Sallal, who was in grey-green uniform, with the crown and three stars of a brigadier-general on his shoulders. Except for Sallal's uniform and their highly polished, black European-style shoes, they looked exactly as the counsellors of a Yemeni Imam must have looked five hundred or a thousand years ago.

When the cabinet meeting broke up at 10.30 p.m. Abdullah Sallal approached the Imam, saluted, and asked to be excused, so as to attend to urgent family matters; and the Imam, with regret and surprise, excused the friend who had spent most evenings with him during the first week of his rule and with whom there would have been many things to discuss on this particular evening, especially the accusations that had been brought by Abdul Wahad. This was a discussion Sallal surely wished to avoid. He had deflected suspicion from himself and he was anxious to leave it at that. Obviously he must have felt uneasy, and he may have suspected something was up. But it is certain that, as he went to his home that night, he did not know that the armoured units he had concentrated in the town were about to go into action under the leadership of Lieutenant al Moghny.

Al Badr turned and walked up the stairs to his private quarters on the third floor, followed by Yahya al Hirsi, his father-in-law, and two servants. Al Hirsi had entered al Badr's service when the Sultan of Lahej in South Arabia, his former sovereign, had turned against the British and sought refuge in Yemen. Al Badr had taken one of al Hirsi's daughters as his second wife, an act for which he was much criticized by other members of the Hamid Eddin family, who not only despised al Hirsi as a commoner but disliked his intriguing ways.

As he mounted the stairs the roar of tanks reverberated from near-by streets. 'Ah yes,' remarked the Imam, 'these are the tanks Sallal asked to move.' As he walked down the third-floor corridor towards his room the Imam heard a 'click'. It was a sound he knew well: the hammer of an unloaded sub-machine-gun released. In this case the weapon was loaded and had simply misfired. The Imam wheeled around and shouted: '*Mahada?*', 'What's that?' As his servants and guards rushed forward in the direction from which the sound had come the Imam hurled himself through the door into his private quarters. He stood inside the door listening to the commotion outside. They had caught the man and were beating him. He was screaming and begging for mercy. The Imam called out to al Hirsi to find out what had happened. A few moments later al Hirsi entered and said: 'The man's name is Sakkari. He is one of your guards, and he seems to be crazy.' The cries in the corridor had subsided. There was a moment of silence.

At 11.45 p.m. a great explosion shook the building. A shell crashed into the wall of the palace just below one of the tall, gracious windows with coloured glass in the top section. Shattered glass scattered across the floor. Pictures on the walls were knocked askew. The lights went out. As more shells began to tear holes in the upper part of the building, al Badr was thrown to the floor. The floor buckled beneath him. Then the young Imam demonstrated his metal. Lurching across the room to a case which contained a light machine-gun, he seized the weapon, thrust it through the window and in a moment was firing back in the direction from which his assailants were shooting. His gesture was hopeless, of course, for the tanks and armoured cars firing at the palace were out of range. But the act was Mohamed al Badr's declaration that he would resist.

27

He could not know that his immediate antagonist was the twenty-five-year-old lieutenant, Ali Abdul al Moghny, who had acquired republican ideals while being trained at a military college in Egypt. Al Moghny considered himself not an Egyptian agent but a friend of the Egyptians, whose help he knew he would need. Egyptian intelligence had spotted him and determined to use his energies.

Al Moghny and his group of officers made their decision to act after Abdul Wahad had warned them that the plot was known. Twenty-four hours later they struck. Al Moghny had succeeded in enlisting the service of six tanks and four armoured cars, almost the entire armoured force, which he combined with the small arsenal he and his friends had accumulated over many months. Whenever there were exercises or manoeuvres they managed to withhold and to hide some part of their arms and ammunition. He deployed some of his vehicles on the road approaching the palace from the great, dusty Sarara Square, others near the al Urdhi headquarters south of the town, from which they could fire over the intervening houses at the palace. From a sports field at the edge of the city other guns were also trained on the palace. One truck-load of men he sent to take over the radio station, another to occupy the airport. They met little resistance. As the shooting started al Moghny sent a fellow officer, Ghalib al Shirai, in an armoured car to Sallal's house and invited him, quite politely, to come in the car to headquarters. Sallal did not hesitate. At headquarters al Moghny told him: 'We have launched the revolution. Your armoured units are with us. What are you going to do? Are you with us?'

Sallal replied briefly: 'I accept, on one condition – that I be President.'

Al Moghny could not have asked for anything better. Sallal would be useful. He had been the Imam's right-hand man, in many respects his first deputy. He knew everything and he had authority. What young al Moghny did not reckon with was that Sallal would take over the revolution and make it his own. Al Moghny might have been the Nasser of this revolution and Sallal the General Naguib, but he was too young, too inexperienced, too impressed by Sallal's higher rank. A few weeks later he allowed Sallal to send him with an inadequate force to the Khawlan tribal area, and he was killed.

But on the night of the *coup* the two men went together to the radio station which al Moghny's men had occupied, and Sallal issued an appeal to the country to be calm, to have faith in the revolution, to know that the corrupt, reactionary régime of the Imam had been overthrown forever.

At that moment there came a message from the besieged Basha'ir palace. The Imam had smuggled a man out with a desperate message to his friend Sallal, asking what had happened and imploring him to bring the army to his assistance. Sallal, still playing a double game, contrived to send a secret messenger back to the Imam with this reply: 'I am against this movement. I am with you.'

Not all of the regular army fell in easily with the revolution. The three hundred officers and men in charge of military stores, ammunition and weapons at al Qalah, on a high point on the eastern side of the town, knew that their supplies should be issued only on direct orders from the Imam himself. That was the system that had been in force since the days of the Imam Ahmed. The men at al Qalah accordingly defied al Moghny and Sallal. Eighty men were killed in the ensuing struggle; it was the bloodiest fight of the *coup*.

Had the Imam made his way from the palace to al Qalah he might have turned the tide of the revolution; but fate took him in another direction. First he moved down from the shattered third floor of Basha'ir palace to the second, to comfort his two wives and thirteen-year-old daughter, who were weeping in an inner room, and tell them that with the first light of morning they must leave the palace. He was sure that even in a revolution he could rely on the traditional Arab respect for women, and that no harm would come to them.[1]

The Imam's blue-uniformed palace guards, known as the *Ugfa*, had almost entirely disappeared. Three men had been killed during

[1] The day after the *coup d'état* the revolutionaries gathered together all the female relatives of the Imam they could find, including his wives, daughter and two sisters, about eighty-five or ninety people, and put them into a single large building, one of the old multi-storeyed structures for which Sana is famous. Forty-two women and children of his father the Imam Ahmed, were brought from Taiz and put into the same house. After one year's captivity they were sent out of Yemen, first to Egypt and later to Saudi Arabia and Lebanon, in exchange for Egyptian and republican prisoners taken by the royalists. When questioned as to whether the family had suffered hardship, a member of the household said that the women were not in the habit of going out in any case, so that they did not suffer particularly from their confinement.

the shooting. The others had slipped away, bought by the revolutionaries or frightened. Still with him were a personal servant, two guards and two black slaves.

All night long sporadic firing continued. The Imam turned on a radio and heard that Basha'ir palace was in ruins and that he was 'dead beneath the rubble'. At this moment he decided that he and those who had stayed with him must try to escape. If he was to fight he must first save his own life.

Towards dawn one of the servants brewed coffee over a brazier in a corridor at the bottom of Basha'ir palace, where they all felt protected from the bombardment which seemed to be damaging only the upper storeys. The Imam decided, as they stood there drinking their coffee, that they should each try to escape from the palace individually and to meet again that night in the village of Gabi al Kaflir, which means 'the grave of the unbeliever', two miles north-west of Sana, in the territory of the Hamdan tribe.

There was a door in the garden wall at the back of the palace that one could reach without being observed from outside. The street was too narrow to permit stationing of an armoured car or tank and the revolutionaries apparently had overlooked this possible route of escape. One by one the five remaining men slipped out. The Imam was the last to go. As he walked nervously through the grass into the unkempt weeds at the back of the garden, where he had never been before, two white rabbits scurried out of his way. He lifted the iron latch on the door in the garden wall and peered out. The street was empty. He stepped quickly outside, leaving the door ajar, and walked to the right. By this time it was morning and the radio had just announced a curfew.

According to the account he gave when he met newspaper correspondents some weeks later al Badr said that a number of people, indeed the whole area, recognized him, but no one informed the revolutionaries. At the first corner to the left beyond the palace he met a woman hurrying home because of the curfew. She was the wife of a man he knew called Mohsin Galala, who remained staunchly loyal. She led him to their house and gave him her husband's army uniform and an empty soldier's scabbard for his dagger, which would be less conspicuous than the big jewelled affair he usually carried. All that day there was very little talking, as the Imam lay low in Mohsin Galala's house, listening to the radio saying that he was dead. After dark, accompanied by a servant and a relative of Mohsin Galala he left the house and walked to the western part of the town.

Because of the curfew the two men guiding the Imam chose a circuitous route through obscure back streets where they were unlikely to meet a military patrol. It was a dark night. The white-washed frames around every window and door reflected the dim light of the stars. They walked past soaring, noble, venerable old houses, many of them eight storeys high, constructed according to a system that pre-dated Islam by many centuries. No one knew exactly who had first worked out the engineering problems in putting up skyscrapers in those ancient times. They scurried through the dark labyrinth of streets of hard-packed earth topped with a layer of dust. Few lights were to be seen for there was no municipal electricity. Only a few of the great houses owned by princes or rich merchants had electric generators of their own. The rest of the town used kerosene lamps. In the dim light the sides of some of the buildings glistened with human excrement. The cold night breeze carried with it the sharp stench of a medieval city in which the only hygienic arrangements consisted of a hole in the wall through which waste was washed down to the street. Only thanks to the abundant sunshine and the clean mountain air could this town have survived so many centuries with a reputation for being healthy.

Avoiding the main streets that led to the twelve gates in the circular medieval wall of the town the Imam and his two companions headed for the western part of the city, where the wall was quite low and often scaled by enterprising urchins. The Imam later recalled that as they stood in the dark beside the wall he prayed: 'Oh Allah, just get me over that wall, then I'll be all right.' He climbed on the shoulders of one of his companions who then got on the second man's shoulders so that the Imam could reach the top of the wall. When he was at the top the Imam pulled his two companions over and all three slid down to the other side. From the bottom of the wall they walked fast for forty-five minutes to the village of Gabi al Kaflir. There, somewhat to their surprise, all those who had escaped from the palace the night before were reunited.

On the second day the Imam made his way on foot to Dolagh Hamdan of the Hamdan al Yaman tribe, but remained for only ten minutes because the sheikh was not at his home. (The sheikh was nonetheless executed a few days later in Sana because his relatives had received and protected the fugitive Imam.) The brother of the sheikh and ten of his men accompanied the Imam to the next town, Amran, one day's journey to the north. From there they moved on to Jabal Miswar in the region of Hajjah, and were there for two days.

On their transistor radios the Imam and his men could hear radio Sana issuing warnings, particularly to the people in the vicinity of Hajjah, not to give shelter to 'fugitives from republican justice and agents of imamic reaction'. Villages that defied the republic would be bombed. Later the Imam recalled with a wry smile: 'I wondered what the republicans were using for aircraft, for I knew that the kingdom had none in operational condition. The ones I had ordered from Russia and Czechoslovakia were no longer flying or had never even been unpacked from their crates. If the republicans had aircraft at their disposal it could only mean that they were supplied and flown by the Egyptians.' It was obvious that the revolutionary authorities suspected that the Imam was in the vicinity of Hajjah, although they did not want to admit yet that he had not perished in the ruins of his palace. The governor of Hajjah had declared for the revolution. It did him no good, because he was executed anyway as the man responsible for incarcerating many republican supporters in the famous prison below the fortress of Hajjah. But his defection put the fortress into the hands of the republican régime, so that this town, the centre from which many an Imam for centuries past had rallied the loyal tribesmen of the Bakil confederation, did not serve the Imam Mohamed al Badr. Had the Imam gone directly to Hajjah instead of delaying in Amran he might have changed the course of the war. It took him three days to get there from Sana.

Though the fortress of Hajjah and many towns were held by the Imam's enemies, the mountains and villages, the tribal country, were surely his. These villages, clinging to the mountain-sides or perched precariously on ridges, are the demographic centre of gravity of Yemen, for the towns are few and small. Here, in the days of Qasim the Great, who rallied the tribesmen against the Turks in the early seventeenth century, the traditional way of life and loyalty to the Imam were deeply rooted. The Imam Ahmed had gone to the region of Hajjah in 1948 to gather support against the followers of his cousin al Wazir, who attempted to seize the throne after the assassination of the Imam Yahya. Young al Badr had gone there too, to rally the Bakil in defence of his father who, in 1955, was for a short time forced from the throne by a usurper.

'His' mountains perhaps – but to a young prince accustomed to an easy, self-indulgent life the journey was hard going. The sun blazed down on the long trails across the waste of grey lava north of Sana. The September nights were cold. The steep trails wound upwards and plunged downwards, and the Imam plodded on among the narrow terraces that furrow every cultivable mountain-side. These terraces were the handiwork of generations of Yemenis, built up painstakingly stone by stone, terrace by terrace, in ledges as narrow as they are high, wherever a man can walk, wherever there is soil.

In the afternoons clouds gathered on the higher mountain-sides, and it rained a soft, misty rain. The Imam pressed on, sometimes on foot, sometimes riding donkeys or mules. Occasionally he and his party heard bombs being dropped in near-by valleys and guessed that their party might be attacked if observed from the air. But the tribesmen seemed undeterred. In each village a great crowd would press closely around the Imam, attempting to kiss his hand, or at least to touch him. Each time a man seized his hand, the Imam, in a kind of reflex action, would withdraw it downwards and backwards to prevent it from being kissed. Some of the tribesmen, still confident of their Imam's powers, even at a moment when he arrived among them as a fugitive, would press into his hand petitions scrawled on tightly-rolled slips of paper. This was their right, in accordance with the immemorial tradition that any man could approach the highest authority and ask for a favour or redress of wrong.

The Imam's force continued to grow. At al Mahabishah, the next stop after Miswar, he had seven hundred men around him. By the time he reached Marwah, in north-western Yemen, he had a force of several thousand men, among whom blue-uniformed members of the palace guard, who had found their way to him in the mountains, formed a hard core. It had taken eight days to travel there, during which time the Imam and his men hardly slept. They settled down around some great caves near Marwah. At night his men built a huge fire and danced the war dances that are so old that no one knows where or how they started, and they sang the songs of the Yemeni mountain warrior, which are unlike ordinary

Arabic music and whose origins are obscure. These songs may well have been the same as those sung by the tribesmen of the Hashid and the Bakil who, in the year 24 B.C., came down from the mountains to serve the King of Saba at Marib against the Roman invasion commanded by Aelius Gallus. Shrilly, they echoed through the mountains towards evening as the tribesmen converged upon the Imam's camping place. And then, while some, still singing, formed a great circle, the rest entered the circle and performed their dances, weaving, writhing and leaping, brandishing their daggers and smiting an imaginary enemy. Dances and songs expressed these men's willingness to be led by their Imam, if he could and would. They showed a faith in the invincibility of their Imam amounting almost to a belief in his supernatural power.

From Marwah, fifteen days after he had left Sana, the Imam sent a man ahead to the Saudi border to announce that he was alive. He himself followed, crossing the border near al Khobar, at the north-western extremity of the kingdom. No geographical or other marking of the border is to be seen here or anywhere else along the frontier between Saudi Arabia and Yemen. There is merely a line on the map which dates from the treaty of 1934, under which the Imam Yahya settled his conflict with the great King Abdul Aziz ibn Saud of Saudi Arabia. In this war the Imam's armies were overwhelmed by a Saudi force under the command of Prince Faisal, who marched down the coast as far as Hodeidah. Faisal's brother Saud was less fortunate against Prince Ahmed, who succeeded in fending off his attack in the north-east. The 1934 settlement of this conflict, in which Ibn Saud is generally given credit for his generosity, awarded to Saudi Arabia the town of Jizan, on the Red Sea coast, and Najran, the oasis town a hundred miles to the east, although they were and are ethnically predominantly Yemeni.

It was this ill-defined frontier which the fugitive Imam crossed in order to reach Jizan; there he was welcomed by the governor, a member of the great family of Sudairis. He spent two days as the governor's guest, resting and sending messages. He sent one to President Nasser of Egypt, denouncing his interference in the internal affairs of Yemen; another to the secretary-general of the Arab League, demanding an emergency meeting of the Arab League Council and asking for 'decisive steps' against the aggressor; a third to King Faisal acknowledging his hospitality and invoking his support; and yet another to King Hussein of Jordan, who at that moment was the most enthusiastic of all his supporters. To the young ruler of Jordan, who is nearly the same age as the Imam, he cabled: 'We have to inform your Majesty that a group of low-ranking officers recently attempted to stage a mutinous movement with a view to annihilating us and taking power in our country, but with the help of God their plan has been thwarted, and we managed to escape death and to leave Sana.' He told King Hussein that he was 'on the verge of suppressing the mutinous movement'. With regret he informed the king that the President of the United Arab Republic, Gamal Abdul Nasser, had supported the rebellion. 'We are sure that this premeditated rebellion was engineered in Cairo,' he said. Finally he asked the Jordanian king to expose to the whole world 'the irresponsible and strange attitude of the invaders'.

Then the Imam, wasting no time, re-crossed the border and headed for Jabal Qara, the mountains above the village of Washhah, some thirty miles south of the point at which he had crossed the border, and there established the headquarters which he maintained until the Egyptian offensive of August 1965. The long hard trek through the mountains had greatly transformed him. When I met him in the mountains on 10 November 1962, the soft, dissipated princeling who had been overthrown in Sana seemed healthy, exhilarated by the unaccustomed physical exertion he had been obliged to make and by the danger to which he had been exposed. In six weeks in the mountains he had acquired a new sense of kinship with his people and of the meaning of his role as Imam.[1]

[1] The details of this account of the night of the *coup* have been compiled from the Imam's press conference in north-western Yemen in October 1962, immediately after his escape; from conversations with the Imam during the other meetings, particularly at Taif in Saudi Arabia in March 1967, and from the account given by the foreign minister of Yemen Ahmed al Shami, during conversations in London at various times since July 1965. Al Shami is largely responsible for the information that the real organizer of the *coup* was al Murny rather than Sallal.

II

Mohamed al Badr

THE young man who carried the title of Imam and symbolized the resistance of traditional Yemen to revolution was the product of a very traditional education and of a wide variety of strong influences. They included a magnificent grandfather, his violently dominant father, a few bright liberals who somehow slipped into the imamic household, and the young man's travels in Europe and Asia.

The Imam looked back with familiarity, half a dozen generations, to Yemen's former rulers; for him it was all very much a family affair. Yemen's greatest hero, Qasim the Great, might be regarded as the founder of the Hamid Eddin family. Early in the seventeenth century the Imam Qasim, when driven from Sana by the Turks, had fled to a hiding-place in the northern mountains of the country and had there gathered strength for a counter-attack. The more troops the Turks brought into the country, the more the tribes rallied to Qasim. Perhaps it would be the same for al Badr.

Qasim had been a great scholar; he carried his books with him even in flight. Al Badr could never equal him in this respect; but he had some ideas he believed he could offer his people, ideas he had acquired during his travels, from Nasser and from others. He believed he could lead his people out of the isolation his father and grandfather and the rulers before them had imposed on Yemen and still preserve the essential virtues of the past. He believed he could show his people how to adapt this, the most profoundly traditional society among all the Arab nations of the Middle East, to the ways of the twentieth century.

Qasim's experience, his flight to the mountains in the face of overwhelming Turkish forces, his rallying of the tribes, and his victorious return, was repeated by al Badr's grandfather, the Imam Yahya. Al Badr could remember the old man with his long white beard, limping and leaning on a stick. In the first part of his extraordinarily long reign, from 1904 to 1948, Yahya was a dashing soldier who exerted a magnetic attraction upon the tribes. He was a kindly man, a firm and good administrator who, having got rid of the Turks at last in 1918, brought a remarkable degree of order and prosperity to his country. He was known also for his niggardliness. He spent nothing unnecessarily on outward appearances; his palaces and his clothing were modest; he built up his treasury partly by insisting on monopolizing a large part of his kingdom's foreign trade. He is said to have broken tradition in the royal harem and put the ladies to work making uniforms for his army. During the greater part of his reign he himself cared only for one wife, a simple woman who called herself a bedouin, Sitt Fatimah.

The dominant characteristic of his rule, its virtue as well as its vice, was the isolation on which Yahya insisted. No one could enter or leave the kingdom without his approval. He excluded foreign technology, foreign investment and above all foreign ideas. There were in Yemen few cars, few factories, few books and no newspapers. He managed to maintain his kingdom, behind the barrier of its mountains and deserts, in a state of traditional purity for a period of forty-four years. While this may have been reprehensible from a modernist's point of view, it was at least consistent. The young al Badr respected his grandfather for it. He was twenty-one years old in 1948 when the Imam Yahya fell victim to an assassin.

That assassination was meant not really to destroy the eighty-one-year-old Imam Yahya but rather to prevent his son Ahmed from succeeding to the throne; for Ahmed was much hated. By the same token, the *coup* that later drove Ahmed's son from Sana was not really against the son but against the hated father.

As a boy Ahmed tried to cultivate a fearsome appearance by drawing a string tightly around his neck until his eyes popped out. His love of authority never left him. As Crown Prince he had his seat in Taiz, the second capital, where the diplomats resided, and he made himself disliked and feared in the region by imposing heavy taxes and ruthlessly imposing the severe penalties of Sharia Law, that is, the law of the Koran. Once his father sent him a message: 'Oh, Ahmed, the people are weary of your cruelties.'

The elements opposing Ahmed's succession were varied. Most important was the al Wazir, a clan of landowning aristocrats headed by Abdullah al Wasir, a sixty-year-old patriarch, who had for generations been the principal rivals in Yemen of the ruling Hamid

Eddin family. In addition to them, an organization of Free Yemenis centred in Aden was at this time working for reform of the imamate; only latterly did it begin to agitate for a republic. One of the Imam's own sons, Ibrahim, who fancied himself a liberal, or who was perhaps merely ambitious, had managed to get out of Yemen on the pretext of seeking medical attention, and had become the titular leader of this group. Then there was another son, Prince Hussein, of whom it can only be said that he was envious of the Crown Prince. A fourth plotter was the Prime Minister of the day, Qadi Abdullah al Amri. With so many conspirators at work it was small wonder that warnings reached the Imam, who immediately sent for his son. As Ahmed approached from Taiz the plotters moved desperately.

On the morning of 17 February 1948, Qadi Abdullah al Amri took advantage of his old friendship with the Imam to make a personal call and inform the ruler that a spring of water had been found on one of his farms. The aged Imam was intrigued and agreed to accompany the Prime Minister to the farm. They set out in the ruler's red 1940 Buick limousine. Just outside the city gates, hired tribesmen waylaid the car. As it pulled up, they called to the Prime Minister to get out; but the Imam clung to Qadi al Amri's wrist. The tribesmen, who may have panicked, or whose courage may have been paid for by more than one of the conspirators, shot them both dead.

All this was observed from a hiding-place by another of the plotters, Yahya's younger son Prince Hussein, who immediately headed for the royal arsenal with the intention of seizing control of the capital and of the government. Outside the palace, however, his way was barred by soldiers in the service of Abdullah al Wazir. Imperiously the prince ordered them aside – and was riddled with bullets.

With two of the conspirators out of the way al Wazir had no difficulty in taking over and having himself proclaimed Imam by a gathering of religious teachers, the ulema, in accordance with tradition. Meanwhile Prince Ibrahim flew from Aden to take the post of Prime Minister.

Al Wazir immediately telegraphed King Ibn Saud of Saudi Arabia seeking recognition and support. The Saudi ruler, however, turned a deaf ear to the al Wazirs and sent a message of support to Prince Ahmed. The Wazirites had underestimated Prince Ahmed.

By-passing the capital, he headed for Hajjah, the north-western fortress town where many an earlier Imam had in times of trouble gone to seek the support of the Hashid and Bakil, the two great tribal confederations, who have been called the wings of the imamate. On his way Prince Ahmed stopped at Hodeidah, the country's principal Red Sea port, whose governor was supposed to be co-operating with the Wazirites. But when Ahmed drew near the governor changed his mind and threw in his support. Within a few days Ahmed was moving with a growing tribal force from Hajjah towards the capital. Word that he was coming spread through the capital and his supporters – including some who stood in fear of him – staged a counter-*coup* and won control of the city. The regular army and the palace guard deserted al Wazir and locked him up. His 'reign' had lasted twenty-six days.

Al Wazir and thirty of his supporters were decapitated in the great square in the centre of Hajjah. The new Imam Ahmed stood by and watched while a grinning negro slave swung the sword and the heads rolled on the ground. The Imam allowed his brother Prince Ibrahim to die in prison 'of a heart attack'.

Against this background the Imam Ahmed preferred to make Taiz rather than Sana his capital. Ahmed was a tyrant in the classic tradition. Quick to strike, to kill and to punish, he succeeded, at a time when the whole Middle East was moving with new ideas, in maintaining the grip of an antique system by sheer terror. One of the keys to his system was the old practice of keeping imamic hostages who were sons of the sheikhs of the more important tribes. The Imam required that these boys be sent to his court, ostensibly for education – and in many cases they were given an education far superior to that which they would have had in their tribal homes – but really to guarantee the good behaviour of their fathers.

Nonetheless, there was opposition. The loyalty of the tribes saved Ahmed in 1955 when an uprising by the regular army took place. The trouble began in the village of Hoban, near Taiz, where some outraged villagers had shot some soldiers who were cutting down their trees for wood. The army demanded exemplary collective punishment of the villagers, but the Imam in this case decreed that it would be sufficient to arrest the ringleaders. The army went ahead anyway, burning, killing and looting in time-honoured fashion. Imam Ahmed dispatched the palace guard to Hoban to restrain the army. But this proved a mistake. The Taiz regular garrison, under a Lieutenant-Colonel Ahmed Yahya al Thalaya, badly mauled the palace guard, then moved into Taiz and besieged the undefended Imam. The Imam's brother Abdullah, then Foreign Minister, supported the insurgent army officers, and it looked for a few days as though he would soon succeed Ahmed as Imam.

Surrounded by a force of six hundred men, and lacking water, electricity and communications in his palace, the Imam was obliged to sign a statement handing over executive powers to his brother. But he refused to abdicate. Abdullah nonetheless assumed the title. Meanwhile, the Imam's eldest son, Mohamed al Badr, had rushed off to Hajjah, rallied the tribes, and begun the march to Taiz.

There are various versions of what happendd next in the capital. But they all agree that the Imam succeeded in liberating himself largely by his own efforts. One story is that he grabbed an automatic rifle from one of the soldiers guarding him, cowed the others and set himself free. When it became known that the Imam had overpowered his guards, the insurrection collapsed. The official account said that the Imam strode through demoralized soldiers, leaped on a white horse, drew his sword and cried 'Allahu Akhbar!' ('God is great.')

After this uprising the Imam Ahmed appeared to have realized that the usual round of executions would not be sufficient to preserve his rule. He must make some concession to the new political forces at work in surrounding countries and, inevitably, in his own. His first major step was to travel to Jeddah – the sixty-four-year-old ruler's first trip outside his own country – to sign a treaty of mutual assistance with King Saud of Saudi Arabia (son of the great Ibn Saud) and President Nasser of Egypt. At this meeting King Saud made him a gift of three million dollars, and the Imam agreed to send his son to Cairo for consultations with President Nasser. From Cairo Prince al Badr went on to London and other European capitals, including Prague and Moscow, and from there to Peking.

These were fateful moves. Every step the Crown Prince took outside Yemen was fraught with consequences for his kingdom. In Cairo he was utterly seduced by President Nasser's charm, to a point where he believed in Nasser's personal friendship and thought that the Egyptian leader understood and sympathized with his problems of reconciling a pre-medieval kingdom with the twentieth century. With President Nasser he arranged a military training mission and later negotiated Yemen's adherence to a Federation of Arab States in which the other partners were Egypt and Syria. In London and elsewhere in Europe the young Crown Prince formed no official ties, but he learned to amuse himself in the European manner. He learned to drink, and alcohol became for him a problem. In Prague and Moscow he spent King Saud's three million dollars on planes and tanks. With the Russians, furthermore, he negotiated a contract for the construction of a deep water port at Hodeidah; and with the communist Chinese he negotiated construction of an asphalt road, from Hodeidah to Sana. (Nasser's military mission became the vehicle through which Egypt introduced the agents who were later to organize Yemen's revolution. The tanks were used against the Imam in the *coup d'état* of 26 September 1962. The port and the road were absolutely essential to the introduction of the Egyptian army which supported the revolution. The alcohol which al Badr began to absorb undoubtedly reduced his ability to cope with the problems that beset him as soon as his father died.)

During the six years between the Jeddah agreement and the revolution the Imam Ahmed tolerated the introduction of a large number of experts and technicians into the country. A German and an American company made unsuccessful searches for oil. An American mission was begun in connection with the so-called Eisenhower doctrine, under which the Americans proposed to help Middle-Eastern countries to defend themselves against communism. The Imam took no interest in the doctrine but, after some delay, in 1958, agreed that the Americans should construct a road from Mocha, the old and almost disused coffee-export port, to Taiz and then through the high mountains up to Sana where it would meet the Chinese road.

In 1957 the Imam Ahmed took the unprecedented step of inviting a group of foreign journalists into the kingdom, largely, it seemed, in order to witness the fighting on the border between the Yemen army and the British of the Aden Protectorate. The initiative hardly had the results the Imam hoped for, for the journalists seem to have considered the Imam an exotic anachronism and not to have taken his war with the British very seriously.

The Imam's attitude towards the modern intrusion and innovations which he had authorized was equivocal. It was exemplified by his treatment of the aircraft al Badr had purchased. Intrigued at first, he sent some young men to Cairo to be trained as pilots. But when a member of the royal household was killed in a crash he immediately grounded all his planes, and some were never removed from the crates in which they had been delivered. From some of the guns he had firing pins removed, and these he had stored separately from the guns, in places which he alone knew. He also tried to immobilize the tanks, and to keep a few of them in operation the Egyptian training mission had to maintain them secretly.

Correctly sensing the dangers involved in equipping his army with murderous weapons – in a world in which armies were often revolutionary – the Imam was nervous about the things his son had bought. He had imagined that he would be able to use the Egyptians, his alliance with them, their arms, and military expertise against the British, with whom he felt it necessary to maintain the historic feud. For more than a hundred years the British had occupied territory which the Yemenis claimed was theirs. No Imam could ever give up Yemeni claims to any of their kingdom's territory; it was a matter of religious faith. It was, after all, the prophet Mohamed who, commissioned by God to rule the Moslems, had sent his son-in-law, Ali Ibn Abi Talib, to rule Yemen; the Zeidi Imams, established in Sana in 885, were Ali's descendants. Qasim the Great had extended his rule over this entire kingdom in accordance with God's will. The Imam Yahya had driven out the Turkish invaders. Ahmed now saw it as his manful duty to insist on his right, confirmed by 'a thousand years' possession', to the British occupied area. His father Yahya had in 1934 come to terms with the British in an agreement for maintenance of the *status quo*. The trouble with this agreement was that while the British interpreted it to mean that the *status quo* should be maintained on the frontier, the Imam took it to mean that the nature of the British relationship with the Protectorate should remain unchanged. What the British read to mean 'the southern Yemeni frontier' the Yemenis read as 'the southern Yemeni area'. From the Yemeni point of view the agreement was violated by the British in the large number of new agreements they concluded with the states of the Hadhramaut and of the western Protectorate, by which the rulers undertook to accept British advice and protection. This was the so-called 'forward policy' by which Britain sought to strengthen the buffer around the Aden base in the 1950s and '60s.

During his visit to London in 1957, Prince al Badr at his father's instruction proposed to accept the British occupation of the southern area until the end of the 1934 treaty. But the British could not accept the implication that their writ would end with the treaty, to be replaced by that of the Imam.

Al Badr had received his formal education almost entirely from tutors, who included religious teachers and three or four Zeidi jurists of some competence. They were able to impart to him the Koranic tradition and much of his nation's history, and they awarded him a degree called the Shebada. But his general education was scanty, and he learned no foreign language, not even Italian, the language of the only foreigners consistently tolerated by his father and grandfather. When al Badr was seventeen years old one of his tutors, for a time, was Ahmed Nomaan, a brilliant young man who had just finished his studies in Cairo and who was to become Prime Minister of a republican Yemen nearly two decades later. Later the young prince fell under the influence of Ibrahim Zahrani, the liberal son of the court poet.

In 1959 al Badr had an opportunity to try his wings as effective ruler of Yemen, with the title of Prime Minister, while his father was absent in Italy for medical treatment. Ahmed had suffered for many years from painful rheumatism and arthritis, not to mention bilharzia and heart disease, and his indulgent Italian doctor, wives and concubines had so thoroughly dosed him with morphine that he became addicted to the drug. His trip to Italy was intended to relieve both his pains and addiction.

When his father departed for Italy the Crown Prince, like many others in the kingdom, assumed that he was near death and would never return, and he began to act as though he had already succeeded to the throne. He had the little Sana radio station broadcast lyrical praise of himself. 'Today', said radio Sana, 'Yemen is in a new era. Today Yemen abounds with hopes, particularly since the people realize the genius of the Crown Prince, who traces the outlines of the enlightened future with far-sighted wisdom. May God preserve his Royal Highness and the hopes of the nation and country.' Al Badr also took to proclaiming a promise of the future at prayer time in the Great Mosque in Taiz. He drew his general inspiration from Nasser in foreign affairs, defining his policy as positive neutralism, pan-Arabism and the advocacy of economic development under State management. He freed a number of slaves on whom his father had particularly relied and he planned thorough reform of both the civil service and the taxation system.

The public reaction to these moves by the young man who was not yet Imam was not at all what he expected. Those whom his father had suppressed sensed his weakness and began to make demands, agitate, demonstrate and even riot. There were demonstrations and disorders in all the main towns. Crowds carried Nasser's portrait through the streets and trampled the portrait of Imam Ahmed. The tribes, distressed by some of the proposed reforms and doubtful of al Badr's qualifications, began to grow restive. The Crown Prince's reaction was to try and buy them off with gifts to the sheikhs, especially to those of the Bakil confederation. He also tried to ensure the loyalty of the army by promising a twenty-five per cent increase in pay and free medical attention. But no one seemed impressed. Al Badr was regarded as a well-meaning but woolly-minded nonentity who could not possibly replace the authority of his father.

Then Ahmed fooled everyone and returned. Like a whirlwind he struck out in every direction, executing, imprisoning, threatening in the old familiar way, and the country lapsed again into uneasy quiescence.

The failure of his attempt to impose his ideas in 1959 left a decisive mark on al Badr's personality. As his father undid the reforms he had ordered and even obliged the tribes to return the gifts they had received from him, al Badr took seriously to drinking. His alcoholism became so serious that a year later the Imam Ahmed sent him, too, to Rome for a cure.

Late in January 1961 a car accident involving the Imam was widely interpreted as an attempted assassination, which it may well have been. But on 26 March a real attempt on the Imam's life took place at the Ahmadi Hospital in Hodeidah. The Imam had gone there for an X-ray examination. He had been expected. The man in charge of internal order and discipline at the hospital, Mohamed al Alafi, had been recruited as a key figure in the plot; this man told the Imam's personal guards, who preceded him to the hospital, that the Imam had said that he did not want them inside the hospital, and they complied. When the Imam arrived al Alafi excluded the guards by closing the outside gates of the hospital. The Imam meanwhile visited some men injured in the January car accident.

As he came down the internal stairs of the hospital to go to the X-ray room three men opened fire on him and his party, which included several princes and four bodyguards. The Imam threw himself on the floor, and his companions fled. The assassins were Abdullah al Qiyal, a twenty-eight-year-old officer of the Hodeidah fire brigade, Mohsin al Hindawam, a forty-year-old army lieutenant, and Mohamed al Alafi. Believing they had killed the Imam, they fled from the hospital; the royal guard outside the gates shot at them, but the three men escaped. Hours later, however, they were rounded up and al Alafi committed suicide.

Hit by five bullets, the Imam was grievously wounded but very much alive. One bullet had gone through his right shoulder and lodged in the left. Two had entered his thigh, broken the bone, and lodged in his bladder. He had hurt his head when he had thrown himself down.

The Imam had escaped once again, but he was slipping. He felt the opposition rising inexorably all around him and realized that his new relationship with Nasser was the channel through which much of this opposition was being organized. Towards the end of the year he composed a sixty-four-line poem which was broadcast by Sana radio and reprinted in the newspapers of Aden. Addressed to 'The Arabs', it was clearly meant for President Nasser. 'Why,' he asked, 'do you pollute the atmosphere with abuse? Why do you shout over the microphone with every inharmonious voice?' He urged the Arabs to move towards 'a unity founded on true principles, a unity whose law is the Sharia of Islam, sacred in its way and its doctrines, free from the defect of innovations prohibited by Islam, such as taking away the property of the people, and the things they have rightly earned, on the pretext of nationalization and of equalization. There is no justification for this in religion, nor is it permitted by common sense.' Thus he denounced Nasser's socialism as irreligious.

President Nasser reacted by terminating Yemen's membership in 'the United Arab States'. For the Egyptians the time for active revolution was now approaching. Cairo radio began to issue its call for revolt in the Yemen. On 29 December 1961, two weeks after the Imam's poem had been broadcast, Cairo's agents began coming into the open. Radio Cairo described Mohamed Mahmoud al Zubairi as leader of the Yemeni Liberation Movement in Cairo, Mohsin al Aini as the Cairo representative of the Aden Trade

Union Congress and Abdurrahman al Baidani as chief spokesman for the revolutionary movement.

In August of that year demonstrations had taken place against the Imam in many parts of the kingdom. Demonstrators dared to march with Nasser's picture in Sana and broke the windows of the Ministry of Education. In September students rioted in Taiz and Sana. On each occasion police suppressed the riots with gunfire, some demonstrators were killed and hundreds were arrested. Twice the Imam ordered villages that had harboured agitators to be destroyed.

By now the Imam was seriously ill and scarcely left his palace in Taiz. Often in arthritic pain, he took refuge in immobility. But his immense appetite remained unaffected. As a result, during his last years he grew extraordinarily fat. David Holden, the British journalist, guessed that he must have weighed 300 pounds. Much as he doubted his son's abilities Imam Ahmed was obliged to turn over most of his power to al Badr. He himself was undoubtedly to blame for much of the weakness with which he taxed his son – a certain diffidence, a lack of self-confidence and a willingness to submit to stronger characters. This was a case of 'too much father' – too much of a father who neither concealed the contempt he felt for his son nor hesitated to humiliate him in public. Herman Eilts, now United States ambassador to Saudi Arabia, remembers an occasion in the late 1940s when as consul in Aden he was visiting the imamic court and was shocked to see the Imam strike his son across the face. On another occasion, recorded by Homer Bigart in a despatch to the *New York Times* after a visit to Yemen in February 1957, the Imam Ahmed in a rage slashed off the tasselled end of the silk turban which hung below his son's shoulder, declaring that 'only Imams wear tassels that low'. Often the Imam referred to his son as 'the handkerchief'.

At 9 p.m. on Tuesday, 18 September 1962 the Imam Ahmed died. His body was flown to Sana on Thursday and buried in the Ridhwani Mosque. Al Badr was proclaimed Imam on the 19th. Not until the 21st did Nasser telegraph to wish the new Imam success in fulfilling the aspirations of his people for a 'future which will realize the dignity that God has given to man'. On the same day, however, radio Cairo declared al Badr 'a ruler made of paper' and warned other Arab monarchs, King Saud and King Hussein, that they were 'just as dead as Ahmed and not yet buried'.

Al Badr tried to rise to the occasion with a speech from the throne promising justice, help for the weak and respect for the rights of all in accordance with modern standards. He promised to improve the material standard of living, to safeguard equality of rights and duties, to work for a 'unified Arab nation'. He offered friendship without alliance to all nations who would assist Yemen. Proclaiming himself Premier as well as head of state, the new Imam also laid down a programme of specific reforms. He issued a general amnesty for political prisoners and exiles, abolished the system of hostages, created an advisory council of forty men, half elected and half nominated, and established municipal councils in all towns, with one representative for every five thousand citizens.

Unfortunately for al Badr, he was no more taken seriously in 1962 than he had been in 1959. Even as he discussed his well-meant reforms the revolutionaries were preparing an assault upon his palace.

III

The Imam's Story

....

On 10 November 1962, the Imam Mohamed al Badr met sixteen foreign correspondents at the foot of Jabal al Nadir in the north-western corner of Yemen. I was the only American present.

Here began my association with Yemen, for behind that press conference was a story. From the day I had first been convinced that the Imam was alive, I had been trying, from my post as Middle East correspondent of the *New York Times* in Beirut, to arrange a meeting with him. My first idea was to try to reach him through the British-protected territory of South Arabia, and through the British Embassy I telegraphed to the press officer attached to the British High Commissioner in Aden. The reply was as follows: 'Prospects seem to me negligible. There is nothing to stop him flying to Beihan by Aden Airways but thereafter motor transport would be practically impossible and the local authorities are not likely to approve his crossing into Yemeni territory in search of royalist forces. In any case it is extremely doubtful whether there is an open overland route from Beihan to the Yemeni/Saudi frontier, where the Imam may be.' How ill-informed or misleading, or both, this message was may be judged from my subsequent experiences.

Because the news about the Imam and royalist activities in the Yemen was at that time coming almost exclusively from radio Amman, to which it was being funnelled by the Saudi Arabian embassy and the royal Yemeni legation, I next tried to arrange in Amman for a trip to royalist Yemen and an exclusive interview with the Imam. Although the Saudis assured me that I would indeed be the first, they delayed so long that their good intentions were overtaken by events.

One reason for my frustration was that King Hussein of Jordan was as aware as I of the value of exposing the Imam of Yemen to the world press. As I had pointed out, in my attempts to arrange an 'exclusive' interview, the world was not convinced at that time that the Imam really still existed, genuinely controlled part of his kingdom and was actually fighting back against the republicans. The King of Jordan, a very sophisticated young man educated at Harrow and Sandhurst, was as aware as anyone that bombastic communiqués emanating from a shadowy royalist headquarters, located no one knew where, were not convincing anyone. It would take live foreign correspondents from Europe and America to establish the fact that this Imam was not just a character in a particularly horrible fairy-tale, not a kind of medieval anachronism who had been wiped out by a long overdue revolution.

Young King Hussein had met Mohamed al Badr during the Crown Prince's travels, and it was said that Hussein took a distinct dislike to al Badr's self-indulgence, liberal talk, and his pose as a friend of President Nasser. That, however, was not important now. What mattered was to try to persuade as many people and governments as possible not to recognize the new republic in Yemen and to prevent President Nasser from getting a foothold on the Arabian Peninsula. If the Egyptians got control of Yemen the young king knew their next targets would be the thrones of Saudi Arabia and Jordan, the only kingdoms left in the eastern Arab world.

But King Hussein did not find the same ready understanding of this situation in Riyadh, the Saudi Arabian capital. In the Saudi government a strong faction was working for acceptance of the republican revolution and Crown Prince Faisal (he did not succeed to the throne until later) had not made up his mind how far he would help the Imam, or whether he would help him at all.

King Hussein was not to be put off. He sent word to Beirut that any foreign correspondents who wanted to visit the Imam of Yemen should come to Amman by 4 November.

At dawn on 5 November, therefore, I was at Amman airport; though the presence of at least a dozen Jordanians and Lebanese and three British journalists made it painfully apparent that my meeting with the Imam was to be anything but 'exclusive'. The British group consisted of Harold A. R. Philby, known as 'Kim', son of the famous Arabist H. St John Philby, then correspondent of the *Observer* and *The Economist*, Eric Downton of the *Daily Telegraph* and Jerome Camenada of *The Times*.

Great was our surprise when we were invited into a shed at the edge of the runway to meet King Hussein. The king, sportingly clad in a heavy sweater to protect him from the intense morning cold, had arisen early to brief us on what we were about to see, and to see us properly on our way. I do not remember the details of the king's remarks about the strength of the royalists and the general state of the conflict. What mattered was that this very engaging young monarch had thrown himself into the fight with typically impulsive, dead serious enthusiasm and that he had lent his personal prestige to our mission. His zeal and sincerity were moving.

When, several hours later, we stepped out of our plane into the dry, burning heat of Riyadh — all of us without visas and some even without passports – the Saudi Arabian authorities were baffled. They ushered us into a VIP reception-room, where chairs were arranged all around the wall; the airport director offered us coffee while he telephoned urgently to town to find out what to do with us. Philby announced that he was going to visit his 'family' – in fact his half-brother, son of his father by a Saudi mother who lived in Riyadh – and he departed somewhat unsteadily, for he had been nipping at a bottle of whisky. This he had carried in his coat pocket from dawn in Amman until a few minutes before we landed, for in 'dry' Riyadh all forms of alcohol are banned. From that point on, however, Kim did not take another drink for three days.[1] After an hour the rest of us were driven to al Yamama, Riyadh's principal hotel. We learned that the Saudi Arabians had been taken completely

---

[1] These were Philby's last days in the Middle East. Soon thereafter, in January 1963, he was confronted by an old associate in the British Secret Service and admitted, we now know, that he was having regular contacts with a councillor at the Soviet embassy in Beirut. About the same time, I later heard, the American Central Intelligence Agency had also found incontrovertible evidence of Philby's role ever since the days when he served in the British embassy in Washington. But neither the British nor the Americans saw fit to kidnap or kill this most brilliant of Soviet agents, and he was able to slip away one stormy night aboard a Soviet freighter in Beirut harbour, and so avoid exposure. I had no inkling at the time that Philby was working for the Russians. Nor do I believe that he can have been a very significant source of information for them during the latter part of his time in Beirut when I knew him. He was too far gone in alcoholism. I rarely saw him sober, and I remember wondering how he could do his job for both the *Observer* and the *Economist*. I heard that he was worried by debts and by demands on him by the families of his two previous marriages. I also heard that he had received several offers to write books, but that he had been unable even to make a start. Under the circumstances, the escape to Russia must have been for him a kind of release.

by surprise by Hussein's action. By sending a plane-load of journalists in one of his own planes to wait, as it were, on King Saud's doorstep for permission to go to Yemen, the King of Jordan was forcing their hand.

Ever since the Yemeni coup on 26 September, the top echelons of Saudi society had been divided on whether to come to terms with the new régime in Sana or whether to support the Imam in the mountains. Six members of the Saudi cabinet, all commoners, had signed a memorandum recommending that Saudi Arabia recognize the republicans. Others, headed by Prince Khaled, were already busy helping the royalists. King Saud, as usual, 'waffled' between ardent support of the royalists and prudent recognition of the revolutionaries.

To this uncertain situation on 24 October, Crown Prince Faisal returned from New York, where he had been heading the Saudi delegation to the United Nations. The Crown Prince found the commoners in the cabinet, who in effect represented the new middle class of Saudi Arabia, a defeatist element. Having little faith in the future of the Saudi monarchy and its ability to reform and defend itself, they were inclined to anticipate that President Nasser would succeed in his evident strategy, which was to use the Yemen revolution combined with a threat of armed force to bring down the structure of the Saudi monarchy. This defeatism was shared by some of the younger members of the royal family. The first among them to defect to Nasser was Prince Tallal, one of King Saud's numerous half-brothers, a former Minister of Finance and a sincere advocate of the reforms and constitutional government of Saudi Arabia. He flew via Beirut to offer his services to President Nasser in Cairo and was soon followed by three other half-brothers of the King, the Princes Abdul Mohsin, Musaad and Abdul Rahman.

I had met Tallal (he had for the time being dropped the title of prince) in the Hotel Saint Georges in Beirut early in October, and had learned that he expected the Saudi kingdom to disintegrate into its component parts, the Hejaz with its holy places in the west, and the Nejd in the centre, the provinces (where most of the oil is) in the north-east, and perhaps fertile Asir, formerly part of Yemen, in the south-west. He believed he had supporters everywhere who at a critical moment would rise to destroy the monarchy. In his mind the Yemeni revolution and revolution in Saudi Arabia were closely interrelated. Aware that I had in July and August of that year made a secret journey into northern Iraq to visit Mullah Mustafa Barzani, the Kurdish leader, he had offered to send me secretly through Saudi Arabia to the Yemen. He had said he would let me know when the time was ripe, but I never heard from him.

Other levels of Saudi society were also infected. Five Saudi pilots who had been ordered to fly military supplies to the Yemen border defected to Egypt. There they found the commander of the Jordanian Air Force, who had defected to Egypt in protest when he was sent to Taif airport, in Saudi Arabia, with a number of Jordanian aircraft to reinforce Saudi defences. Although the Jordanian government insisted that this was a strictly defensive move, a precaution against Egyptian attack, he believed it was the first step towards carrying the war into Yemen with a combined Jordanian and Saudi force.

President Nasser reinforced the evident disarray among the Saudis with military threats and several pin-prick raids on Saudi territory. The first Egyptian raid was an attack on the town of Najran around 25 October, followed by raids on five villages near Jizan during the first week of November, and a fourteen-hour air and sea bombardment of a village called Mowasem, on the Red Sea coast north of Jizan, on 5 November. During the first week of November Egyptian aircraft again dropped bombs in the area of Najran. The Egyptians allowed President Sallal of Yemen, meanwhile, to threaten on 4 November to march into Jizan and Najran. Sallal's deputy, Abdurrahman Baidini, as early as 11 October had spoken of a 'state of war' with Saudi Arabia, alleging that the Saudis were helping the Yemeni royalists. In other broadcasts, Baidani threatened that Saudi airports, towns and palaces would be bombed if the Saudis did not refrain from helping the royalists, or, as he put it, from 'infiltrating' Yemen. Speakers on Sana radio at the same time began to talk about a future 'republic of the Arabian peninsula'. These threats were followed by a bold Egyptian attempt to provoke an insurrection inside Saudi Arabia. On the basis, presumably, of reports of internal disaffection Egyptian aircraft in a night flight dropped arms on the road between Jeddah and Mecca. But the revolutionaries the Egyptians hoped for did not appear, and the weapons were collected by the Saudi Arabian army.

As on other occasions when the Saudi régime was under pressure, King Saud at this point turned to his brother Faisal. He gave up the post of Prime Minister, which he had himself filled for some months, and he asked the Crown Prince to form a new government.

It was our good fortune as journalists to arrive in Riyadh just in time to witness Faisal's vigorous counter-attack as Prime Minister. On 6 November, the day after our arrival, Prince Faisal received us and announced that Saudi Arabia had broken off relations with Cairo in protest against the Egyptian bombardments culminating in the attack of Mowasem.

Prince Faisal also announced a series of internal reforms, and these were probably his most significant counter to the revolutionary threat fomented by Egypt. The reforms he announced were the following.

1. All remaining slaves in the kingdom would be freed immediately; the government would compensate their masters financially. In fact, most of the remaining slaves in the kingdom were Negro household servants who had little desire to leave the families with whom they lived. Many among them had achieved positions of trust and had eventually been freed. Mohamed Sursur, for instance, the Finance Minister of Saudi Arabia for many years, had been born a slave. Slaves had been imported into Arabia from Africa for as long as anyone could remember, but for many years it had been illegal to buy and sell slaves. Faisal's proclamation merely stimulated a reform already in progress.

2. The so-called 'public morality committees' were to be reformed. This was Prince Faisal's first move to limit the excessive zeal of the religious police in combating activities regarded by the puritanical Wahabi sect of Saudi Arabian Moslems as antireligious, including smoking, drinking and the making of music. The Wahabis had risen to great influence in the time of King Abdul Aziz ibn Saud, father of Crown Prince Faisal and King Saud. Ibn Saud gathered the warlike tribes who followed this faith into a force with which he united the greater part of the Arabian peninsula. Since his time the remnants of the Wahabi movement had been organized into the so-called 'white army', a tribal force whose camps were to be seen on the outskirts of Jeddah and Riyadh, and who were one of the principal supports of the ruling family.

In the other towns, meanwhile, Wahabi influence had become oppressive. Directed by the Public Morality Committee, the Society for the Promotion of Virtue and the Prevention of Vice operated a religious police who felt free to interfere in every aspect of the people's lives. Men in khaki uniforms carrying bamboo staves patrolled the market-places, and closed the shops at prayer time. In Riyadh they made attempts to prevent smoking and sometimes even knocked cigarettes from the mouths of unwary foreign visitors walking in the bazaar. They also spasmodically conducted a campaign against what they regarded as the irreligious practice of reproducing man's image, namely the making of photographs or other pictures of the human form. On one occasion they raided an airline office and removed a life-size cardboard image of an airline hostess; on another they confiscated pedestrian stop-signs, made in the shape of the human body, which had been placed at intersections in Riyadh. Their yellow jeeps could be seen patrolling everywhere and they were widely feared.

3. The rule of law was to be generally strengthened by the creation of a Supreme Court, a Ministry of Justice and an attorney-general.

4. While the government remained based in Islamic principles, a committee was to be formed to study the development of a constitution providing for national and regional consultative councils.

5. Administration, particularly in provincial areas, was to be reorganized.

6. New legislation for the development of education and social security and for the regulation of labour was to be promulgated.

7. Retroactive payments due from the Arabian-American Oil Company (ARAMCO) were to be used to establish a petroleum authority and to set up industrial and agricultural banks for the promotion of the country's economic development. This retroactive payment amounted to several hundred million dollars.

8. Finally, the government was to permit what it called 'innocent pleasures'. This was taken to be a promise that cinemas, entirely banned in the kingdom, were to be authorized and that television, then available only in the north-eastern corner of the kingdom, where ARAMCO transmitted programmes for its employees, would soon be allowed throughout the country.

Prince Faisal told the group of journalists from Amman that they were welcome to traverse the kingdom to visit Imam Mohamed al Badr in Yemen, but that he must first obtain al Badr's approval. In a land where the art of delay is highly developed this sounded like an excuse, and the correspondents were impatient. The next day, however, King Saud himself received us in one of the magnificent multi-chandeliered halls of Nasiriyah and informed us that he had received word from the Imam, and that there would be a plane to fly us to the Yemeni border next day. This may have been the last occasion when King Saud received a large group of foreign newsmen. Walking stiff-legged and wearily to his throne at one end of the room, he seemed distinctly unwell. The strain of the conflict unleashed by the Yemeni revolution already showed in his face and his movement. These were signs of the illness which was to culminate in his abdication in Faisal's favour in 1964.

King Saud told us that his government would be 'obliged to take other measures' if a rupture of diplomatic relations with the United Arab Republic was not sufficient to halt aggression against Saudi territory. But no one really believed that the Saudi Arabians were capable of putting an army in the field against the Egyptians. Their most effective defence, like that of the Soviet Union, was the immensity of their country, for it was hardly conceivable that the Egyptians would master logistically the formidable mountains and deserts that lay between their army in Yemen and the main centres of Saudi Arabia. Apart from this, King Saud stated that the Imam had a force of 30,000 men under his command (King Hussein had said 15,000) and that some of his units were operating within twenty-five miles of Sana, the capital.

In the morning we were flown to Jizan in an aircraft of the Saudi Arabian airline, which was piloted by an American. There we first stowed our baggage in a new customs building, where a whole floor with rows of beds had been set aside for us. Then the Saudis took us on an exhausting search for the traces of the Egyptian bombardment of Mowasem. This turned out to be a frustrating experience, and somewhat embarrassing to our Saudi hosts. For we could find no evidence of actual damage at Mowasem. At each village we were directed to, it turned out to be the next village which, it was supposed, had been heavily damaged. In fact, it seemed that the Egyptians had fired their shells from warships in the Red Sea and had dropped bombs from aircraft more or less at random in the open countryside. It was the noise of the explosions, rather than any damage, which had frightened the tribesmen into abandoning their villages and hurrying into the interior. We saw them on the roads, all distinctly African, very black and in many cases naked to the waist. These were of primitive Negro tribes identical with those who live in the sandy, malarial, low-lying coastal region of the Yemen known as the Tihama. Quite unlike the mountain-dwellers of the interior, who wear turbans and build stone houses, these Negroes wear a conical head-dress of straw and live in circular straw huts.

Although we were exhausted by the search for bomb damage, we then had to attend an all too copious dinner with the governor. After this we returned to our frigid and unsalubrious customs-house for a short night on extremely uncomfortable beds. It is odd how the fatigue of such occasions makes people snappish and unreasonable. It seemed that we were constantly quarrelling among ourselves and with our Saudi hosts about what we should do, where we should go and when. The Saudi in charge of us, who was called Galib, tried to compensate for the primitiveness and discomfort of our environment by asserting that he was more accustomed to living on an expense account in $40-a-day New York hotel suites, a remark whose relevance I never really understood.

After this appropriate period of confusion and argument, our fleet of Saudi government vehicles got started the next morning, several hours later than the appointed time; we drove to the end of the asphalt at Abu Arish and from there over more rudimentary roads to the border at al Jabri. That is what it looked like when I consulted a map later; but at the time we did not know where the border lay, nor which of the tiny villages we passed was al Jabri. Gradually the road deteriorated into what appeared to be a river bed; this we had to circumnavigate, climbing over huge boulders and fallen trees which alternated with short stretches of pebbles, soft sand and mud.

We could feel that we had entered here a new climatic zone. Unlike the sharp cold of the high plateau where Riyadh is located, here on the Red Sea coastal plain the weather was mild and steamy. Our route led from the plain towards the mountains. Towards noon we stopped at a shack in one of the villages, where we bought boxes of imported biscuits and cans of pineapple from Kenya, presumably imported via Saudi Arabia. Here and there along the trail we also saw piles of bags of commercially imported American flour, apparently awaiting transportation farther into the interior.

After six exhausting hours we came upon a great crowd of Yemenis, who we thought at first had gathered for some kind of market day. They stood at the foot of a mountain cliff 2,000 feet high, at the top of which, silhouetted against the sky, stood the fortress-like stone houses of a Yemeni highland village, which, we were told, had been bombed by five Egyptian aircraft half an hour before our arrival. It turned out that the crowd was there because of the proximity of the Imam.

We found the Imam in an open field, surrounded by his courtiers. Around him, in a vibrant, throbbing circle, his subjects waved their rifles and curved daggers in the air in a tribal war dance, chanting, shouting and clapping. From time to time they broke into wild warrior songs, very shrill and on a rising, almost hysterical inflection, echoing weirdly from the mountains.

The Imam made no attempt to restrain the hubbub and tolerantly allowed some tribesmen to break through the circle of his courtiers and guards to kiss, or try to kiss, his hands and feet. Clad in a green turban, a khaki shirt with rolled-up sleeves and a short kilt that is part of Yemeni national dress, he seemed youthful, enthusiastic and in perfect health. His clean clothes, small trimmed beard and gold watch made it hard to believe that he had just escaped death in Sana and completed a forced march through the mountains on foot and on muleback.

He led the way to a white tent at one side of the field where he sat down, cross-legged, with a new rifle across his knees. Across his chest he wore a double bandolier of cartridges. 'As you see, here I am,' he said in Arabic; a Jordanian journalist translated for him. This was, in sum, the main point he had to make, that he had in fact escaped uninjured and was ready to fight. He told us the story of his escape, pouring out his bitterness and sense of outrage at the betrayal he had suffered at the hands of President Gamal Abdul Nasser, whom he had considered his friend. 'I placed all my hopes in Nasser, whom I considered a friend and brother, and who I thought was right in everything he was saying,' the Imam declared. 'But facts have proved the contrary. He does not keep his promises.' He addressed himself to the Egyptian people: 'Had you come as friends, we would have opened to you our homes and our hearts. But since you came as invaders we can open for you only your graves. No one is really fighting me any more except the Egyptians,' he added.

The warlike cries outside the tent became so loud that it was difficult to hear the Imam speak; but he paid no attention to them. He smoked cigarettes and picked his teeth with a toothpick.

His men had already captured some Egyptians, he said, but he could not show any prisoners. He was sorry to say that 'whenever tribesmen took prisoners they never brought them in alive, because

57

they were so enraged. They were all annihilated.' The planes that were raiding his men were certainly not Yemeni; they must there-fore be Egyptian. He should know, for he had himself purchased Yemen's aeroplanes. There had once been an air force of twenty planes, but it had been grounded many years ago. As for the Yemeni navy, it consisted of two coastguard craft in all, each mounting only one machine-gun. So the shelling of the Saudi coast, as well as the bombing, must have been done by the Egyptians.

The Imam commented bitterly on the speed with which some nations had recognized the republicans. 'Apparently all you need to make a government these days is a radio station.' He expressed pity for the states who would soon have to come to him humbly and 'put their recognitions on my desk'. He appealed to the nations of the world to 'help me spare innocent blood', and to help save Yemen from the troops of the United Arab Republic. He said he would not make a formal protest to the United Nations, but he had taken steps to 'draw its attention' to the fact that Yemen, 'a member of the United Nations, had been occupied by another member'. He said that he had appealed to the Arab League. But there was no use 'shouting in the ear of the dead', he added.

The Imam was then asked whether he had appealed for help from foreign governments; he replied that if he needed help he could apply to Jordan or Saudi Arabia. In fact, although the Imam didn't say so, they were already helping with supplies and training, but not with troops.

On the question of the reforms he would introduce if he were victorious, the Imam seemed to be evasive. It was perhaps not an appropriate time to broach this matter. He replied that 'building a nation is not a simple matter', and that the reforms he would carry out would be those he had announced. He predicted that within two weeks he would be leading his men back into Sana. He hoped to meet the correspondents there after his arrival.

The Imam went on to describe the military situation. He had formed two royalist armies, one under his uncle Prince Hassan in the east, and one under his own direct command in the west. The two armies were in control of most of the north and east of the country including Harib in the south-east, Marib in the east and Sadah in the north. In the area of Hajjah, he said, his men controlled the mountains, but the town and fort were still held by the republicans.

The Imam was later proved wrong in reporting that the royalists had occupied Sadah. Had he been able to hold it, it would have been a splendid prize, for it was the ancient seat of the first imams and the natural capital of the northern part of his country. This fact, and his prediction that he would return to Sana within two weeks, demonstrated the extent of his optimism and his miscalculation of the rival forces in Yemen.

Behind the Imam in the tent stood several princes and officers and guards who, in addition to their rifles and Yemeni daggers, wore United States army Colt pistols in their belts. Some of the guards wore the bright blue tribal costume of the Imam's personal guard. They had, I was told, made their way from Sana to be with him. But I never saw them wear that blue costume again. Perhaps the colour was later deemed too flamboyant and lacking in camouflage for a fugitive monarch.

Some of us asked the Imam to allow us to stay with him a few days in the mountains. But he refused categorically, maintaining that it was 'too dangerous'. We had now spent about two hours with him and it was around three o'clock in the afternoon. During our stay clouds had been gathering around the cliff above us, and as we left a thunderstorm broke over our heads. A fine, warm rain descended like mist, and a splendid rainbow arched through the sky. As we drove back, we came upon a group of tribesmen driving Egyptian armoured cars, which they said they had captured from an Egyptian column whom they had ambushed near Haradh. With childish excitement the tribesmen displayed Egyptian military caps taken from their victims, and I suspect that had we stayed with them a little longer they would have showed us some of the Egyptian heads as well. Decapitation of captured enemy soldiers is an old Yemeni custom.

Galib, the Saudi official escorting us, said he was willing to fly us from Jizan across to Najran and from there to the eastern front in Yemen where we might visit the royalist Prime Minister, Prince Hassan. Nevertheless we were eager to write the story we already had and insisted on returning to Jeddah. However, I assured Galib that I myself would return to visit Prince Hassan and the eastern front within a month.

During that month a burst of fighting swiftly enveloped Yemen. As the Egyptians penetrated, they were met by increasing resistance the farther they went north and east.

IV

The Princes in Action

WHILE the fugitive Imam was still struggling through the mountains towards the Saudi Arabian border and the world remained in
doubt as to whether he was alive or dead, the princes of the house of
Hamid Eddin were already beginning their own campaign. They
gathered first at Najran, an oasis town on the southern border of
Saudi Arabia, and from there fanned out to engage the enemy in the
north and the north-west and especially on the eastern desert side of
Yemen. How it started was described to me by Prince Abdurrahman
bin Yahya, the youngest brother of the late Imam Ahmed, in the
course of several meetings at Beirut, Jeddah and at the royalist
headquarters in north-eastern Yemen.

Prince Abdurrahman was the last son of the old Imam Yahya,
whom he remembers with affection. 'I was twelve years old when
my father died,' he recalled. We were riding together in a jeep on
our way to the royalist military headquarters in north-eastern
Yemen, early one morning in May 1965. 'I was quite lost without
him,' he continued, 'so many people began giving me advice.' Since
he was the son of the Imam Yahya, Abdurrahman became the
uncle of the Imam al Badr, although in fact he was only seven years
his junior. One might regard him as a personal link between the
Yemen of his father's time, when Yemen was fighting the Turks,
and the Yemen of the present, which has been fighting the
Egyptians.

'It is exactly the same thing as in my father's time,' he said to me.
'Then it was Yemeni 'jambiyas' (daggers) against Turkish artillery;
today it is Yemeni automatic weapons against Egyptian tanks
and aircraft. My father fought for seven years until he won
back Sana. We are quite prepared to fight much longer than
that.'

Prince Abdurrahman had no use for his brother, the former

Imam Ahmed. 'In his thirteen years of rule he did not do any good thing,' said the prince.

One of the most sophisticated of all the princes, he spoke fluent English and a smattering of German and Italian, had studied at the University of Heidelberg and was studying in Italy when his brother the Imam Ahmed died. He had no illusions about himself as a military leader, although he did for a while hold a command in the western part of the country. Usually when he went to the fighting fronts he did not even trouble to wear tribal dress. Although he put on a khaki Yemeni kilt he also wore a most urban looking jacket. Unlike all the other Yemenis, of high and low estate, he did not usually carry arms. As deputy Prime Minister, the rank to which he was eventually promoted, he deemed it his duty mainly to handle royalist affairs in foreign countries, and to travel constantly on both sides of the Atlantic and between Riyadh, Jeddah, the Imam's headquarters, and the head-quarters of the Prime Minister, Prince Hassan bin Yahya, his elder brother.

Immediately upon the death of the Imam Ahmed the new Imam sent Prince Abdurrahman a telegram asking him to come as soon as possible and take over the post of Minister of Health. This was a post to which the Imam Ahmed had named him some years earlier, but he had not accepted because he was aware that Ahmed was chronically suspicious of all his near relatives and did not really want them in Sana. Now, however, he was determined to join the government.

'I arrived in Aden by air at six o'clock on the morning of Tuesday, 27 September,' he recalled. 'As there were nine of us in my party, and only three places on the plane to Sana, we decided that none of us would go that day and returned to our hotel. It was when we arrived at the hotel that we heard about the *coup d'état* in Sana. By sheer luck, thanks to the fact that there was no room on the plane, I had escaped falling into the hands of the republicans. We stayed in Aden and I telephoned to New York to my brother Hassan. Hassan, twenty-two years my elder, was the Yemeni delegate to the United Nations, a post he had held for six years because he, like me, knew that our brother the Imam did not welcome us in Sana.

'Prince Hassan set out at once and a few days later we flew to meet him in Jeddah, the Saudi Arabian Red Sea port. From there we went to Riyadh, to see King Saud and Crown Prince Faisal, and then we continued to Najran.'

Of the nine persons aboard that plane to Najran five were to play key roles in the royalist camp. They were: Prince Hassan bin Yahya, from New York, whom all immediately recognized as Imam when they thought al Badr was dead; Prince Mohamed bin Hussein, Prince Mohamed bin Ismail, Ibrahim al Kipsy, a student, and Prince Abdurrahman himself. These were the men who, together with others who soon joined them, including Mohamed Ahmed al Shami, who had been head of the Imam's legation in London and who was named Foreign Minister, met in this oasis town at the cross-roads between the mountains of Yemen, the plains of Saudi Arabia and the Rub al Khali desert, in order to lay their plans to regain the kingdom. Here in Najran, where much Yemeni history has been made in the past, a new chapter of history was beginning. Here, or at least near by, had stood the ancient city of Main, capital of the Minaean kingdom, the oldest of the five pre-Islamic kingdoms of Yemen which were founded three or four thousand years before Christ. Here, for hundreds of years before and after the birth of Christ, had been a prosperous city, famed for its cloth, silk and leather goods. The pre-Islamic inhabitants of Najran had a Kaaba, a great black stone similar to that in Mecca, around which they worshipped; it was here that the Christian community, founded in the first few centuries of the Christian era, built a famous cathedral. It was here, too, that 20,000 Christians are said to have been massacred by Dhu Nuwas, early in the sixth century, and from here that Abraha, the Christian Abyssinian ruler of Yemen, set out on his white elephant hoping to conquer Mecca and destroy the pagan Kaaba; the road Abraha took northwards is still called Tariq al Fil, the 'road of the elephant'.

Most of the royalist leaders who gathered here were young men in their twenties, most, though not all, of the Hamid Eddin family. These were no effete princelings, spoiled by luxurious living. They had been shaped by Imam Ahmed's suspicion of all his relatives; he was happy to send them abroad to be educated just to keep them away, but he kept them on modest allowances. Most of the princes had picked up liberal ideas along with their education, but retained an inbred sense of their position and rights. They were, as someone has said, 'a fighting tribe of cousins'. It was their fighting spirit and their ability to lead their own people that turned the course of

history in Yemen. Without them the Imam al Badr would soon
have been lost; without them Saudi help in gold and arms would
have been meaningless.

The oldest and most distinguished among them was Prince
Hassan bin Yahya; he was fifty-six, but looked older. He was well
known to the tribes, many of whom would have preferred him to
young Mohamed al Badr as successor to Imam Ahmed. Although
not a particularly brilliant or forceful personality he had a benign
and likeable way which inspired confidence. Most of his life he had
been thoroughly provincial, conservative and old-fashioned; but
thanks to his exile he had learned some English, had observed
something of western methods of government and was able to
agree with the reform-minded young princes on steps to liberalize
and modernize Yemeni society. At the same time he kept the
support of the religious element and of the tribal leaders. He had
assumed the title of 'Imam al Watheq Bizzah', 'the believer in God',
but he renounced it immediately when he learned, twelve days
after the *coup*, that the Imam al Badr was still alive. The young
princes made Prince Hassan Prime Minister and Commander-in-
Chief. The Saudi army equipped him with a radio telephone, a
fair supply of gold sovereigns and silver Maria Theresa thalers,
some rifles and machine-guns. First from Najran, then from the
headquarters in a cave in the mountains east of Sadah, he deployed
the men who gathered around him, tribesmen, sheikhs and princes.
The best leaders he found were his own two sons and six nephews.

The names of the princes were often confusingly similar and
could sometimes be distinguished only by the addition of the name
of the father to each young man's name. The Imam Yahya had
many sons, two of whom were Hassan and Hussein. Hassan bin
Yahya, the first, had two sons, Abdullah bin Hassan and Hassan
bin Hassan. The second, Hussein bin Yahya, had six sons, Mohamed, Abdullah, Hassan, Ahmed, Ali and Yahya, to each of whose
names the words 'bin Hussein' could be added for clarity of
identification. The 'bin' is often used in the form of 'ben' or 'ibn';
frequently it is dropped, so that Mohamed bin Hussein becomes
merely Mohamed Hussein.

The Prime Minister immediately dispatched Prince Mohamed
Hussein and his cousin, Mohamed Ismail, to Sadah, the principal city
of northern Yemen and the seat of the first Imams in the eighth
century. Prince Mohamed arrived there on 1 October 1962. But

his move proved a miscalculation. The royalists were not yet in any position to hold a large town. The republicans, backed by Egyptian troops were soon on their way from the capital to occupy Sadah, and within a week Mohamed was betrayed, as he later put it, 'by a treasonable sheikh'. He and his cousin escaped back to the eastern deserts, where he soon found employment organizing the training of the tribesmen who rallied round old Prince Hassan.

Mohamed Ismail, a handsome, pleasant-looking man in his early twenties, moved off after a pause at the Prime Minister's headquarters to the western part of the country, where he became commander in a vast area extending from the vicinity of Hajjah, to the Imam's headquarters at Qara, all the way to Haradh and Sadah. At various times Prince Mohamed Ismail shared this area with other princes, including Prince Abdurrahman. In 1964 Prince Hassan bin Hussein, one of the younger Hussein brothers, whose half-truculent, half-humourous demeanour contained something of that 'tough guy' pose, became the dominant military commander in the west. At all times the commanders in the west played the role of deputy to the Imam, who rarely took an active part in directing operations; the commanders were responsible for the Imam's personal safety.

Another of the Hussein brothers, Abdullah, aged twenty-eight, a third-year student at the American University of Beirut, was sent by the Prime Minister to the Jawf, the great semi-desert region of the north-east, notable for its magnificent scenery and Minaean inscriptions. Although not in good health Abdullah proved versatile and indefatigable, though not as successful in battle as some of the others. He had under his command two more of the Hussein brothers, Ahmed, and Ali, who was later killed in battle. Ahmed had been trained at a military school in Egypt where he attained the rank of lieutenant. Ali, who had been studying political science at the A.U.B., played a role in drafting a constitutional proposal.

The remaining Hussein brother, Yahya, somewhat older than the rest, had held a post in the royalist legation in Beirut. He served for a time as a liaison with the Saudis.

One of the first things the Prime Minister did was to send his sons, Abdullah and Hassan, to the southernmost part of the area which the royalists hoped to keep under their control. First to arrive on the scene, Prince Hassan bin Hassan led a tribal force into the town of Marib and scored a useful *coup* in capturing a helicopter with three Russian technicians aboard, which landed outside the town under the impression that it was in the hands of republicans. The Russians, who were later sent out of the country via Aden, left behind a detailed map of Yemen which has proved valuable to the royalists. When Hassan bin Hassan fell ill and was evacuated to Europe, his brother Abdullah took over and established himself in the key area between Marib, Harib and Sana, the importance of which was that it covered the line of communications from British-controlled South Arabia and was the royalists' nearest approach to the capital.

To halt a mixed Egyptian armoured and republican infantry force attempting to reach Sirwah and retake Marib, Prince Abdullah Hassan fought one of the first big battles of the war against a mixed Egyptian and republican force at Jabal[1] al Urush, half-way between Jihanah and Sirwah. Having inflicted severe casualties on his enemy at Jabal al Urush, Abdullah Hassan moved on in an attempt to occupy Sirwah, which was held by a strong Egyptian force. The Egyptians tried to relieve it early in November 1962 with four drops of sixty paratroopers each. The first three were dropped from too great a height and most of them were killed by Abdullah Hassan's sharp-shooters before they reached the ground. The fourth group fell wide of the town on a mountain-top.

In competence and personality, and certainly in vanity, Abdullah bin Hassan rivalled Mohamed bin Hussein. Both princes were mentioned from time to time as possible successors to al Badr as Imam. I shall describe Prince Mohamed more fully in Chapter Fifteen. Prince Abdullah, who had been educated in Cairo, was a young man of delicate appearance about whom Sanche de Gramont, who visited him in the mountains early in 1964, wrote in an article for the *New York Herald Tribune* that he was an unlikely-looking guerilla sheikh 'with the aquiline features and large sloe eyes of a Byzantine icon'. Prince Abdullah had an exalted sense of his role as prince and guerilla leader. 'My family have been ruling for seventy years,' he once said, 'and there are not many Yemenis who have known any other rule. We represent the legitimate power. The Egyptians are like the Turks, usurpers, the people hate them.'

De Gramont said that Prince Abdullah had a manservant who was always at his side and slept at his feet. At night the manservant

[1] The word *jabal*, which recurs frequently, is Arabic for mountain.

would inflate a pneumatic mattress for the prince and massage his feet with aromatic oils. In the morning he would bring an incense burner with sandalwood, over which the prince would stand to let the fragrant fumes rise through his clothing. The servant carried a cellophane bag containing choice *qat* leaves, and during marches would run alongside the prince's camel with a thermos of cool water.

Just before the revolution in Yemen Abdullah Hassan had served as a member of the Yemeni delegation to the United Nations in New York, and he recalled this time nostalgically. To George di Carvalho of *Life* Magazine he once remarked: 'I wake up in the cave sometimes aching and dirty, with no shower or toilet, no nothing. And I think about New York. I will never forget Fifth Avenue and Times Square.'

All the tribes around Sana at one time or another addressed to him letters declaring their loyalty. These included the Khawlan, the Hamdan, the Arhab, the Bani Matar, the Bani al Harith, the Bani Hushaysh and the Nahm. From these tribes he was able, most of the time up to 1967, to draw about 600 men for his front line, with about 2,000 more on call within twenty-four hours, and 7,000 within five days. The tribes looked up to him as 'their' prince: they expected him to act as a supreme arbiter in their disputes and to be able to supply them with guns and money. Because his positions were difficult of access, at the far end of the main supply line from Saudi Arabia and of the secondary one from South Arabia, there were times when he had difficulty in living up to his tribesmen's expectations. Then he had also to be a wiley prince, not without a sense of humour. Once, when the secret caves where he stored arms and ammunition were bare and his purse was empty, a deputation of sheikhs arrived in the early morning when he was still asleep. Abdullah's servant shook him, crying, 'Sidi Abdullah goum goum!', meaning 'My Lord Abdullah, get up, get up!' But the prince was sufficiently awake to be aware of the situation and refused to be roused. His servant had to go out and announce that the prince appeared to be ill. The sheikhs sat around most of the day. But still the prince did not emerge from his cave, and at last they went away. The next night an ammunition train arrived and the prince's prestige was saved.

He gained a reputation for magnanimity, as on the occasion when two republican agents were caught trying to set an explosive charge in a house he sometimes occupied. He let them off with a lecture, declaring, 'If I worried about being blown up I would never go out at all.' There were stories also about his daring. Once, it was said, he slipped through Egyptian lines in disguise into Sana and walked through the streets of the capital to visit friends, and to return still unrecognized.

With the Egyptians he dealt as often by diplomacy as by force of arms. It was in their interest to avoid ambushes and trouble and in his interest to maintain freedom of movement. Thus he was able to maintain tacit or even formal truces for long periods which enabled him repeatedly to travel eastwards to Beihan and Aden for a rest and to return with a supply caravan that passed within sight of the Egyptian positions at Marib. A regular camel caravan operated between Beihan and the mountains of the Khawlan, sometimes with Egyptian consent and sometimes in spite of them. There were stories that Prince Abdullah also received supplies parachuted by aircraft, flown secretly in the night from bases in South Arabia; but I was never able to confirm them.

He had a wife and children who were held captive by the Egyptians in Cairo, and he often threatened that if any harm came to them the prisoners he had would pay in blood.

Within the area of Abdullah bin Hassan's authority, two teenage princes, Sharaf bin Mutahar and Mohamed bin Mohsin, held lesser commands. Sharaf bin Mutahar, with curly brown hair half-way down to his shoulders, large almond-shaped hazel eyes widely spaced in his rather sallow face, long lashes, hooked nose and classic profile, indeed looked the part of a Himyaritic prince out of Yemen's pre-Islamic past. He had refused education abroad and instead steeped himself in the 'Yellow Books', the manuscripts of the early days of Islam preserved in the great mosques at Sana and Sadah. Prince Abdullah once observed: 'My cousin of the Yellow Book thinks he is an independent power in Nahm, but actually he is too young and lacks the means, so I am looking after him secretly.'

The only commoner in the top echelon of the royalist leaders at this time was Qadi Ahmed al Sayaghi, a man of exceptional capacity, both intellectually and as an administrator and politician, who had served as the Imam Ahmed's viceroy in the town of Ibb. His critical attitude towards the Imam al Badr led him eventually to become the advocate of a 'Third Force' — neither republican nor royalist – and made him suspect among members of both sides. Towards the end of 1963, after a period of inactivity in Lahej, he was killed while travelling near the border line between royalist and republican territory.

V

Roots of a Republic

THE Yemeni Arab Republic was the child of the old Arab nationalist
ideology and the newer Nasserism. Through Nasser the Yemeni
revolutionaries are linked to the Arab nationalist movement, whose
origins go all the way back to Napoleon's invasion of Egypt
in 1798. It was then that Egyptians began to think not just
as Moslems but in the European manner, as nationalists, and
the first Arab nationalist philosopher, Jamal ad-Din al Afghani,
was born. By the time of the Arab revolt against Turkey during
the First World War, nationalism, both as it applied to individual nations and of the pan-Arab variety, was firmly implanted
not only in Egypt but in Syria, Lebanon, Iraq and North
Africa.

The Yemenis, too, fought the Turks and were indeed among the
chief beneficiaries of the Turkish defeat. Their concern was to
liberate their kingdom from centuries of Turkish occupation.
Nasser's association with Yemen resulted from a marvellous con-
currence of national interests. The Imam Ahmed needed Nasser to
back his claims on the British-occupied territory of what the Yemenis
called Southern Yemen; furthermore, sensing that the appeal of
Nasserism would eventually exceed the appeal of his own national
claims as Zeidi Imam, he thought it expedient to come to terms
with the Egyptian leader.

Nasser was interested in Yemen because he had to encourage all
forces opposing the imperialist British. But he – or at least the
anonymous advisers who worked behind the scenes in Cairo – had a
more devious motive, namely oil. There was oil, not in Yemen, but
in the Persian Gulf and Saudi Arabia, and Yemen might serve as
the stepping-stone towards it. Partly for this reason, and partly
also because the idealistic socialist elements among them could not
for long stomach alliance with the most medieval and anachronistic

ruler in the Middle East, the Nasserites soon began to undermine the Imam.

It was, then, the Imam's flirtation with Nasser which let the Arab nationalist virus into his kingdom. As Egyptian military missions and technicians, and later Russians, Czechs, Bulgarians and Chinese communists crowded into Yemen, the spell of the isolation cultivated by his father, the Imam Yahya, was broken beyond repair. For a few years, however, the Imam Ahmed's extraordinary personal toughness, alertness and combativeness kept the flood in check.

For a time Nasser appears to have been willing to wait for the Imam Ahmed to die, anticipating that he would then be able to work through his son, al Badr. But in the course of 1961 he became impatient. It seemed as though the tough old man would never die, and Nasser's political agents determined to force the pace by revolution. At first Nasser had been content to manipulate the nationalist forces in Yemen and South Arabia, much as Stalinist communists have at certain times manipulated what they call bourgeois nationalists with the ultimate objective of taking power for themselves. At this stage he worked through an alliance with Imam Ahmed in Yemen; in South Arabia he favoured the South Arabian League, in whose ranks were gathered a number of disaffected sultans, emirs and sheikhs. But during the period between the attempt on the Imam's life at Hodeidah in March 1961 and the publication in December of the Imam's poem denouncing Nasser's socialism, Nasser moved towards outright revolution. He chose the men who would be his revolutionary instruments in Yemen, and shifted his favour in South Arabia to left-wing political elements such as the trade union congress, headed by Abdullah al Asnag.

The chosen men in Yemen were Mohamed Mahmoud al Zubairi, Mohsin al Aini, Dr Abdurrahman al Baidini and Colonel, later Brigadier, Abdullah al Sallal. Zubairi, who later became a minister of the republican government, was a liberal deeply concerned with finding a basis for reconciliation between republicans and royalists; he was mysteriously assassinated in 1964. Al Aini is a Zeidi from the north of Yemen. He was one of the few who, in the days of the Imam Yahya's rule, managed to get out of the country to study in Cairo and later at the Sorbonne. In 1958 he was a school-teacher in Aden, where he became secretary-general of the teacher's union.

As one of Abdullah al Asnag's followers he took part in political strikes and was deported from Aden in 1960.

Baidani, the son of an Indian mother and a Sunni father, had migrated from Yemen to Cairo, where he married an Egyptian woman. After meeting young Mohamed al Badr, who was on his first visit to Cairo in 1956, Baidani returned to Yemen. Always a smooth talker, he convinced the Imam Ahmed as well as al Badr of his potential usefulness, and was sent to Bonn as a Yemeni minister. In the German capital he continued his studies and acquired the degree of doctor of political economy. He returned to Sana during the brief period while al Badr, during his father's absence in 1961, was in control as premier. He hoped to become the kingdom's economic planner. But soon thereafter, disillusioned no doubt by the longevity of the old Imam Ahmed, he quit his post in Bonn amidst charges that he had embezzled government funds, and moved to Cairo. There he began actively campaigning against the Imam Ahmed, first identifying the Imam with imperialism and then calling for revolution. On radio Cairo's 'Enemy of God' programme he was introduced as 'The Yemeni Revolutionary'. For six months before the *coup d'état* of September 1962 he was in touch with some of the young officers in Sana. Arriving in Sana with the first group of Egyptians who flew in to support the revolution, he looked, acted and talked like a smart young Egyptian university teacher. Few Yemenis understood him.

The most important of the men marked by Cairo, however, was Abdullah Sallal, whose supreme value to the revolutionaries was that he had Mohamed al Badr's confidence and that he was firmly situated in Sana. Born in 1922, the son of a blacksmith[1] in Sana, Abdullah Sallal was orphaned at an early age and had the good fortune to be picked for education in one of the few schools in existence in the capital. The Imam Yahya chose him for further military education, after which, in the late thirties, he was sent to Baghdad for advanced military training. Why this particular young man was so favoured by the old Imam Yahya can only be guessed. Apart from the fact that he was of passable, though not brilliant, intelligence, it may have been because he did not belong to any group likely to become disaffected. He did not belong to the privileged class of the sayeds, nor did he come from any tribe, nor

[1] Probably because blacksmiths, along with barbers, are considered socially inferior in this part of the Arab world, official republican biographies say Sallal was the son of a farmer.

was he identified with any family of merchants or intellectuals.

Returning to Sana in 1939 Sallal began a career as a regular army officer. His experience in Baghdad and subsequent contact with the Iraqi military mission had opened his mind to political ideas and awareness of the oppressive nature of the régime under which he lived, and very soon he was involved in conspiracy and trouble. He began to display an extraordinary capacity not only for getting into but for getting out of trouble. Repeatedly he was thrown into prison, but always he succeeded in being released and in returning to the army. In the late thirties he was in prison for eight months, for subversive activities; in the early forties he spent three years in a Sana prison, on similar charges; in 1948 he was sentenced to death on a charge that he had participated in the conspiracy that brought about the assassination of the Imam Yahya. Reprieved by the Imam Ahmed, he spent seven years in the prisons of the fortress at Hajjah, first in a dungeon called Nafie where he had chains on his legs, later in a prison called Cairo, which was reserved for politicians and where the conditions were more tolerable. His political thinking was undoubtedly stimulated by contact in prison at Hajjah with leading liberals of Yemen, including Mohamed Ahmed Nomaan, Abdurrahman al Iryani and Mohamed Ahmed al Shami, all of whom had been associated with the Free Yemeni movement in Aden and had, like himself, made the mistake of backing the Wazir family against the Imam Yahya in 1948. Among them, Nomaan was the most skilful political operator; he corresponded with the Imam Ahmed, who appears to have respected his intellect and released him in 1951. Al Shami was released in 1953, Iryani in 1954 and Sallal in 1955.

Whether Sallal ever did any really serious studying is open to question. He is a practical man of action and certainly no theoretician or scholar. His supporters say, however, that during the latter part of his imprisonment in Hajjah he was able to acquire some books, including some on the French revolution, as well as a copy of Nasser's *Philosophy of the Revolution.*

It is astonishing yet revealing that Mohamed al Badr should have been instrumental in introducing to high office in the kingdom both Baidani and Sallal. Much as he had persuaded the Imam Ahmed to send Baidani to Bonn as minister, he now persuaded him to release Sallal from prison and to appoint him harbour-master at Hodeidah. The kingdom's principal port proved an admirable place for Sallal to resume his conspiracy, particularly with the Egyptians who in the ensuing years began to infiltrate the country.

The Egyptians handled Sallal with care. They did not attempt to recruit him directly as an agent, for that might have cast a pall upon his relationship with al Badr. Instead, they allowed him to indulge his own vague scheming. The precise role of military leader of the *coup* they allocated to a younger, less valuable man, al Moghny.[1]

Probably Sallal was still in prison at the time of the 1955 plot against Imam Ahmed; probably he was involved in the attempt on the Imam Ahmed's life at Hodeidah in March 1961. The evidence is not clear. The Imam was sufficiently suspicious to dismiss him from his post as harbour-master, but raised no objection when al Badr appointed him chief of his personal guard and got him the post of inspector of the military airport.

Indeed, there seems to have been no limit to the Crown Prince's solicitude for Sallal's career. Through al Badr's interventions, Sallal was for a time put in charge of the military academy at Sana and was returned to his former post as harbour-master in Hodeidah. Immediately after the Imam Ahmed's death, al Badr pushed Sallal into the highest military post in the land, as his Chief of Staff. Undoubtedly al Badr regarded Sallal as a like-minded liberal who, if suitably rewarded, would help him realize his own liberal aspirations. It seems that they were also personally quite intimate. But the confidence he placed in his supposed friend in fact admitted the Nasserites to the most sensitive inner structure of imamic power, and prepared its destruction.

By the late summer of 1962 Cairo radio propaganda was having its effect. Students were rioting; the army's loyalty was questionable. The stage was well set for the *coup* which took place on 26 September.

The republic's first order of business after the *coup* was revenge, or, depending on how one looked at it, purge. The new régime offered the equivalent of £1,500 sterling for every member of the royal family who was killed or captured. At least twenty persons were executed in the first two days, fifty in the first two weeks. Among them were three royal princes, Ismail bin Yahya, an uncle of al Badr, Ali bin Yahya, another uncle, and Hassan bin Ali, a

[1] See Chapter One for a full account of the *coup*.

cousin; also Amhed Abdurrahman al Shami, Minister of Justice, Abdul Rahman Abu Taleb, former ambassador to Washington, Qadi Mohamed Armuli, a mufti and at least two leading tribal sheikhs, including the sheikh of Hamdan whose relatives helped the Imam to escape. On 19 October, eight members of the royal family were sentenced to death *in absentia* by a special military court in Sana. Among six other members of the former régime sentenced *in absentia* was Ahmed al Shami, the Imam's minister in London who became the royalist Foreign Minister and was already playing an important role in resisting the revolution.

The seventy-year-old Qadi Abdullah al Shami, one of Yemen's most distinguished elder statesmen, was the first dignitary of the old régime put on trial before a people's tribunal in Sana. On 27 November he was charged with misuse of office, amassing wealth at the expense of the poor and betraying his country by conniving with the British. Later the tribunal tried and sentenced to death eighty-five-year-old Sayed Ali bin Ahmed Ibrahim, a former army chief of staff who was accused of misuse of office, bribery, neglect, waste of public money and selling on the black market arms imported through official channels. President Sallal commuted the death sentences passed on both these men. But by the beginning of December seventy-five royalists had been executed by firing squads, including the former Foreign Minister Hassan Ibrahim. Others sentenced to death in the first six months of the régime included Hussein ibn Ali Waisy, Minister of Education and Public Order, and Yahya al Ajja, the Imam Ahmed's treasurer. Women and children of al Badr's and the former Imam Ahmed's families, as well as their close relatives, were brought together in a building in Sana, as already described, and several years later exchanged for Egyptian prisoners through the good offices of the International Red Cross.

The first journalistic visitors to Sana, who made the arduous trip by jeep from Aden at the end of October, found President Abdullah Sallal, the new head of state of a republican government, installed with his revolutionary council in a tall central building which until a few weeks before had been the royal guest-house. Brigadier Sallal had taken over a room on one of the higher floors as his personal quarters; there he had an office, with a camp bed in one corner, and worked a large part of every night.

After sunset on 29 October, Brigadier Sallal received the correspondent of the *New York Times*, Jay Walz, in a reception room adjoining the revolutionary council's chambers. The brigadier looked weary. His drawn face was covered by a growth of black stubby beard and he slouched across a settee. He wore a crudely cut uniform of heavy coarse khaki, and a peaked service cap. Mr Walz thought that Sallal might pass as an older brother of Nasser, who was just a year younger and whom he slightly resembled.

Speaking through an interpreter, Sallal said his government was determined to work for the people. 'This is the first time in one thousand years,' he declared, 'that anyone has ever worked for them. We need help and have no established credits; nevertheless we shall do our best to get help from abroad – any and all kinds of help we can use – credits, gifts, technical assistance.' He would be glad if the United States would continue work on the 313-mile highway linking Sana, Taiz and the port of Mocha, which it had undertaken during the Imam's reign and which at the time was one-third complete. 'Most certainly we want the United States to go ahead,' he declared.

Under the rule of the Imams, Sallal continued, oppressive taxes had discouraged people from working; 'but we shall encourage them to work,' he said. Land taxes and other assessments imposed by the Imams and tribal chiefs had been so exorbitant that 'people just gave up' and many fled from the country. Other officials pointed out that Yemen relied heavily on money sent home to relatives by men who emigrated. They estimated that about 500,000 men, women and children out of Yemen's total population of four million had left the country in the previous ten years.

On the floor of the building below President Sallal, Doctor Baidani, his deputy, was busy fashioning a new two-year economic plan. In the days when he was a protégé of the Imam Ahmed, he had aspired in vain to become the kingdom's economic adviser. Now he had his chance. Although he was obviously the spearhead of Egyptian influence in Yemen and his political ideas were radical, Baidani did not reflect Nasser's socialism. He explained that there was no need for land reform such as had been carried out in Egypt, because 'Yemen does not have Egypt's population and land pressures'. He spoke about the need for tax reform, for eliminating burdensome road tolls, and the desirability of re-routing the flow of trade from the port of Hodeidah. He complained that Adeni merchants charged twenty-five per cent commission and twenty-five per cent for transport. 'This survival from the feudal past must be expunged,' he said.

In challenging the royalists and the Saudis, Baidani always managed to be a little more extreme than anyone else. It was he who, soon after the republic had been established, began talking over radio Sana about plans for a republic of the Arabian peninsula. His talk alarmed the Saudis and other governments in Arabia and went too far even for Cairo. He was sharply called to order by Cairo and no more was heard about his plan.

Inevitably, Sallal and Baidani quarrelled. They were an ill-assorted team; the rough-hewn, slow-spoken Zeidi, son of a blacksmith, distrusted the fast-talking intellectual from Cairo. Of the key men whom Cairo backed in the first revolutionary government proclaimed on 27 September 1962, Sallal has proved politically the most durable. A few months after Cairo had complained of his Baathist sympathies, Mohsin al Aini, the first Foreign Minister, was sent off to New York as Yemeni delegate to the United Nations. There he remained until October 1966, when he joined the Anti-Egyptian 'third force' opposition. Mohamed Zubairi, the Education Minister was, as already mentioned, assassinated. Finally, during the third week of January 1963, Baidani himself was relieved of his post and Sallal accused him of attempting to undermine his leadership. There had been a clash of personalities; Cairo had withdrawn Baidani so as to maintain the viability of the government. After some months of mysterious silence Dr Baidani reappeared in Aden, where he claimed to be setting up a new commercial bank and was rumoured to be trying to organize exiled Yemenis of the Shaffei Moslem sect against the government in their homeland. He complained that he had been forced out of the government because he was a Shaffei rather than a member of the dominant Zeidi sect.

The government in Sana responded by depriving Baidani of his nationality. But Cairo kept silent and a few weeks later, at the end of August 1963, he was persuaded to return to Egypt. A reconciliation between him and President Sallal took place at a hospital in Alexandria, where the Yemeni president had gone for treatment of an ulcer. A few years later Dr Baidani was sent by the republican government to Beirut as minister in charge of the legation.

In spite of the political divisions among the Yemeni republicans and the lack of men trained for the tasks of government, the new régime did manage to get some things done. It could draw on 200 Cairo-trained officers in the army and about fifty individuals with university educations. But government operations depended very largely on Egyptian advisers, who were stationed in every ministry and every important office.

During the first year there were a number of reforms. It was announced that 'the executioner's sword is broken' and that there would be no more public beheading, an activity which for generations had been ghoulish entertainment for the people of Sana and Taiz. Often the heads were displayed on sticks at the city gates. When I visited Taiz in October 1964, the old foreign ministry, in front of which executions used to take place, was being used by the Egyptian army as a youth centre, and one of the Egyptian officers in charge showed me a pile of photographs of executions and severed heads, which he had found in a forgotten drawer. The irony of the new announcement, which stated that executions would in future take place privately and by firing squad, was that the republic has been responsible for infinitely more killing than any imamic régime.

President Sallal ordered the confiscation of the former Imam's estates, said to include one-quarter of the best farm land in the kingdom. He directed that it should be converted into state farms.

The new régime also abolished slavery. The impact of this move, however, was not as drastic as might be imagined. Slaves had been almost exclusively household servants in the homes of the well-to-do and were generally well-treated. As in Saudi Arabia, some of them had risen to positions of high responsibility in their masters' service, and were eventually freed. While most were Negroes, some were children, usually girls, sold by poor villagers as household servants.

Other innovations of the first year included educational and municipal reforms. The number of children in schools was doubled, from one in twenty to about one in ten of those of school age in the republican areas. (Or so the government claimed. I suspect that the real proportion attending school was somewhat smaller.) The paving of streets in Sana, Taiz and other towns was begun. Gravel and tar was spread on streets which for centuries had been rutted dust-traps in summer and bogs of mud in winter. There was even talk of street lights. In place of the two bi-weeklies published in the Imam's day, the country now had a daily newspaper printed in Taiz and flown to the capital. Sana radio stepped up its broadcasts from two and a half hours daily to fourteen hours.

On 13 April, President Sallal proclaimed an interim constitution modelled on that of the United Arab Republic. Under the constitution he became head of state, Commander-in-Chief of the armed forces and chairman of a presidential council. The presidential council was to be responsible for the state's political, economic, social and administrative policies, and an executive council was appointed to put these policies into effect. The state's official religion was declared to be Islam, all laws to be in conformity with Islamic tenets. The constitution provided for equality of privileges and opportunities, fair trial and the sanctity of the home. Civil liberties were guaranteed, and the independence of the judiciary was proclaimed. Free enterprise and private property were protected but monopoly outlawed. Finally, conscription was introduced.

The new régime established a national bank and introduced a silver coin in place of the silver thaler, showing the face of Maria Theresa of Austria, which had circulated in Yemen for 150 years. Always dated 1780, the thaler's silver content is five parts in six and its worth about one United States dollar. Although the coin, which originated in Austria, was not struck for the Arabs, this was the emblem the tribesmen had grown accustomed to; they did not take kindly to the replacement of these big silver cartwheels by a coin which, though equally large, had lost not only the empress but some of its weight as well. The thaler continues in circulation today in the royalist areas, and covertly in the republic. In addition, gold sovereigns introduced from Saudi Arabia, Saudi Arabian paper rials, pounds sterling, the East African pounds used in Aden, and American dollars all circulate in the country. The more the Yemeni tribesmen question the value of coins and paper money produced by the Egyptians, the more avidly sought are these foreign currencies. When I arrived in Sana from Cairo in October 1964, more than two years after the revolution, I handed the porter who carried my bags to my room a handful of Egyptian coins. Opening my door a few minutes later, I found that he had contemptuously hurled them all on the floor.

One of the problems that worried the republican régime in its early days was diplomatic recognition. Apart from the United

States, which did recognize the republic on 19 December 1962, the only two western countries to take this step were the German Federal Republic and Italy. But Britain did not follow the American example and on 13 February the republican government asked the British legation to close its offices within seven days. The American legation took over representation of British interests.

In the first days of the republic thousands of the Yemenis established in Aden, Saudi Arabia and many other places swarmed back to the homeland. It is estimated that there were 120,000 in Aden, 100,000 in Saudi Arabia (including Hadhramis, who, once they are abroad, seem indistinguishable from other Yemenis) and about a million others scattered around the world. So great was the rush of returning Yemenis that radio Sana during the month after the revolution repeatedly broadcast appeals to Yemenis not to return prematurely. 'When new industries have been established,' the broadcast said, 'we will call you.' Two brothers named Rashid and Shaber Abdulhak and their uncle Abdul Jabar, who flew to Sana from Nairobi, succeeded in getting a lease on the Imam al Badr's old palace and establishing there the Liberty Hotel. They were assisted in their enterprise by the fact that the United Nations observer teams, who arrived in Sana in the summer of 1963, took over the greater part of the hotel and made the most necessary improvements in the plumbing. But no one could do much to alleviate the basic discomfort of this damaged pile of masonry from which looters had removed every scrap of imamic furnishing – the dank darkness of the hallways, the low portals, the steep, narrow staircases with their enormously high steps.

Very reasonably, but a little prematurely, the founders of the Liberty Hotel were in the summer of 1963 anticipating the arrival of tourists, who would doubtless be more interested in the past than the present and future of Yemen. They would enjoy the rich panoply of native costumes still to be seen every day on every street of Yemen, the saffron and magenta turbans, the violet, purple, green, blue and yellow of the men's shirts and jackets, the women's dresses and the clothes of the children, the colours of all of them being decorated with gold and silver *lamé*. Outside the towns the roads built by the Chinese, being built by the Americans and being planned by the Russians would enable the tourists, it was thought, to appreciate the marvellous scenery and a still-to-be-discovered archaeological wonderland. Nowhere else in the Middle East could a tourist find lush valleys, some of them subtropical, populated by herds of chattering baboons, or see such dramatically soaring mountains, lined with terraces piled so steeply one upon another, as many as five hundred on a single slope, that they had to be narrower than the walls supporting them. At Marib could be seen the ruins of the capital of the Queen of Sheba's capital, the temple of the moon god and the great dam of Marib, 2,700 years old; further north, in the region of the Jawf, were the almost unexplored remains of the Minaean kingdom, where cliff-sides outside the former capital had been left covered with crude paintings and still undeciphered inscriptions.

At the military academy outside Sana I found Egyptian soldiers, all seemingly twice as large as the Yemenis, engaged in training the new Yemeni army. In fact, they were just continuing what had been begun under the Imam. The only changes I could observe were that cadets who formerly had to sleep on the floor now had camp beds. The school directors explained with some pride that they received far more applicants from all parts of Yemen than they could possibly accommodate. A chart on the commanding officer's wall showed the number of applicants from each district.

At all times the Egyptians were at once the republic's mainstay and its greatest handicap. The republic needed Egyptian help and protection, but the condescension of Egyptian teachers, experts and officials infuriated the quick, intelligent Yemenis; the Egyptian soldiers, though well-behaved and docile, were increasingly resented. In Sana the Egyptians entirely dominated the scene; on the out-skirts stood acres and acres of tents surrounded by barbed wire; in the streets their fleshy bodies, clad in yellow-brown uniforms, forever bent over counters, broad buttocks facing the streets, endlessly choosing rolls of cloth to send home to their wives, examining transistor radios, and fingering a thousand things that might be bought with the extra pound in Egyptian money they received as a bonus for serving in Yemen. If a soldier chose to save his money, in fact, by the time he got home he might have enough to buy a small farm, or perhaps a taxi cab.

Russians, too, were prominent in the street scene of the capital, for they had a part in military training, in demonstrating Russian-built weapons; they were building a new military airfield at Rawdah, north of Sana, and they were developing by far the largest of all foreign aid programmes in Yemen. The greatest Russian centre, however, was Hodeidah, the deep-water port they had already constructed during the reign of Imam Ahmed. Their presence soon stimulated a boom in the construction of offices and blocks of flats. A young Yemeni from Hodeidah being interviewed for an American scholarship was once asked whether he could be trusted to return to Yemen at the end of his studies. '*Da*,' he replied.

In Sana, during the first year after the revolution, whole streets of characterless, modern concrete and plaster blocks of flats went up, an architectural blight on the pure, classic lines of the old city. But most of the town remained unchanged, especially the stately four-, five-, six- and more storeyed structures, built of stone to the second or third floor, then mud brick above, looking down from equally partitioned windows: the lower halves of each window had shutters, while the upper part was closed decoratively, with alabaster foil in older homes, or elaborately coloured glass in newer ones. The divisions of the windows, each accentuated by a frame of whitewash, made every storey seem like two, so that the whole structure more than ever resembled a skyscraper.

In the soft and gracious light behind the windows life went on unchanged for most people. Revolutions in politics and in ways of living are, after all, matters for a tiny minority of the young and enterprising. To the rest change comes slowly.

A year after the revolution I went to a *qat* party in one of these old houses. *Qat* parties are nothing special in Yemen. They are not exceptional occasions, but take place every day, beginning very soon after noon, so that for most people the working day is even shorter than in other Arab countries, where work goes on until one or two o'clock, followed by lunch and afternoon siesta. For many Yemenis the *qat* leaf is a substitute for food; 'a man can live without food, but not one day without *qat*,' runs an old Yemeni proverb. This was the time of day when, in Imam Yahya's day, Crown Prince Ahmed used to emerge from his palace at the head of a party of courtiers and head for Jabal Nuqum, the mountain overlooking Sana, a servant running along at his side skilfully holding an umbrella over his head as he worked up his thirst for the afternoon *qat*. It is still fashionable, today, to go for a brisk walk so that *qat* may be better appreciated.

Having left our shoes at the door of the house, we sat cross-legged on the floor, propped on cushions and against the wall. The sprigs of *qat* branches, ranging from a few inches to a foot or so in length, were thrown upon the floor and the guests helped themselves, stripping off leaves, rolling them up into wads and chewing them. When the jaws become tired, the chewer holds the great wad of leaves in his cheek as though suffering from one-sided mumps. Tall thermoses of water stood conveniently to hand and the *qat*-chewers, their thirst stimulated by the bitter taste of the leaves, helped themselves to long draughts from the thermos, which they then passed on to their neighbour. A tall narghile, the traditional water pipe of the East, also stood on the floor, its long flexible hose and mouthpiece extended invitingly to the guests, who took it in turn, breathing long cool draughts of smoke from tobacco burned over a charcoal brazier and filtered through water to the smoker. As the hours went by the conversation became livelier. Eyes glistened and good humour was general, for the *qat* leaf is mildly narcotic. Doctors have told me that the sense of well-being, of intelligence and understanding, indeed of expanded consciousness, which the leaf imparts is accompanied by loss of appetite and sexual desire. In the long run its effects are debilitating. But this fact did not seem to worry the republicans any more than it did the royalists; they had no plans to limit the acreage devoted to *qat* in the republic, even though it was generally recognized that cultivation of the *qat* bushes was progressively undermining the cultivation of coffee trees. *Qat*, which could be sold at high prices at home or exported to Aden, was less trouble to grow and more profitable than coffee, it seemed.

Qat-chewing went on every day in the republic, as though Yemen would never change. Young and old, rich and poor, republicans and royalists seemed equally addicted. But I remember one young man whom I met in Sana about a year after the revolution who was disgusted by this old habit. He had been educated in France and the United States, and to him the chewing of *qat* symbolized the psychological fetters with which the Yemeni people are bound to their old ways. Vibrantly patriotic, he believed ardently in the idea of a republic. He would not consider return to imamic rule as a possible solution to his country's problems. But he could not, on the other hand, abide the Egyptians who were the republic's main bulwark. He worked in a government office under the supervision of an Egyptian whom he despised; he considered himself much more intelligent than his boss.

This young man was like a great many others in Yemen – a

revolutionary in revolt not only against the past but against the present of his country. The real problem was to find a compromise.

The Egyptian way of making friends and influencing people was illustrated to me in Sadah, to which I was flown by the Egyptian air force in October 1964, one of the few American correspondents ever to visit this remote and romantic place. I travelled with the American consul in Sana, Pat Quinlan, and an American freelance photographer named William Carter. Sadah was the town where the Zeidi religious movement in Yemen started. Here the first Imams, fugitives from Persia, began to preach in about 740; for centuries it was the Zeidi capital of Yemen. A large, long-disused slag heap on the outskirts of the town bore witness to centuries during which iron ore was mined here and transformed into metal, thence into swords that were famous throughout the Arab world. Sadah is architecturally as beautiful as Sana, but in a simpler, more primitive way. Filled with mosques and haunted by memories, the town is to all Zeidis a sacred place.

At the edge of Sadah, Brigadier Ali al Sheikh of the Egyptian army had established his headquarters in a farmhouse compound surrounded by a high mud wall. A friendly, warm-hearted man, the brigadier welcomed the opportunity to tell his American visitors about the wonderful things he was doing for the Yemenis, and how well he got along with them. Although I knew that Egyptian tanks were in operation at that time south of Haradh to the west, the brigadier maintained that in his sector there was no fighting at all. He told us he was able to devote more than half his time to civilian activities. These included a field hospital, thirty per cent of whose beds were allocated to civilians, a school where Egyptian soldiers were teaching a hundred boys and fifty girls, and the distribution of tractors, water-pumps and seeds among the farmers of the region. All this was additional to the Egyptian government's help in providing experts and supplies to Yemeni government departments.

In the school which the Egyptians had improvised in an old army barracks we came upon a rare sight – little Yemeni girls, loaded with necklaces and bracelets, experiencing their first lessons, their brown eyes large with curiosity and wonder. In the hospital many of the Yemenis were experiencing twentieth-century medical care for the first time. A hut near the hospital had been allocated to the mayor of the town of Harf and swarmed with his relatives and servants. Given confidence, kindness and care, a doctor told me, the Yemenis quickly overcame their fears and suspicions.

As we walked through the streets of Sadah we saw that we were in a ghost town. The narrow cobbled streets were flanked by houses five or six storeys high, stone on the lower levels, mud farther up, with multi-coloured glass above the windows and white-wash round window-frames and doors. They differed from those of Sana only in their more modest proportions and in that, it seemed, they tapered noticeably towards the top. No modern cement and plaster monsters were there to mar the town's architectural purity, and unlike Sana, whose wall has been torn down in places, Sadah's beautiful turreted wall stood proudly intact. Buildings damaged during the fighting when the Egyptians arrived in October 1962 were not, on the other hand, repaired for two years afterwards. The poor shops of Sadah's bazaar displayed hardly any goods, for commerce was almost at a standstill. In time of peace this had been a cross-roads for trade with Saudi Arabia to the north; now the border was shut from one side, and from the other hardly any vehicles managed to make the four-day road journey through royalist-dominated territory northwards from Sana.

Two-thirds or more of Sadah's 15,000 inhabitants had fled in 1962 to escape first Egyptian bombs and then Egyptian occupation. Most of them took refuge in Najran, on the Saudi Arabian side of the border, where the old *élite* of sheikhs and ulema could still be safe. Sadah retained the very old, the very poor, the men without pride; and, it seemed, a vast number of urchins, who scrambled about the ruins and among the borrow-pits between the houses where clay had been removed to make bricks.

As darkness fell hardly any lights went on in the windows. Perhaps because he noticed my reaction to the eerie scene, the brigadier remarked cheerfully that he was planning to bring in a generator with which to begin lighting the streets at night. He said that he generally kept Egyptian soldiers out of the town to avoid any possible friction – not that there was much to attract soldiers in Sadah.

Back at the compound a group of tribal leaders and farmers were waiting outside the gate. They had come to petition the topmost authority of the region for help with their various problems. 'First of all,' said the brigadier, 'they want safety. Then they want pumps, tractors, seeds and money.' He said he had given away three pumps and six tractors. After that he found himself settling disputes about the distribution of water, the use of the tractors, and a thousand other things.

I felt he was enjoying his role as dispenser of largesse in a primitive community. Dealing with the supplicants at his gate with a mixture of condescension and affection, he may have imagined himself in the role the British played for so many years in his own home in Egypt. The slightly contemptuous stories he told about the Yemenis were rather like the talk one used to hear in a British officers' mess in the Middle East in the days before the Suez war of 1956. Recalling the operations of the previous August, he observed that the Yemenis 'think that tanks are very horrible; they think tanks are something from Shattan (the devil). And so we make use of this opinion'. Because they lacked training in modern warfare, the brigadier explained, the Yemenis 'have to fight the primitive way – from behind the rocks – like thieves'. He had noted, however, that a certain element of organization had appeared in royalist operations in the last six months, and he found it implausible that the Yemenis could have done this for themselves. They must have obtained foreign experts.

The brigadier's contempt was reflected in a fund of stories about the royalists. He said that the former Imam Ahmed, father of al Badr, used to carry on his belt the keys to the royal stores of kerosene, coffee and ammunition. These were dispensed only at his express desire. As fast as his son went out and bought aeroplanes, guns and tanks, the Imam had them taken apart and distributed in secret, scattered hiding-places. All this, according to the brigadier, was because he not only feared these modern toys but 'feared his own people'. The Egyptian army was still finding 'pieces of weapons stored in caves, here and there, lacking bolts or sights, the locations of which only the Imam knew'.

Al Badr had fortunately 'fled away' since the fighting in August, the brigadier told me, claiming (quite incorrectly) that the Imam had gone to Jizan and that the tribesmen in the Razih mountains were preventing his return. According to the brigadier, most of his guards and people abandoned him; only ten per cent, in fact, remained. Prince Hassan was in the same dire straits in the mountains near Najran; 'even his princes, his own boys, have left him,' the brigadier said. He doubted that either the Imam or Prince

Hassan would ever be able to mount any more operations of consequence. 'I am assured that the borders are completely blocked and loyal tribesmen on guard on all the passes.' Asked whether there were Egyptians stationed in these places he observed that 'the terrain is very difficult for us, especially at these altitudes'. But, he added, the Egyptian army included commando units, known as *saaker*, the first of whom had trained with American Rangers in 1954. These men, selected for high intelligence and physical fitness, 'could go two days with only a cup of water', he said, 'and could be relied upon to carry out special jobs in any environment'.

The brigadier also had a collection of implausible stories about the Imam al Badr. He said that the Imam had put a story among the tribesmen that on certain days of the year his body became luminous, although actually he had covered it with phosphorescent paint. In another minor fraud, he said, the Imam had maintained that he was protected by God from any harm that could be inflicted by bullets. To prove it, so the story went, he had a guard fire at him with blanks. The brigadier said that when he heard these stories he ordered a demonstration before a gathering of tribesmen. 'We covered a soldier with phosphorescent paint and demonstrated how we could shoot at him with blanks.'

The afternoon after our walk through the town, as we were resting in our quarters in the Egyptian compound late in the afternoon, we heard a burst of shooting outside. It was not a royalist raid but tribesmen from the surrounding villages, the Sahar tribe, who had arrived with gifts for the visiting Americans. Shooting in the air was their way of announcing this joyous event. Three dignified sheikhs asked and were given admission, bringing with them five sheep and a cow. Our consul, Mr Quinlan, rose to the occasion and, in eloquent Arabic , which apparently delighted the sheikhs, persuaded them to take back the cow. He proposed that they should regard the cow as a symbol of the American aid which he hoped they would soon receive. He had in fact broached to the Egyptian commander and the local republican Yemeni authorities his desire to begin the distribution of American wheat in Sadah. That night we all dined on mutton, with the Egyptian brigadier and his officers. The rest of the sheep were left with the Egyptian troops – bar one, which we took back to Sana with us, locked in the W.C. of the Egyptian military plane. (When last seen, it was nibbling grass in the courtyard of the United States embassy, under the protective eye of the consul's wife.)

The gift of five sheep and one cow did not surprise the brigadier at all. He observed that when Field Marshal Amer came to Sadah he got twenty sheep and eight cows. In return, he said, the field marshal would distribute packets of cotton and woollen clothing, each packet containing clothes for five persons, and radios. A cow he estimated to be worth the equivalent of $80 or $90, and a sheep $12 or $15.

In the evening, during the intervals between failures of the Egyptian army's electric generator, we were presented with a group of seven young defectors from the royalist army who, the brigadier asserted, were typical cases. They said they had left the republic and volunteered for service with the Imam simply in order to get rifles and then return. While they were in northern Yemen, near the Saudi frontier, they had taken the opportunity to go on a pilgrimage to Mecca; returning then to the headquarters of Prince Hassan, the Prime Minister, they had been given sub-machine-guns. These they were now anxious to exchange for what they called 'German rifles', this being their description of the old-fashioned German Mausers to which they were accustomed and which they prized for their long-range accuracy. They said, to the brigadier's evident satisfaction, that at Prince Hassan's headquarters they had seen French, English and American technicians. The brigadier said he would give them the rifles they wanted and send them off to their villages. The leader of this group was from the district of Dhamar, a town south of Sana, noted as a royalist stronghold; another, somewhat surprisingly, was a Shaffei from south Yemen.

The next morning Brigadier Ali Sheikh took us to visit the farm of Faid Magali, a farm which had prospered, apparently, thanks to Egyptian equipment and advice. The farmer invited us into his house to eat. The brigadier, who led the way, observed brusquely that he would not take off his shoes when he went into the Yemeni's house and we should likewise refrain from doing so; 'because,' he said simply, 'I have taught them not to take off shoes.' In he clumped fully shod, and we rather shamefacedly followed.

Slightly shocked by this lesson in modernity I wondered whether this brigadier born in the Nile delta, who could speak to the Yemenis in their own language, was really any closer to the Yemenis than we Europeans, and whether he was really succeeding in his 'hearts and minds' campaign. Egyptian modernity – their schools, hospitals, and advice – was undoubtedly reaching the Yemenis' minds. But I had my doubts about the effect on their hearts.

PART
TWO

••

Modern War,
Ancient Ruins

VI

The Incense Trail

WHEN I try to understand the present struggle for Yemen the romance of the country's history looms large in my mind. The Yemenis behave as they do because their geology, their climate and their ethnology have made them unique in the Middle East. Modern Yemen is the projection of an incredible past.

Millions of years ago, when the earth's crust was still forming, the African continent and the Arabian peninsula were one. Then, in a series of gigantic eruptions, the crust split to form a great rift extending from what are now the Taurus mountains of Turkey, southwards through the Sea of Galilee, the Jordan valley, the Dead Sea and the Wadi Araba to the Gulf of Aqaba and the Red Sea, and thence down to the straits of Bab al Mandab. Arabia was separated forever from Africa. At the same time as the rift valley sank, the corner of Arabia that was to become Yemen was forced up on its eastern side, so that the geological strata stood exposed like the layers of a cake. That is why today the eastern slopes of Yemen plunge precipitously down from craggy peaks to the eastern desert, while the western slopes towards the sea are more gradual.

The original link between Africa and Arabia survives in geological formations on both sides of the Red Sea, and in related flora, fauna and climatic conditions. For many centuries lions and giraffes similar to those in Africa roamed in Yemen and much of the rest of the Arabian peninsula; still today baboons abound in the well-watered jungle growth of Yemen's southern-most mountains. In this south-western corner of the Arabian peninsula, closest to Africa and along the Arabian coast as far as Dhofar, the climate retained its East African pattern: monsoon rains in spring and autumn, and a splattering of African equatorial summer rains. Gradually, over many centuries, the heavy rains which once nourished jungle growth in Yemen and South Arabia diminished.

Then, much much later, no one is quite sure when, people arrived. They came probably from southern Asia, down into the Arabian peninsula, across the Red Sea into East Africa, and across the northern part of Africa as far as the Atlantic. While little is known for sure about these early inhabitants some ethnologists believe they were the ancestors of some of the Berbers of North Africa, and of the Minaeans, Sabaeans and other peoples who formed the five pre-Islamic kingdoms of Yemen. Carleton S. Coon, the American ethnologist, calls these people Hamites. He classifies them as belonging to a Mediterranean race, with narrow, low-crowned heads, narrow faces and light complexions of a kind which still predominates in the towns of Yemen's highlands. Other authorities have noted fuzzy hair and almost beardless faces, frequently seen especially in the eastern Hadhramaut and the Qara mountains of Dhofar, as Hamitic characteristics.

A thousand years before Christ, a Semitic intrusion began from the north. The Semites crowded aside or mingled with the original people, sometimes displacing, but more often enriching, the old culture. They included two dominant types: big, broad-shouldered men with wavy hair of a kind still seen in the Yemeni countryside; and tall, long-headed, long-faced, sometimes Nordic-looking people, of a type now mainly found among the sheikhs. With these came also Jews, accompanying the caravans and ships of King Solomon and Hiram of Tyre.[1] The hot, malarial plain between the Red Sea coast and the mountains was settled partly by negroid people who had crossed the Red Sea in fishing boats. Their clothing, or lack of it, conical hats and circular straw huts were and are indistinguishable from those of African tribes on the other side of the water.

Very early in the development of these people, perhaps even before the arrival of the Hamites, trade had begun to supplement agriculture and to hasten the growth of civilization, for the people inhabited the area between the mountains and the desert where communications are easiest. The coast was malarial and hot and the mountains difficult of access but at the edge of a sea, and the people could still enjoy the fresh water and vegetation of the mountains. At first, no doubt, the inhabitants were tempted to raid passing caravans; these were composed in earliest times of trains of donkeys, until, about a thousand years before Christ,

[1] See the account of Jewish history in Chapter Seven.

camels were domesticated, thereby vastly expanding the trading horizon, for they could carry a great load over long waterless stretches of desert. But as time went on some inhabitants found it more profitable to create safe havens for the traders, with food and water, to protect them, and in return to receive taxes in the form of tolls. It was in this way that the Incense Trail developed, and along the trail towns and kingdoms.

When and how the first kingdoms were formed is uncertain, for the work of archaeologists in this part of the world has only just begun. Some of them believe that the earliest kingdom was called Main. Evidence has been found that the Minaeans lived there between 950 and 650 B.C., dominating a fork in the Incense Trail. It is possible that the Minaeans lived there for thousands of years, though of this no archaeological evidence has yet been found. Wendell Phillips, the American archaeologist, believes that the Sabaean kingdom, whose capital at Marib[1] he excavated in 1951, may be the oldest of all, and may have continued throughout the period during which other kingdoms rose and fell around it. Phillips found evidence of continuous habitation from the eighth century B.C. until well after the destruction of the great dam of Marib around A.D. 600. But this kingdom seems to have moved its capital from the region of Sirwah to Marib and may therefore be much older.

The kingdom of Qataban, with its capital at Timna in Wadi Beihan, now the northern fringe of the South Arabian Federation, was one of the places excavated by Wendell Phillips, and where he found traces of habitation dating back to 1000 B.C. Somewhat later a fourth South Arabian kingdom seems to have been centred at Shabwa, in the Hadhramaut, in the eastern part of what has been the British-protected area of South Arabia. But this kingdom, inhabited by a tribe known as the Atramitae, may have been part of the kingdom of the Sabaeans. The latest of the kingdoms was the Himyaritic, which, according to Harold Ingrams, the great British authority on South Arabia, in his book *Arabia and the Isles*, had a capital at Maipha, in a wadi by that name, where its ruins can still be seen in the modern Arab state of Qaiti. Ingrams says that the kingdom had its port at Cana, near the modern village of Bir Ali, and that this was one of the gateways of the Incense Trail. Other authorities, however, mention a Himyaritic capital at Zofar

[1] See the account of Marib in Chapter Ten.

in the hill country of Yemen, which may be the place to which the Himyarites moved after they had conquered the Sabaeans and after the trade in incense along the desert caravan trail had begun to collapse.

The known history of the pre-Islamic kingdoms lasted for a thousand years before the time of Christ, and for about six hundred years afterwards. But for several thousand years before that, while the Incense Trail was in formation, the economic and cultural foundations of the kingdoms were developing. It was at this time that the South Arabians were developing their terraced agriculture and irrigation system, which astonishes the world to this day. Intricately and painstakingly pieced together by generations upon generations of labour, following the contours around and around the mountains, the rock-walled terraces are an aesthetic as well as an economic marvel. From springs high on the mountain-side stone watercourses carry water for many miles, while dams, the most extraordinary of which was the great dam of Marib, ensure that the seasonal floods are not entirely wasted.

In these pre-Islamic times the inhabitants of the future Yemen and South Arabia developed their peculiar music and architecture, which suggest a link with the Berbers of North Africa and a common Hamitic origin. Their music, quite different from the Arabic, has been preserved in traditional soldier songs. A German writer [1] Hans Helfritz brought back more than a hundred recordings of South Arabian music from his travels in the 1930s. He observed that Yemeni soldiers' songs differed radically from the usual Arabian music and bedouin songs. In particular he mentioned the wide range of melody exemplified in the bedouin songs of the Bani Ismail and Bani Matar, in the 'Samel', the Yemeni national anthem, and in the genuine soldier songs heard in the regions of Sana and the Jabal Harraz, whose population provides a great part of the Imam's army. He noted a great similarity between the harmony of the South Arabian songs and the songs of the Berbers of the Kabil in North Africa. Some of the melodies, he said, were absolutely identical and also bore marked similarity with some Mongolian music.

Hans Helfritz also observed that buildings like those in South Arabia also exist in centres of Berber civilization. South Arabian architecture, implying extraordinary engineering ability, was chiefly

[1] *The Yemen – A Secret Journey*, George Allen & Unwin Ltd, London, 1958.

expressed in tall buildings, which could serve as forts in a time when enemy raids were to be expected. Animals were housed on the lower floors, fodder was stored on the floors above them, and the people lived on the top floors. The same basic style may be seen in the villages, and in more sophisticated forms in the towns. In the villages the windows are mere slits in the sides of thick mud walls, while in the cities, where at least the lower floors were likely to be built of stone, the windows are larger and often surmounted by intricately arranged coloured glass. Window frames are white-washed in a fashion that makes the windows appear much larger to the casual observer.

The inhabitants of the early kingdoms borrowed an alphabet from the Canaanites and adapted it to their own needs. For their South Arabian tongue they developed an elegant rectilinear alphabet of twenty-nine letters, which is linked through the Sinaitic to the cursive Egyptian and Phoenician. The temple of the moon god at Marib was built in a style derived from the Hamitic past, in circular patterns; this style was abandoned in about 1000 B.C., when the Semitic influence from the north imposed a new rectangular, geometric style.

Economic foundations for this culture were laid even before the arrival of the Semites by the Incense Trail. Over the trail a multitude of products was transported from points as far distant as China and Western Europe. There were silks, ointments and dyes from China; pepper and cinnamon, fabrics and swords from India; spices from south-east Asia; pearls from the Persian Gulf; and cosmetics, frankincense and myrrh from Arabia. Ivory, ostrich feathers, monkeys, panther skins and Negro slaves from East Africa were in demand in both East and West. In payment, the western world of those days could offer few things desired in the East, except some copperware and leather goods of a manufacture superior to that available in the Orient. But for the most part the West paid for these luxuries in gold, which then, as now, was in great demand in the Orient.

Of all the things that were traded, the most valuable was incense. The idea of making sacrifices to gods must be as old as religion itself, and somewhere near the beginning of religious thinking someone must have discovered that resin from the frankincense tree could be burned with the sacrifices; the thought took hold that incense could carry to heaven both sacrifice and prayer.

Frankincense, whose technical description is *boswellia carterii*, is a straggly shrub or tree which grows wild to a height of eight or nine feet. Its greyish-white branches, bearing tiny leaves, extend from a thin trunk. During the months of March, April and May, before the summer monsoons, the trees may be tapped to give off a fragrant gum-resin, in the form of a milky liquid which dries in pearly droplets. In antiquity frankincense probably grew only in Dhofar, in the arid hills some four days' journey from the coast, and in the eastern half of northern Somaliland. But in later years it appears to have spread to other parts of South Arabia, particularly to the hill country inland from Shabwa.

Myrrh, often mentioned along with frankincense, is obtained from a tree found in most of the hills to the east of Yemen. It sometimes grows as high as fifteen feet with a trunk as much as a foot in diameter. The sap of the tree is red in colour and tastes bitter. While frankincense is mainly desired for its aroma, myrrh is used in embalming and the making of perfumes, and as a pain-killer.

The origin of the use of frankincense and myrrh is lost in the mists of pre-history. We know, however, that long before the birth of Christ the Egyptians sought to break the South Arabians' caravan monopoly by use of the sea route to the land of Punt or Ophir in East Africa. They built a canal from the Nile to the Red Sea near the modern town of Suez. At Leuchos Limen they launched ships to sail upon the Red Sea. Pharaoh Sesostris III of the twelfth dynasty (1878–1842 B.C.) used this canal and port for expeditions to Punt. So did Queen Hatshephet of Egypt, who in 1500 B.C. sent five vessels to bring back myrrh trees for the temple terraces. Balls of incense were found in the tomb of King Tutankhamen. The ancient Israelites kept a store-house for incense in the temple and the Song of Solomon mentions 'the hill of frankincense'; in Matthew ii. 2, we read that the Wise Men brought to the infant Jesus gifts of 'gold, frankincense and myrrh'. And the analgesic given Jesus on the cross may have been a mixture of wine and myrrh. In Rome, the use of frankincense developed in domestic life as well as in religious ceremonials and on state occasions. It was burned to mark weddings, births and funerals. Among the Romans, as among later peoples, the incense doubtless served to disguise the smells that, before the invention of refrigeration, were an inevitable part of daily life. When the second wife of the Roman Emperor Nero died, in A.D. 66, he mourned her by burning an amount of frankincense greater than a whole year's imports from Arabia.

Such Roman writers as Ptolemy and Pliny speak of mountains where the incense was grown, but they did not know exactly where the frankincense and myrrh came from; the South Arabians, custodians of this trade, deliberately kept its secret. Secrecy was facilitated by the fact that cultivation of frankincense was a privilege according to Pliny, reserved to three thousand families of one Sabaean tribe. They guarded their privilege as some similar tribes in South Arabia in modern times guard the cultivation of betel and areca nuts. At the present time frankincense is produced in Dhofar by the Beit Khathir tribe, within whose boundaries each family has its own marked incense trees. They store it in caves until it is carried to the coast during the winter. This is said to be the highest quality incense. Pliny described the incense traffic as follows:

'The incense, after being collected, is carried on camels' backs to Sabota [Shabwa], of which place a single gate is left open for its admission. To deviate from the high road while carrying it, the laws have made a capital offence. At this place the priests take, by measure and not by weight, a tenth part in honour of their god, whom they call Sabia; indeed it is not allowable to dispose of it before this has been done; out of this tenth the public expenses are defrayed for the divinity generously entertains all those strangers who have made a certain number of days' journey in coming thither. The incense can only be exported through the country of the Gebanitae and for this reason it is that a certain tax is paid to their king as well. . . . The whole trade is an immense machine, delicately adjusted. . . . There are certain portions also of frankincense which are given to the priests and king's secretaries, and in addition to these the keepers of it, as well as the soldiers who guard it, the gatekeepers and various other employees, have their share as well. And then, besides, all along the route there is at one place water to pay for, at another fodder, lodging of the stations, and various taxes and imposts besides; the consequence of which is that the expense for each camel before it arrives at the shore of our sea [the Mediterranean] is 688 denarii.'

While it is true that the Sabaeans and others tried to keep the caravan traffic in controlled routes there were in fact several shifting

incense trails and feeder routes. From Dhofar some of the incense
went to ports on the bay of Sachalites, in particular Sumhuram
(the port of the province now known as Dhofar), where sea routes
from the Orient converged. From Sumhuram the ships followed
the coast westwards to the port of Cana, near the modern Bir Ali,

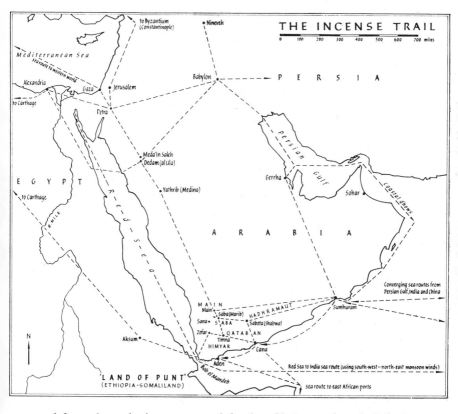

and from there the incense went inland to Shabwa, where it linked
up with the overland route from Dhofar. From Shabwa the caravans
moved between the desert sands and the hills westwards to Timna,
Marib, Main, Yathrib (the modern Medina), Dedam (the modern
al Ula), Meda'in Saleh, Petra, and on to the Mediterranean ports,
particularly Gaza.

From the Hadhramaut another route headed straight across the
great Rub al Khali desert, the 'Empty Quarter', a forty-five-day
camel journey to Gerrha on the Persian Gulf. From Gerrha the

YEMEN: THE UNKNOWN WAR

route led to Mesopotamia and thence to Palestine, where it linked
up with the classic Incense Trail between Marib and Jerusalem.
At Main, near the modern Najran, the trail forked, one branch
going due north towards the Mediterranean ports, the other north-
east to Mesopotamia. Yet another branch, which linked Mesopotamia and Egypt, went roughly from east to west, making a cross-
roads at Meda'in Saleh. A further route linked Arabia with Egypt
and North Africa. The caravans unloaded at ports in the vicinity
of the straits of Bab al Mandab, into ships which moved across the
Red Sea to such centres as Aksum. From the Red Sea coast new
caravans carried the precious goods on to Egypt, and across the
western desert to Carthage, which, like Gaza in the eastern Mediterranean, is a major maritime distribution point.

An important part of the old trail was paralleled in more recent
times by the Pilgrim Railway, built by the Ottoman government of
Turkey, much of which was demolished by Lawrence of Arabia
during the First World War. In the last few years the Saudi and
Jordanian governments have begun to rebuild the old railway and
the Saudis have constructed a good asphalt road all the way
from Jeddah through Medina and Tobouk to the Jordanian
border.

The American ambassador in Saudi Arabia, Parker T. Hart,
who travelled along part of this route in 1964, described it in an
account published in a Saudi Arabian newspaper. As he approached
Meda'in Saleh, the ambassador said, the route 'cuts across vast
and bottomless sumps and through the great basalt lava flow known
as the Harrat al Khaybar, a waterless, treeless, shrubless waste
elevated above the surrounding terrain like a Scottish moorland,
but infinitely more forbidding and totally without life'. The trail
passed near the mosquito-infested date gardens of Harrat, known
in Arabic history as a Jewish centre in the time of Mohamed.
Beyond Harrat Ambassador Hart came upon a spectacular rock
formation, 'granite, infused with green fluorite, salmon-granite and
halaban andesite, all bare of growth and gleaming in the slanting
rays'. He found much of the 'long thread of steel' of the Turkish
railway still intact, more damaged by desert torrents and wind
erosion than by dynamite; tie and bolts remained solid; the stone-
work of bridges and culverts remained intact. Here and there an
old locomotive sat quietly on a siding and an old freight-car,
stripped of its planking, lay overturned. In the railway station at

Meda'in Saleh several locomotives stood at the platform as though waiting to be recalled to life.

Harold Ingrams in *Arabia and the Isles* described another part of the trail, the part between Cana and Shabwa. He says he was the first European to travel this part of the Incense Trail. After travelling more than four hours from the sea coast over a desert of sand and black basalt known as al Khabt, or 'the wilderness', he passed a multitude of 'Himyaritic scratchings' hammered into rocks and cliff-sides, isolated letters, words and phrases, sometimes whole messages, mostly still undeciphered, around the camping places of the ancient travellers. Then he passed an extraordinary masonry wall some two hundred yards long, which extended from a mountain-side to a steep wadi wall, blocking all passages except one about seven feet wide. This was a Himyaritic wall, whose ancient name, according to Ptolemy, was the Bana, originally constructed in order to control the passage of caravans, who would be obliged to use the seven-foot-wide opening. Constructed of shaped stones, four or five feet thick and about twenty feet high, the wall effectively prevented travellers from using any other route. According to Pliny, it was in fact a capital offence to circumvent it. In ancient times the wall marked the boundary between Himyarites and Sabaeans, between the modern tribes of Hajur and Wahidi; a section of the Wahidi are still called Himyar.

Alerted to the existence of dangerous snakes along this route, Ingrams recalled a story told by Herodotus of winged serpents who guarded the incense trees. According to the account of Artemidorus, quoted by Strabo, these serpents were a span long, red in colour, and could spring as high as the thigh to inflict a bite that caused instant death. Ingrams had no doubt that these were the same serpents described by Herodotus.

Further along the trail Ingrams discovered the white marble plinth of a small temple in the midst of a freshly ploughed field, and at the head of a pass he found a quarry used in ancient times by the people of Shabwa. From there a road sixteen feet wide led down for three miles to the site of the ancient town. This was the route over which the Atramitae tribe, the ancestors of the Hadhramis, whose territory formed part of the kingdom of Sabaea, hauled the blocks of stone out of which they built their city. The sight started him dreaming: 'Gleaming white in the sun, set in the middle of green fields with its desert background, the hill of Shabwa, crowned with its citadel, the king's palace and marble temple . . . must have presented a fair sight to the incense caravans of old as they approached.' Like survivors of some cataclysm the poor villagers were using the remaining walls of the ancient town as parts of their own dwellings. As he entered Shabwa Ingrams recalled Pliny's story that the gate was always left open for incense caravans, with a secretary of the king in attendance. He reflected that just as the ancient kingdom – Himyar on the coast and Saba in the interior – lived on the incense trade which supplemented their poor agriculture, the modern Hadhramaut also derived its wealth from outside. The modern Hadhramis migrated to Java and Singapore and sent back their earnings; when that source of income was cut off by political upheavals in south-east Asia, they began to migrate to the burgeoning economy of Saudi Arabia.

Trade between the East and the West, above all trade in incense, brought wealth to the ancient South Arabia for the first time. Incense was to ancient Arabia what oil has become to the modern Arabia, a source of wealth, of discord, of progress and of destruction. As we have seen, thousands of years before Christ the Egyptians sought to use ships to evade South Arabian control of the Incense Trail.

Incense brought the Romans into Yemen in 24 B.C., as oil brought the Egyptians in 1962. Weary of the heavy tolls imposed on trade by the Sabaeans the Romans sent Aelius Gallus with a legion of Roman soldiers to open up the route. He got as far as Marsiaba in the country of the Mafabi tribe in the valley of the Minaeans, which was probably Wadi Beihan. The Roman legion was there decimated by the raids of the ancestors of today's Hashid and Bakil tribesmen, as well as by disease and thirst. Native guides are said to have misled them deliberately in the mountains and deserts, to which the Romans were no more accustomed than the Egyptians were in 1962. In their military enterprise, therefore, the Romans failed. But they succeeded in undermining South Arabian control of the Incense Trail in quite another way. A Greek sailor named Hippalus had discovered that it was possible to use the monsoon winds to travel from East Africa to India and back without ever touching the South Arabian coast. So the Romans concentrated on clearing the sea lanes of the Red Sea of pirates; they obtained their frankincense and myrrh from the land of Punt, which we know today as Ethiopia and Somaliland, and carried East-West trade by sea rather than by camel caravan. Arabic historians usually attribute the decline of South Arabian civilizations to the bursting of the dam at Marib in the seventh century. But the effects on trade and the Incense Trail of maritime competition were probably more important.

In the end it was probably the spread of Christianity that led to the final decline of the Incense Trail and the kingdoms of South Arabia. The new religion, it seems, had less need than pagan faiths for incense as a means of reaching heaven. The pre-Islamic inhabitants of these ancient kingdoms worshipped a moon god and other deities.[1] But soon after the time of Jesus some of the earliest apostles penetrated to this part of the world. The Emperor Constantine sent missionaries, and the apostles Thomas (who was on his way to India) and Bartholomew converted the Himyaritic kings to Christianity. By the beginning of the fourth century a great many of the Himyarites had been converted. Meanwhile the Jewish community was also growing in size and influence, and between the fourth and sixth centuries a Jewish dynasty emerged unique in the annals of Jewish history.[2] The Christianized Himyarites later obtained help against their Jewish rulers from an Abyssinian expeditionary force, which defeated Dhu Nuwas, the Jewish leader, in the year 525. Under the ensuing Abyssinian rule the Christian Church developed rapidly. There were bishops at Najran and Zofar, and a great church called Kalis, whose foundation-stones are incorporated in the present Great Mosque, was built at Sana by the Abyssinian viceroy, Abraha.

According to legend Abraha conducted a great campaign against the pagans, who, even before Islam, worshipped at the great black stone known as the Kaaba, in Mecca. Abraha was defeated in 570 in a battle known as 'the battle of the Elephant', so called because his army included a train of elephants. The story recounted in the Koran is that in this year of Mohamed's birth the future holy place of Islam was saved from the Christians by a multitude of birds, who dropped stones on the invaders and routed them.

Meanwhile the descendants of the old Himyaritic rulers had appealed to the King of Persia for help against the Abyssinians. King Chosroes I responded and his troops drove out the Abyssinians, who had been much weakened by the failure of their expedi-

[1] See Chapter Ten.
[2] See Chapter Seven.

tion into the heart of Arabia. But the Persians, like the Abyssinians before them, also remained in Yemen as rulers. The remaining Himyaritic princes were caught between their Abyssinian enemies on one side and their Persian allies on the other, just as the Yemenis of the 1960s were to be caught between the Egyptians and the Saudis. It would seem as though the Himyarites' appeal for help, first to the Abyssinians against the Jewish dynasty, then to King Chosroes against the Abyssinians, set a historical pattern in Yemen. Much later, the Imam Ahmed was to try to use the force of the Egyptians against the British. They undermined his régime and remained for a time, in effect, as conquerors.

Unable to solve their dilemma, the Himyarites, who had ruled from 115 B.C. until A.D. 525, never regained power. Their attempts to rid themselves of Persian rule were ended by the conversion of the Persian governor Badhan to Islam, following which Yemen became part of an Islamic empire. From then until the tenth century Yemen was under the Omayyid caliphs. The prophet Mohamed despatched his son-in-law Ali to Yemen as governor, an event which shaped the Yemeni's approach to Islam for ever after. The adherents of the Zeidi sect of the Shia branch of Islam, which believes that Ali was the true successor to the prophet and the first caliph, became dominant in Yemen.

VII

Jewish Kingdom and Zeidi Imams

••

THE Jews of Yemen, almost all of whom have now migrated to Israel, are the only ones who ever formed a Jewish kingdom outside Palestine. They were the oldest community in the Diaspora, the community of Jews dispersed from Palestine.

The ancestors of the Yemeni Jews were one of the Semitic elements that penetrated into Yemen and South Arabia during the thousand years before Christ. How they came or why they came is largely a matter of legend. At first they probably came as merchants, sent out by King Solomon in about 1000 B.C., in caravans and by ship, in co-operation with the Phoenician King Hiram of Tyre. It is said that some came as followers in the train of the Queen of Sheba, after she had visited King Solomon in Jerusalem.

As trading expanded, Jewish colonies sprang up in such places as Medina in the Hejaz province of what is now Saudi Arabia, at Najran on the north-eastern fringe of Yemen, at Aksum on the African side of the Red Sea and many other places, all of which were way-stations on the Incense Trail. There is a legend that 75,000 Jews migrated from Palestine to Yemen forty-two years before the destruction of the first temple in Jerusalem in the year 586 B.C. While the number is certainly exaggerated, it is quite likely that a group did move in response to the warning of the prophet Jeremiah, who said: 'He that remaineth in this city shall die by the sword, by the famine and by the pestilence, but those going forth shall live.' According to the legend which may well have an historical foundation, the emigrants included the twenty-five noblest families of Jerusalem.

A larger infusion of Jews probably took place after the destruction of the temple. It was natural that some of the Jews seeking new homes outside Palestine would go to the trading posts in Arabia. Gradually they gained wealth and influence, representing not only a mercantile community but a community of warriors fully capable of defending themselves or imposing themselves on others. A well-organized community of Jews appears to have existed in the second century A.D., and in the fourth century the ruler, then known as the Tubba, As'ad Kamil and his court were converted to Judaism, according to some historians. There is more general agreement that early in the sixth century the Tubba Dhu Yuseph Nuwas embraced the Jewish faith and attempted to exterminate the Christians of Yemen. He is said to have been responsible for the massacre at Najran of 20,000 Christians, who were buried in a mass grave. The figure was undoubtedly exaggerated but the event was sufficient to induce the Christians among the Himyaritic princes to appeal to the Emperor of Byzantium for help. The Byzantine emperor brought in a Christian Abyssinian army which defeated Dhu Nuwas in A.D. 525. This period of the Jewish kingdom ended melodramatically, according to the legend, with Dhu Nuwas riding to his death into the waves of the Mediterranean.

A community of about 3,000 Jews appears to have lived peacefully enough in Yemen until the twelfth century when intermittent persecution began in spite of the official tolerance of Judaism by the dominant Moslems. In the midst of their period of prosperity, according to tradition, Ezra, the scribe, returned to Judaea and sent word back to Yemen that the Jews should return to help rebuild the temple in their homeland. But the Jews of Yemen so much loved their new homeland in the valley of Sana that they scorned Ezra. Ezra, it is said, cursed them, thereby dooming them to a future of poverty and suffering; the Yemeni Jews, in turn, excommunicated him and refrained from naming their children Ezra.

President Itzhak Ben Zvi, in *The Exiled and the Redeemed*, has written that the Jews in Yemen in the fourth century strongly resisted Christian missionary propaganda and wielded considerable influence over the royal house. He says that stone tablets discovered in Yemen indicate a gradual Judaization of the royal household, which reached its peak when the Jewish Tubba Dhu Nuwas, 'Lord of the Forelock', ascended the throne.

The relative freedom from persecution which the Jews of Yemen enjoyed for many centuries is explained in Jewish history by the order issued by Mohamed that they should not be forced to adopt Islam. While the original of Mohamed's order has been lost Jewish sources have preserved the following text:

This is the letter of protection which the prophet Mohamed, may peace and mercy and God's blessing be with him, caused to be written for the children of Israel.

When the heathen were pressing hard against the prophet, may peace be with him, the children of Israel came to him saying, 'We are with you and on your side; we will fight against the unbelievers and you will have peace with them.' And thus they did, fighting all the week until at noon on Friday the prophet said to them, 'Children of Israel, go and keep your Sabbath. With God's help we will fight off the enemy alone, though it be hard.' But the children of Israel answered, 'Prophet of God, dearer to us than life or possessions, for us there is no Sabbath whilst you have no peace.' So they joined battle again. The sun went down and the children of Israel desecrated the Sabbath, fighting on until they had conquered the heathen. When the prophet heard of this his joy was great, and he said, 'Men of Israel, by God's grace I will reward you for your goodness and for all time give you my protection and my vow, until the Day of Resurrection.'

The prophet is said to have dictated to his son-in-law, Ali, an order putting the Jews under his protection and declaring, 'Let no insults, abuse, accusations and hostile acts take place in any town, village or market place of Moslems and true believers. Illegal levies, fines and special taxes of any kind may not be demanded of them; their fields and vineyards must be free of tithe; they have only to pay the head tax, and the rich who ride on horse-back must pay three pieces of silver a year.' The order went on to say that the protected Jews were not forbidden to enter mosques or Koran schools, nor prevented from riding horse-back, nor to be disturbed in their religious observances.

Unfortunately the things that were forbidden were exactly the things that were done to the Jews in subsequent years. During the periods of Turkish rule, which lasted some four hundred years beginning in the sixteenth century, the Jews only sometimes enjoyed the protection of the occupying power. For a time after 1677 the Jews of Sana were banished from the Yemeni hill country to Mauza, in the malarial coastal districts. After their homes had been plundered and the Moslems had realized the inconvenience of removing them as the nation's craftsmen, they were allowed to return – but were confined to special quarters outside the city gates.

In 1906 the Imam Yahya followed his triumph over the Turks by renewing the persecution of the Jews. He prescribed the taxes Jews should pay and declared that Jews were forbidden to do the following things:

1. To raise their voices in front of Moslems.
2. To build higher than the houses of Moslems.
3. To touch a Moslem passing on his way.
4. To engage in the traditional trades and occupations of Moslems.
5. To cast obloquy upon the religion of Islam.
6. To curse the prophets.
7. To discuss religion with Moslems.
8. To ride an animal cross-saddle.
9. To laugh or make remarks at the sight of a naked Moslem.
10. To study their books outside the synagogue.
11. To raise their voices when praying.
12. To sound the ram's horn loudly.
13. To lend money on interest, which leads to the destruction of the world.
14. Jews must always stand up in the presence of Moslems and show them honour and respect on all occasions.

In their misery, aggravated by periodical famines, the Jews of Yemen were much given to mysticism. A succession of false messiahs and precursors of messiahs arose among them. Their religious life was based upon the Talmud, and until recent times they took a lively part in the production of scholarly, poetical and mystical works, as they had done throughout the Middle Ages.

The rabbi Jacob Saphir of Jerusalem who made a two-year visit to Yemen in 1859 found the Jews in a miserable condition. He wrote that the native Yemenis considered the Jews unclean, that a Jew could not prosecute a Moslem in a court of law and that a Jew was not admissible as a witness, as his oath was considered without validity.

In 1863, letters alleging that the Jews of Sana were being subjected to hideous atrocities were received by the Jewish board of deputies in London, from a Yemenite rabbi who had taken refuge in Aden. The board appealed to Earl Russell, who asked the Indian government to instruct the governor of Aden 'to take such steps in the matter as may be in his power'. But the British governor was in no position to help these Jews.

According to a pamphlet of the American Jewish Congress, called 'The End of Galut Yemen',[1] the situation of the Jews of Yemen became more abject than ever after the end of Turkish rule, following the First World War. The old Islamic code replaced the Turkish judicial code and the Jews became legally the property of the Imam. They were not permitted to serve in the army or carry arms, even though Jewish smiths were particularly skilled in arms making. Instead of a belt they were required to wear a rope around their waists. A Jew was not allowed to ride a horse or a mule; he had to use donkeys. When he met a Moslem he must dismount as a sign of respect. A Jew was not permitted to walk on the same side of the street or to touch food to be used by Moslems. He was forbidden to wear coloured clothes, or to leave the ghetto at night. Lights were forbidden on the streets of the Jewish quarter. A Jew could not enter a public bath except to stir the fires. The Jewish community of Sana was required to clean the city latrines and the streets. If a Christian died in the Yemen the Jews were required to bury him. They were forbidden to build houses more than two storeys high. Jewish orphans, according to a law promulgated in 1922, were to be taken from the ghetto and converted to Islam as 'children of the Imam'.

Physically different from other Jews, including those of the Orient, the Jews of Yemen were generally long-bearded, small, slender and wiry, with coal black hair and eyes, and fine features. Very probably as a result of the inter-marriage that seems to take place in spite of even the most rigorous taboos, the country Jews seemed relatively darker and more heavily built, the city Jews short, more slender and light complexioned, with long, narrow faces. The men shaved the crowns of their heads, which they covered with little black skull-caps. Their long curling ear-locks were similar to those of the Polish Jews. The women wore over their heads a black, peaked cowl and over their shoulders a long shawl which they might throw over their faces at the approach of strangers.

The Jewish community in Yemen was split into a complex of castes. The patrician families of Sana, who considered themselves the descendants of the twenty-four temple guards, regarded them-

[1] *Galut* is the Hebrew for exile.

selves as far superior to the Jews in the small villages, whom they believed descended from converts and slaves.

Persecution notwithstanding, there was a pleasant side to the life of the Jews in Yemen. Ameen Rihani, in *Arabian Peak and Desert Travels in the Yemen*, offered the following description of the ghetto in Sana:

> My idea of the ghetto, as it exists on the East side of Manhattan or even in the Bronx, is totally upset, but happily upset. I looked for clothes-lines, rags, for overflowing garbage cans, for accumulated filth, for babble and confusion, ragamuffin children, for slatterns with infants at their breasts, for dingy and smelling doorways; but I found instead a labyrinth of incredibly clean lanes, narrowing in places into footpaths, with little doors on either side, far apart, a few people going sluggishly and quietly hither and thither, a woman's face in a window, a flower-pot, a sweet basil plant. . . . No cries, no noise, no confusion, no smells. . . . The little terraces are whitewashed and hedged with flower-pots; in the principal street, a broad thoroughfare leading to the outer gate, the children play; and neither the dense crowd, nor the unctuous raggedness of the slums is evident except in its business section.

The Jews maintained a high level of religious education and many could make themselves understood in Hebrew. Their concern with education had won for them the tag of 'Lithuanians of the East'. Beginning in early childhood the boys spent many hours in the synagogue from before daybreak until the end of the service. Indeed, so onerous was the regime imposed on the boys that Jewish girls and women were generally bigger and healthier than the boys and men. Except in cases where the father had no sons, the girls were rarely exposed to rigorous formal religious education.

The Jews concentrated on handicrafts and became blacksmiths, potters, basket weavers, embroiderers, arms manufacturers, gold and silversmiths. They produced some of the finest delicate silver filigree jewellery in the world, as well as colourful exotic embroidery and basket work, in patterns similar to those of the American Indians. Some were active in the cloth industry and owned silk factories, iron foundries and wood-working shops. A few practised agriculture until barred from this pursuit, while others wandered with the bedouin in the desert. After the departure of the Turks at the end of the First World War the Imam Yahya attempted to oblige the Jews to teach their skills to the Arabs.

Like the South Arabian Arabs the Jews married early. Parents arranged matches. The girls were ten or twelve and the boys in their early teens, ostensibly in order to prevent extra-marital intercourse among young people. One consequence was that in middle life many Jewish men sought second wives. Polygamy was not unusual.

Interest in migration to the Holy Land among these people was of long standing. The first group of Yemenis reached Palestine in 1882, only two years after the first pioneers from Russia. A trickle of Jews continued to reach Israel in spite of all difficulties. By the time the state of Israel was proclaimed in 1948 the Yemeni community totalled 35,000. The death in that year of the Imam Yahya, who in 1921 had ordered the confiscation of the property of any Jew emigrating to Palestine and had later banned emigration altogether, opened the way to a massive movement of the Jewish community.

The pressure for emigration was heightened by a malicious story early in 1948 that six Jews of Sana had been arrested on a charge of having murdered, for ritual purposes, two Arab girls whose bodies they had thrown into a well. Violence against the Jewish community ensued. As the press of migrants into Aden increased, the British High Commissioner, Sir Reginald Champion, attempted to stem the influx. He asked the Imam Ahmed, who had succeeded Yahya, to prevent Jews from leaving Yemen, and the Imam at once decreed that Yemen's Jews must register themselves and their property. But although he had a great reputation for cruelty the Imam Ahmed was willing to allow the Jews to depart, and, to the dismay of the British, Jews from more than a thousand communities in large numbers poured into Sana to pay the head-tax of three Maria Theresa thalers which would allow them to travel to Aden. In hired trucks, on donkeys and on foot, the migrating groups made their way through mountains and deserts, paying additional head-taxes to the various sultanates and sheikhdoms until they reached the Aden colony border. Some died of exhaustion and disease on the way, and many of those who reached the transit camps organized by the American Joint Distribution Committee in Aden were sick. They suffered from malaria, tropical ulcers, trachoma, tuberculosis and malnutrition. Their average weight was about eighty-six pounds. The DC-3s of the Alaska airline and later the C-54 Skymasters of the Near East Air Transport Company were able to pack in more than twice the usual number of passengers. 'Operation Magic Carpet', which had begun as a secret airlift during the Arab–Israeli war, became an open exodus during the reign of the Imam Ahmed. From December 1948 to February 1949, 33,750 Yemeni Jews were flown to Israel and another 15,000 followed in 1950. In the words of the prophecy often quoted by the Yemenis themselves from Exodus xix. 4:

> You have seen what I did to the Egyptians, and how I bore you on eagles' wings and brought you to myself.

As they were flown to the Promised Land it seemed to the Yemenis that the prophecy had been fulfilled.

This remarkable Jewish community, so different in many ways from any other, brought valuable talents to the new state. Their skill in a multitude of handicrafts made them easily adaptable to new occupations in agriculture and industry. Israel's gain was Yemen's loss. In all my travels on royalist and republican sides in Yemen I did not once come across a Jew who had remained behind, although I know that there are a few in remote villages. The silver filigree jewellery with its semi-precious stones, which the Jewish craftsmen in Yemen had made so well, was made no more. In Israel, the few Jews who attempted to continue their old crafts modified their styles in imitation of European models. In Yemen the old jewellery, much sought after, mounted in price. A tradition was ended.

The Yemenis are proud of their historical heritage. Even the most uneducated among them are aware of their long tradition of independence, and not a few know the dual origins of their Imam. On the one hand, these go back to the pre-Islamic kings of Himyar; on the other, back through the first Imam to the prophet Mohamed himself. These religious origins are especially important to the mountain warriors who for many centuries have dominated Yemen, for they belong to the Zeidi sect of the Shia branch of Islam. Their Zeidi faith distinguishes them from the rest of the inhabitants of the Arabian peninsula and lends to their lives a special quality.

The Zeidi are not particularly fanatical in religious observance. Indeed, they make less of a fetish of praying five times a day than

do the fanatical Sunni sect, known as the Wahabis, who are dominant in Saudi Arabia; they do not insist as fanatically as the Wahabis
on enforcing the pitiless code of the Koran, with its penalties of
hand-chopping for thieves and stoning for adulterers, and its
prohibition of tobacco and music as well as alcohol. But they are
fanatically attached to their Imam, whose rule in their religious
observance they consider vital.

The Islamic religion has two main branches – the Sunni and the
Shia. The distinction between them is that the Shia regard Ali, the
son-in-law of the prophet, as the successor to Mohamed. According
to their doctrine Ali became the first Imam or holder of the highest
spiritual office. This was passed on to his two sons, Hassan and
Hussein, and later to the descendants of the latter, for Hassan had
no children. This line ended with the twelfth Imam, Mohamed
al Mahdi, 'the messenger', who was killed by the Abbasid caliph,
the leader of the faith of Constantinople. The Shia of Persia and of
Yemen believe that Mohamed al Mahdi ascended to heaven,
whence he will return some day as a Messiah; others say that one
of his descendants will be the Messiah.

Yemen, which became the first country to separate itself from the
vast caliphate, had an early connection with Ali, the son-in-law
of the prophet, when the prophet sent him to Yemen as governor
to re-establish order. A great-grandson of Ali, Zeid Ibn Ali Zein
al Abidin, founded a group who not only regarded Ali as the true
successor of the prophet, that is to the caliphate, but believed that
one of *his* descendants would some day reappear on earth as the
'Mahdi' or Messiah. Because of his heretical belief Zeid was
considered a rebel and was killed by the army of the Omayyid
caliph near Kufa, in Iraq, in about the year 740. After that the
followers of Zeid scattered, and some, led by Yahya ibn al Hussein
al Qasim ar Rassi, who claimed he was the eighth-generation
descendant of Fatimah and Ali, the daughter and son-in-law of
Mohamed, migrated to Yemen and settled at Sadah. That is why
the Zeidi rulers of Yemen are known as the Rassid dynasty.

Although this line always returned to the throne and the present
Imam is of the Rassid dynasty, for periods of several centuries at a
time there were departures from this house. There was for instance
the great Queen Sayida, who ruled about the time of William the
Conqueror, at the beginning of the eleventh century, and founded
the branch in Yemen of the Ismaili sect, the followers of Aga Khan;

a small group of Ismailis have survived to this day. Queen Sayida was famous for her good works. She built roads, some of which are still to be seen today. Their surface was made of painstakingly dressed, carefully graded blocks of stone, and fountains and water troughs, for animals as well as humans, were set up in convenient places along the roadside.

The Egyptians also in the twelfth century, in the first of their four invasions, under the command of an elder brother of Saladin (Salaheddin), installed governors representing Saladin's Ayyubid dynasty. These governors asserted their independence and founded the Rassulid dynasty, which lasted for two centuries; as the Egyptian influence weakened, the dynasty's greatest representative, the Sultan al Muzaffar, brought under his rule, towards the end of the thirteenth century, the entire area from Mecca to the Hadhramaut, including Aden.

At first the Zeidi Imams ruled from Sadah, the town at the northern end of the Yemeni mountain massif, at a point where it dips down into the plain towards Asir, the fertile province which now forms the south-western corner of Saudi Arabia. The line of Imams did not follow necessarily from father to son. According to Zeidi tradition the Imam was elected by the notables of the land and by the ulema. He bore the title of Al Muta Wakil al Allah, meaning 'He who relies on God'; hence the kingdom was known as the Mutawakilite kingdom. The Imams also used the title of Commander of the Faithful, and their princes were known as Said al Islam, 'the sword of Islam'.

The first of the Rassid house to rule from Sana was the seventeenth-century Imam Mansur al Qasim, usually called 'the Great'. But both before and after his time some of the imams were reduced to the role of spiritual head without temporal power. Rival dynasties sprang up in various parts of the country.

The mountain tribes of the north and centre of Yemen embraced the Zeidi faith, while those of the south and the western seaboard remained faithful to the Sunni branch of Islam. The Zeidis, numbering probably about forty per cent of the population, have always been less sophisticated but more warlike and vigorous than the Sunnis. They have succeeded in maintaining a dominant position in the governments centred in Sana, even in the present republican régime.

In 1538 the Turks invaded Yemen, staying there until 1630.

This invasion set off the great revolution led by Qasim the Great, seven of whose ancestors had been Zeidi Imams. In his struggle against the Turks Qasim succeeded in uniting the Shia and the Sunnis of Yemen for the first time. Like the Egyptians, who recently devoted themselves to trying to capture the Imam Mohamed al Badr, the Turks concentrated all their efforts on capturing Qasim But he always slipped away. He was not only a warrior but a noted scholar, who used to carry a supply of books to his mountain caves and hide-outs.

Although Qasim, after eight years of rule, had eleven provinces supporting him, he was overwhelmed by large Turkish reinforcements in 1598 and forced to withdraw to a remote hiding-place in the east of Yemen. Little by little the tribes rallied to his support until in 1608 the Turks were obliged to conclude a ten-year truce – the kind of compromise which might be possible in the present conflict. The truce provided that the Imam remain in control of the provinces he held; the Turks would conduct the foreign affairs of the whole country, but its inhabitants would have freedom of movement.

In 1629 the Turks surrendered Sana, and by 1636 they had left Yemen entirely. For more than two hundred years thereafter there were no Turks in Yemen. The second Turkish invasion in 1849 proved disastrous, for the Turks were unable to hold Sana. After the construction of the Suez Canal, however, the Turks returned a third time and occupied Sana in 1871. But they were never able to control the whole of the country.

A new war of liberation got under way after the election in 1891 of the Imam Mohamed bin Yahya, who was descended from Qasim the Great. The legendary stature of Qasim and the arrival of more and more Turkish troops made Mohamed bin Yahya a focus for growing support, but it was not until the time of his son, Yahya bin Yahya, that the revolt achieved any marked success. In 1904 the Turks were crushingly defeated at Shaharah. A large Turkish force under the command of Saidhi Pasha, totalling 10,000 men, composed of their best European and Anatolian troops, and supported by artillery and cavalry, was caught in a narrow mountain pass as it attempted to make its way northwards from Sana in the direction of Sadah. It is said that only 400 men escaped. Capitalizing on this great victory, Yahya went on to besiege Sana in 1911. Though we may doubt the precision of their figure, Arab historians say that he concentrated 150,000 men around the city. Of this force, the Turkish General Izzet Pasha is said to have observed that 'all Europe could be conquered by such men'. In consequence the Turks were obliged, in 1911 as in 1608, to compromise. They concluded an agreement providing that religious law as understood by the Zeidis and the traditional system of taxation should prevail throughout the land, that religious endowments should not be used for non-religious purposes, and that posts of authority should go only to religious leaders. In effect, this agreement established Yemeni sovereignty internally. Foreign affairs, however, were once again left to the Turks.

The original Turkish interest in the Yemen was probably stimulated by the Ottoman rulers, who had controlled traffic through the Red Sea to the East. The Ottomans lost interest when communications around the Cape of Good Hope became common, which may explain their first withdrawal. After the construction of the Suez Canal, not only did access to Yemen become easier, but the Turks may have considered it strategically more important for its position flanking the Red Sea and for the gateway it provided to Aden, which was first occupied by the British in 1713.

The Turks made their greatest effort towards the end, when the strength of their empire was failing. They feared that a rebellious movement in the south might spread northwards into what is now Saudi Arabia, threatening the holy places. One cannot fail to notice the parallel between the Turks then and King Faisal of Saudi Arabia at present. Like the Turks, King Faisal feels that he cannot tolerate a hostile régime in Yemen.

The Egyptian impact on Yemen was not as traumatic as that of the Turks, although, while the Turkish invaders came back three times, the Egyptians have now returned a fourth time. The first Egyptian invasion was that conducted by Saladin's elder brother in the twelfth century; the second was in 1515, and the third under Ibrahim Pasha at the beginning of the nineteenth century. Only after both the second and third Egyptian intrusions did the Turks take over and replace them as the occupying power. Finally, in 1962, there came the fourth invasion, the most destructive, and socially and politically the most revolutionary in Yemen's history.

VIII

The Prime Minister in His Cave

++

DURING the first week of December 1962, I travelled overland from Najran in Saudi Arabia to Aden, at the southern tip of the peninsula, right through royalist-held Yemen and close to the fighting fronts.

To get to Yemen I had to pass through Saudi Arabia, and in Riyadh, the Saudi capital, I fell in with a group of four French correspondents and a Spaniard, who were fighting the usual battle against official delay to get permission to go to Yemen. I remember especially tall, gaunt Georges Herbouze of the Agence France-Presse, who had been trained in French government service in Morocco and who spoke fluent Arabic; also fat and jolly Camille Menassa, one of two assistants to Jean Lefèvre, chief of a French radio network team; and the gloomy correspondent of the Spanish newspaper *A.B.C.* of Barcelona, Salvador Lopez della Torre, whom, I don't know why, we called George.

Together, we at last boarded an American-piloted plane of the Saudi Arabian airline, with a dozen soldiers and a Saudi Arabian prince who was organizing help for the royalists. Our first stop was at Taif, the Saudi summer capital in the mountains behind Jeddah, to which we had to make a detour to suit the convenience of our Saudi prince. At Taif we heard that a squadron of Jordanian planes had been stationed there until a few days before we arrived. The sharp cold reminded some of us that we had better acquire some warm clothes for our expedition into Yemen, and Herbouze and I proceeded to the *souk* to buy enormous woollen shepherd cloaks, each weighing fifteen pounds of thickly woven wool. It seemed a joke at the time, but a few days later I was most grateful for the warmth of that cloak.

Landing at Najran the next day, we felt immediately that we were in a war zone. Both Saudis and Jordanians had training officers there and we saw a group of Jordanians as we landed. The Yemeni camp, under the command of the bright and forceful young Prince Mohamed Hussein, was populated by thousands of Yemenis, led by their sheikhs, who had swarmed in to declare their loyalty to the Imam, to receive arms and be trained in their use. From a purely military point of view, it is understandable that this was the first target the Egyptians bombed inside Saudi Arabia.

In Najran we declined the invitation of local officials to leave our luggage in the big whitewashed guest-house. Already well acquainted with the delays of Saudi Arabia we insisted on keeping our things in the jeep and pushing on into Yemen the same day. And the local officials, much more co-operative than those of Riyadh, readily agreed. We bought ourselves a meal in a restaurant near the central market-place, loaded our jeeps with tinned goods, chocolate and biscuits, and marvelled a while at the skyscraper architecture of the town. Then we set off with a Saudi driver who, although he demonstrated an alarming inability to take corners or change gear on hills, was said to know his way to the headquarters of the Prime Minister, Prince Hassan, inside Yemen.

Our route followed a great arc, first due east, out into the edge of the Rub al Khali desert, then gradually southwards and eventually westwards through the desert back into the Yemen. We followed no road, merely heading across the open desert. We travelled fast. Off to the south-west great black rocks jutted out of the sand, higher and higher until they rose into a mountain range. We followed this route as a stratagem to avoid the most travelled direct way where we were most likely to be spotted by Egyptian aircraft.

After two hours' driving we came upon an extraordinary Yemeni camp at the lower end of a wadi that led westwards to the small town of Amlah. Hundreds of tribesmen, in a wide variety of tribal costumes mixed with pieces of European clothing and uniforms, swarmed out to meet us. I saw tennis shoes, plastic sandals and, of course, bare feet; Arab long shirts, Yemeni short kilts and European trousers; and here and there a U.S. army greatcoat. Some, having been used to the ways of regular armies, tried to form a line, a kind of guard of honour, on the assumption, I suppose, that we were important visitors. But this hardly succeeded.

Somehow, although no one seemed to be in charge, we were escorted to one of the two tents in the camp, while the tribesmen continued to mill around, chatting and crowding, and attempting to squeeze into the tent to catch a glimpse of us. There was no one who could be called an officer. These were just a conglomeration of tribesmen who had gathered to offer their services to their Imam. Some seemed to be confused about whether Imam al Badr was still alive; they called Prince Hassan 'Imam'. Elderly Prince Hassan was clearly popular and appeared to be a kind of father figure to them.

Towards evening, and later by the light of bonfires, the tribesmen danced and sang wildly and the photographers exercised their talents in trying to get night pictures of them. This dancing was entirely spontaneous and traditional, to music every tribesman had known since childhood. But they sang new words to the songs, such as: 'We will die for the Imam . . . we will cut off the Egyptians' noses . . . Sallal has betrayed us . . . the Sahar are powerful . . . they will fight for Badr.' And there was one I liked especially which began: 'A bird flies round the throne.'

A man and his twelve-year-old son, Saleh, who said they had come from the tribal area of Khawlan to volunteer, automatically attached themselves to us and guarded the entrance of our tent against all but selected visitors. Some of those who were allowed in were eager to tell stories, especially about alleged Egyptian atrocities and Yemeni revenge. A man named Rashid Lauthi of Khawlan, for example, claimed that he had, with his own rifle, shot down an Egyptian plane. This was, of course, possible but unlikely, and one may similarly assess his story about an Egyptian commander who had called together the sheikhs near the town of Jihana and had demanded forty girls for his 175 men. According to the story the sheikhs pretended to agree. But that night when the Egyptians were all asleep, the sheikhs, with 2,000 men, surrounded the Egyptians and in a sudden assault killed them, every one. 'We cut off their noses and ears, and took out their eyes, and put them in a box and sent them to Sallal. After that the Egyptian planes bombed our villages.'

I asked the tribesmen how they were fed. Someone explained that they got their food from rich farmers or by paying from their own pocket. 'The Imam will repay us and them, when he regains the throne,' they said. It sounded a bit disorganized.

We discovered a man they called 'the secretary', who was handling correspondence with Prince Hassan, who, we learned, occupied a cave about four hours from where we were by donkey. In this part of the country there were no mules, only donkeys, and small ones at that. We told the secretary that we must have donkeys to go to Prince Hassan next morning, and he promised to do his best. He said he had been taken prisoner while serving with the republicans at Sadah, and had been allowed, presumably because he could write, to volunteer for service with the royalists. He showed us some of his correspondence with Prince Hassan. One of the messages from the prince, I recall, went something like this: 'I sent you sixteen camels with supplies and you have not returned the camels. Please see to this at once.'

In the morning, to our surprise, the donkeys we had asked for were actually there. But they were not much larger than Great Danes and, when I sat on one, my feet almost touched the ground. I found these little donkeys erratic and harder to manage than the more deliberate mules I had become acquainted with in Kurdistan, and after I had twice slid off the tail of mine I decided to walk.

We were now in the real Yemen and the villages through which we passed as we climbed higher into the mountains were an architectural revelation. It seemed extraordinary that here in these remote villages such primitive people should construct such marvellous houses, like little fortresses of mud bricks four, five and even more storeys high. We were filled with admiration also for the pumps operated by oxen, with great wheels turned by a system of pulleys which the oxen worked by walking in a circle. I cannot say how they worked mechanically, but they did produce a fine flow of sparkling water, from deep cemented wells which they called 'mijals'. These are said to have been introduced by the Persians when they came first as allies and then as rulers in the sixth century A.D.

In every village the people turned out to greet us, regarding us as an important foreign delegation on our way to see the Prime Minister. We found him at the head of a long valley, called after the village of Amlah near by, about fifteen miles east of Sadah, in a deep cave whose existence one would never suspect from the outside, a place known only to local inhabitants and probably not all of these. We could hear in the distance a dull booming – either bombs or guns fired in the vicinity of Sadah. At this time the royalists occupied some high ground to the west of Sadah airport, from which they hoped to bring gunfire to bear on the airfield.

Among the Yemenis hanging around outside the cave was a young boy in a black woman's coat with a black astrakan collar, who carried a sword-stick wrapped in black, gold and green material. This extraordinary get-up belonged to a prince, aged sixteen, named Sharaf bin Modagha, a nephew of Prince Hassan, who had been in hospital in Beirut when the war began. Although still unwell and certainly of questionable military value, he had come to Yemen to offer his services.

We were ushered into the Prime Minister's cave. As we greeted him he took off his turban, revealing that he was quite bald. Wrinkled and gnarled as an old olive tree, he looked considerably older than his fifty-six years. Having spent many years in the Plaza hotel in New York he was suffering from the effects of life in a cave, and he coughed a good deal. Already, for reasons of safety, he had changed caves three or four times. But he was as friendly, good-natured, and courteous as if he were receiving us in the hotel in New York.

I must add that I also found him a slightly confused old man. His thinking was done for him by a young secretary named Ibrahim al Kipsy, one of those in the first planeload of royalist leaders who had flown to Najran in the first days of October. At that time Ibrahim did not want to disclose his full name, for he was the son of one of the highest functionaries of the old régime and still had a father and mother in Sana. He had been studying at the American University in Beirut when he volunteered for service. He said that when we arrived he had been composing a letter to his former professor of political science at the A.U.B. explaining why he had chosen to fight. A small, wiry, thin-faced young man, he was physically a typical Yemeni and one of the most intelligent of his people I ever met. I have no doubt he has a brilliant future in the affairs of his country.

We talked to the Prime Minister in his cave all afternoon and to Ibrahim, in a tent in the valley below the cave, far into the night. Inside the Prime Minister's cave, which was about twenty feet deep and ten feet wide, rugs and quilts covered the floor. All kinds of supplies, papers, tinned goods and baggage were piled in the back, and Ibrahim had a corner for his special papers. Around the Imam on the quilt where he was squatting, I saw a thermos bottle, a Japanese Sony transistor radio, some silver paper from a chocolate bar, a bottle of ink, a pile of envelopes on a suitcase, some glue, an umbrella and a Beretta automatic rifle – a collection suitable for a Salvador Dali.

As we talked to the prince we became aware of a hubbub outside and Ibrahim motioned to us to come to the mouth of the cave. Below us in the valley we could see tribesmen come sweeping along in an enormous procession, first three or four abreast, then ten or twenty, then fifty or sixty. Eventually they spread out and formed an immense circle within which some of them performed wild war-dances. These were men of the Wayila and the al Amalisa tribes. Four different groups came to present their respects to the Prime Minister in this way with song and dance.

Everywhere, Prince Hassan maintained, the people refused to support the republicans, who were the Egyptians' agents. He accused the Egyptians of burning the harvest in places where the people had refused their support. He said the Egyptian army had fanned out across the country and occupied strong-points which they later used against the Yemeni people. He said that if the Egyptians withdrew the people would rise and deal with the republicans themselves.

Prince Hassan also said he had asked for bazookas from an unnamed European country. Until his forces had received these weapons they could not destroy the Egyptians. He complained that Saudi and Jordanian help had been 'nominal, almost *pro forma*. Some people may think that the Saudis and Jordanians have intervened, but they have given little.' He was clearly not satisfied with their aid. He maintained nonetheless that the arms he needed to fight Egyptian tanks and armoured cars were on their way. He said he had asked for four Saudi guards but they had not been sent. (It is odd that he should have made this request – as though he could depend better on the Saudis than on his own people. He was oblivious, apparently, of its political implications, for it would have meant the direct military involvement of Saudi Arabia.) He pointed out that he had received help from the Saudis only after the Egyptians had entered Sana. 'I asked for planes,' he said, 'but they were not sent. My idea was that they would be piloted by volunteers.'

The prince argued that it was logical that the countries of the world would want a few days to observe the reaction of the people after the Egyptians had withdrawn, before they decided to recognize the republic. He argued that United States recognition of the republic would be contrary to the interests of Yemen and of the United States also. He said that if Sallal remained in Yemen he would turn the country over to the communists. Already there were four hundred Russian technicians in economic and military missions to the republic. He argued, a little lamely, that, although the Russians who had helped the royal régime had been without political influence, the Russians now in the republic, who were sometimes the same men, would be subversive.

Asked whether, if the Imam regained power, he would undertake reform, he replied: 'In everything. First,' he said, 'the Imam would repair what Sallal destroyed. Then he would continue the projects already begun and undertake economic projects.'

Prince Hassan said that many people were being shot in Sana and even more killed by Egyptian planes in Yemen. He wanted the United Nations to send observers to Yemen. They should find out if he had told the truth about the war, stop the fighting, and give the people a chance to have their say in a referendum. Prince Hassan said that if the United Nations could not oust the Egyptians he would ask for international volunteers. 'Why,' he asked, 'doesn't the American people help us to obtain a referendum?' He said he had written to the American Secretary of State as well as to the United Nations. 'How,' he complained, 'can everyone be taken in by Nasser's claim to be neutral?' He offered the opinion that the Americans opposed a referendum 'because they don't know what is going on in the Middle East'. He said that he had submitted his proposal for a referendum to the United Nations 'by private telegram'. He was planning to write a letter to President Kennedy.

While we were there, Prince Hassan sent a simple message to the world from his cave. 'Let the whole world recognize Sallal,' he declared. 'But let the Egyptians withdraw. Only the Egyptians are stopping us. If they withdrew we would be in Sana in a week.'

He said he had addressed telegrams along these lines to President Kennedy and to Mr Macmillan, the British Prime Minister, and he had protested to the British and American leaders about their plan to hold a conference to discuss the problem of Yemen without consulting any of its representatives. The problem was caused, he insisted, entirely by Egyptian intervention.

Prince Hassan said that he believed that there were 100 Egyptians in the town of Sadah and 200 in the castle of Sinnara, which dominated the town. His own men had mined the road to the airport and had occupied the mountain above it. 'Two days ago,' he explained, 'the Egyptians tried to drive my people off this mountain. My forces knocked out two tanks, two armoured cars and four trucks with the only two bazookas we possessed in the area, and from the Egyptian dead they collected forty Berettas.' According to Prince Hassan, his forces on the eastern side of the mountains had come closest to Sana at Sinwan, which was fifty miles from the capital. The Imam, on the western side of the mountains, was closest to Sana at al Gafla, about seventy miles from the capital.

Prince Hassan believed that three-quarters of the Yemeni people supported the royalist cause. He admitted that the townsmen in the west and the south supported the republicans. 'But these,' he said, 'are Shaffei and they are not fighters. They ask only to be left alone.'

In our talks with him, Ibrahim, the Prime Minister's secretary, admitted quite frankly that there had been trouble in the past between Mohamed al Badr and Prince Hassan. He felt that most of the tribes had really wanted Prince Hassan as successor to the throne in 1956 when the Imam Ahmed persuaded the ulema to elect his son al Badr, because Hassan was older and more learned.

Ibrahim said there were 15,000 Egyptians in the country, 7,000 of them in Sana. He said the royalists had captured sixty-five members of the republican National Guard, many of them literate men from the towns, and that the royalists had persuaded many of them to serve with the Imam's forces as clerks and secretaries.

One of the correspondents asked Ibrahim why the royalists did not engage in more commando-type raids. He rejoined that thirteen days before 'we attacked the airport at Sana and the radio station. We killed fifty Egyptians and put the station off the air for one hour. They struck back by attacking two villages from which they believed the attack had come.' Ibrahim said that they had seized the sons of the local sheikhs and sent them to Egypt as hostages.

Ibrahim estimated the regular army at the time of the *coup* at 30,000 men. Of these, 200 were in the 'Badr unit'; most of the rest merged into the tribes. 2,000 were estimated to be on each of the four fronts at this time, and there were many others who could be called up from the tribes at any time. Royalist leaders often used a total figure of 100,000. Ibrahim calculated that if they could take Hajja, where the fort held 200 republicans, it would open the way for an attack on the road between Sana and Hodeidah. In the east, the objective was to approach Sana via Amran and the Arhab region; it was reported, however, that an attempt to send ammunition to the Arhab tribe had gone wrong and the ammunition had fallen into Egyptian hands. Nevertheless, seventy-five tribal sheikhs, including all the tribes around Sana, had written declaring their loyalty and willingness to fight. 'As soon as your forces come we will rally to you,' said one letter, 'but for the moment we are at the mercy of armoured cars. Many of our sheikhs are prisoners in the hands of the Egyptians and our villages are threatened with destruction.'

My French colleagues insisted after this interview on returning to Najran, from where they planned to fly to Jizan, thence to travel into the western mountains to see the Imam. I had already seen the Imam a month earlier and my plan was in any case to keep going southwards, to visit other sections of the royalist army and traverse the whole royalist area. I therefore asked Prince Hassan for two things: firstly, a *laissez-passer* — a piece of paper I could show if challenged, authorizing me to travel in royalist territory; and secondly, transportation. The Prime Minister wrote out the *laissez-passer* forthwith, and dictated a message to the Saudi authorities in Najran requesting 'a vehicle for the American correspondent'.

The Prime Minister had a radio telephone connection to Najran and could relay messages through Najran to the Imam on the other side of the mountains. His radio communications were intended also to link him to the various forces in the east under his command. But I gathered that they did not work very well at that time.

That night I sat up with a flash-light in our tent tap-tapping on my typewriter until about two o'clock, so that the French correspondents could take back with them a story to be filed for the *New York Times*.

We were up at dawn, which proved a good deal earlier than any of the Yemenis were ready. There was nothing for us to eat and there was nothing for us to ride on. The man who was supposed to prepare breakfast did not show up until eight o'clock. The man who had been sent to requisition some donkeys for us had gone into the village during the night and had not returned. When he did arrive at about nine o'clock, he confessed that, instead of rounding up donkeys during the night as he had been ordered to do, he had decided, because it was cold, to get a good sleep in the village and find donkeys in the morning!

The confusion was compounded by the inability of the tribesmen in charge to figure out a way to attach our various suitcases, type-writers and photo and sound equipment to the backs of the donkeys. Somehow it had all been brought up the valley the day before; but now it seemed impossible to get it down again. Our donkey-master said he needed rope, but no one could find any; someone went off to the village to look for it, but did not return. All this to the accompaniment of shouting, imprecations, gesticulations by the Yemenis and, of course, protests from the increasingly short-tempered correspondents.

Ibrahim took it all lightly and humorously. He knew how to handle his people and get from them as much effort as was possible. And he understood their limitations. 'That is their habit,' he observed calmly, 'you order something at six o'clock and it comes at nine o'clock.'

By noon, partly on donkeys, partly on foot, we struggled to the bottom of the valley again to that extraordinary inchoate camp, where I parted company with the other correspondents. To my great joy the transportation I had requested through Prince Hassan had actually arrived from Najran. At the most unexpected times things really seemed to work.

They left me beside a big red three-quarter-ton Ford truck — it seemed that most of the vehicles the Saudis used to help the Yemenis were red – with a Saudi driver and four guards in the back. I had no way of communicating with my crew except by muttering the name of the prince to whom they were supposed to take me. I sat in the cab of the truck with the driver, while the four guards crouched in the open and clung to the back. We drove several hours across country, sometimes on a trail, sometimes navigating the desert as though at sea. Shortly before dusk, in the midst of a great expanse of sand, the trucks halted and my crew hauled out from the back of the truck a tethered goat, which they slaughtered. They then built a fire and roasted the goat's meat. Although I had food of my own, they offered me some delicacies, a piece of the heart and the liver which I, of course, accepted. They were friendly fellows, and we amused ourselves by trying to communicate by sign language. I learned that two of the guards were Yemenis and the others Saudis. The Yemeni guards were Aziz, from the Jawf, and Mohamed from Marib. The Saudi guards were Hassan and Hashan, and the driver Hamid.

Soon after we had eaten we stopped again, under a cliff face where I could see that we would be sheltered from aircraft and where clumps of trees offered hiding-places for the trucks. It was dark by then, for the twilight lasts but a few minutes at this latitude. I observed my crew were getting ready to settle down for the night. By sign language they gave me to understand that their intention was first to sleep, then to spend the entire next day in the shelter of the rocks, and to go on in the cool of the evening safe from air attacks. This would have lost me a whole day. I was furious, and conveyed my anger by banging on the hood of the truck and shouting, 'Amir Hussein, Amir Abdullah Hussein.' They understood well enough and, with a shrug and a grin, gathered up their equipment and we set off again in the dark.

As we drove along I realized that we were by no means alone on this track. Many others had apparently waited for the safe obscurity of the night. Supplies from Saudi Arabia were on the move. We passed several small camps that had apparently been set up along the line. This trail alternating between deep ruts and areas where the trucks had left scores upon scores of parallel tracks in the sand, followed the same route between the desert and the mountains that had been used two and three thousand years before by the caravans of the Incense Trail. The cliffs that jutted out of the desert bore inscriptions made by those ancient travellers – drawings and paintings of camels, gazelles and of some animals that are today extinct in the area, including lions, giraffes and ostriches.

It seemed weird to be alone with four bedouin in the lonely desert, unable to speak to them except by sign language, in a strange and wild land, out of communication with the world. For all I knew my crew might imagine that I carried a lot of money. They could easily have killed and robbed me and reported that I had suffered some sort of accident. As was my invariable habit on such journeys, I carried no weapon, for the unarmed traveller is often safer than the one who presumes to defend himself by force.

It occurred to me that the Kurds with whom I had travelled in the region controlled by Mullah Mustafa Barzani, in northern Iraq the previous summer, would never have sent off a visiting American journalist without some sort of literate guide and interpreter. The Kurds had more feeling than the Yemenis of the value to them of a visit from a European or American journalist.

Towards dawn we got lost for an hour or so but at last, as the horizon was beginning to brighten, we drove into the camp of Prince Abdullah Hussein in the Wadi Ashia, which is a continuation of Wadi Hirran. I could see a few tents but no one seemed to be awake, so I rolled up in my Saudi bedouin shepherd's cloak, and slept on the ground next to our truck for the few remaining hours until the sun came up.

IX

A Royalist Headquarters

••

IN the morning I was delighted to be awakened by someone addressing me in English. It was Bruce Condé, one of the most remarkable characters of the Yemeni war. He had attached himself to this particular part of the royalist forces as combination public relations officer, political adviser, and most notably, as I was soon to discover, adviser on postal affairs. In appearance Condé might have been a Yemeni – thin, wiry, quite good-looking and friendly in demeanour. He wore typical Yemeni dress, which included a black turban and the khaki-coloured kilt affected by many of those in the fighting services.

I had, of course, heard about Conde before I went to Yemen and I was hoping that I would find him, partly because he is a fascinating character, and partly because he could be so helpful. I shall digress to tell more about him.

Born in San Juan Capistrano, California – a tenth-generation American, as he put it, 'in some branches of my family' – Bruce Condé developed early in life an interest in stamps of remote places. As a teenager he wrote a letter to the government of Yemen asking for stamps and, to his surprise, received in reply a letter from the Crown Prince, Mohamed al Badr. His contact with the prince remained postal for some years.

In the meantime Condé joined the American army and became an intelligence major in the 82nd Airborne Division in North Africa. Towards the end of the war he was sent for a time to Japan, where he studied Japanese; but his first love remained the Arab Middle East. When he was demobilized he went to Beirut to study Arabic and Arab affairs with the help of the 'G.I. Bill of Rights', which provided a system of scholarships for student veterans. His continuing correspondence with Yemen led to an invitation to visit the country. There, in 1953, he found favour with the Imam Ahmed, who honoured him with a gift of an enormous bag of coffee.

In Sana he found that he could make a business of exporting Yemeni stamps to collectors around the world. He settled down and began to 'go native'. Having learned Arabic and adopted Yemeni dress, his next step, in 1958, was to adopt the Moslem religion. (Later, in June 1962, while photographing the holy places of Mecca and Medina for a Saudi commemorative stamp issue, he even went through the rites of the minor pilgrimage of 'Umrah' to the Kaaba of Mecca.) Dropping the 'Bruce', he renamed himself Abdurrahman Condé, and after that, to ensure his permanence in Yemen, renounced his American citizenship and in 1958 became a Yemeni subject. He did not give up his American citizenship in any spirit of antagonism towards the United States. He merely thought he would be better off as a Yemeni, and during the trips he often made to Jeddah and Beirut he was in friendly contact with members of the American as well as the British embassies.

Condé then took a job with the Yemeni ministry of communications as postal adviser. His ambition was to become not only the expert on postal affairs in Yemen but its director of antiquities. American and British correspondents who in 1957 visited Yemen, at the Imam Ahmed's invitation, to witness his war against the British, found Condé acting as public relations man for the imamic army and an indefatigable propagandist for the Yemen cause. They found him also a convinced Arab nationalist and staunch supporter of Gamal Abdul Nasser. He was one of those who took seriously the Imam's federation with Nasser's Egypt. But, as he dug himself in in Sana, he made enemies as well as friends. Just what happened I never did discover, but in 1959, his Moslem faith and Yemeni citizenship notwithstanding, Bruce Condé was expelled from Yemen.

He flew to Lebanon, where the authorities allowed him to stay for a time without either American or valid Yemeni citizenship. But then, with bureaucratic heartlessness, they told him he would have to leave. At this time he gained some notoriety as a stateless and passportless individual who was stranded at Cairo airport for three weeks.

Eventually Condé took refuge in the sheikhdom of Sharjah in the Persian Gulf, where he gained the favour of the ruling sheikh by showing him how he could make money out of postage stamps. Gratefully the sheikh made Condé a citizen of Sharjah, and he thus gained a passport, and the status of a 'British-protected person', Sharjah being one of the seven British-protected Trucial States of the Persian Gulf.

On his Sharjah passport Condé travelled freely in the Middle East. In April 1962 in Cairo he was approached by Dr Abdurrahman al Baidani, a former Yemeni diplomat who had become a leading anti-royalist propagandist in the services of President Nasser and who was to become the deputy Prime Minister of republican Yemen. In a Christmas letter to his friends in 1964, Condé reported that Baidani 'invited me to collaborate with him in publicity and propaganda work as a fellow exile from Yemen; but I did not trust him and managed to excuse myself for "urgent work" in Beirut.'

In Lebanon Condé became devoted to a family who lived on the top floor of one of the very old houses overlooking the sea in Beirut. Their name was Saide Muawwad and they had four children, George, Elie, Yussef and Bruce, whose ages in 1964 ran from a few months to seven years. After the beginning of the Yemeni war Condé moved this family to Sharjah for a year, but after the experience of a Persian Gulf summer, they decided to return to Beirut. Late in 1963, a relative of the family named Tony went with him to the Imam's headquarters at Qara for several months.

When the Yemeni revolution took place Condé saw his opportunity to regain favour. He made his way to Najran and joined the fighting princes. They welcomed him back gratefully. At first he was much preoccupied with the stamp business, and had 40,000 old stamps of the Imam Ahmed's reign overprinted with the slogan 'Free Yemen fights for God, Imam and Country', and issued these as from the Jawf and Mishriq districts of Yemen. He appointed provincial postmasters in both Marib and Harib.

Two months after I met him, in February 1963, he told me in a letter that he was 'in the little-known province of Arhab, thirty to forty miles north of Sana, where the brave young Prince Seif al Islam Sharafuddin al Mutahar was acting as Prince Abdullah's deputy commander for the first army's Arhab sector'. Condé said that at Haifeh, in the Arhab province, he had photographed a scene 'where sixty royal Arhabi volunteers had ambushed an

Egyptian column, killing 205 in twenty-four hours and knocking out sixteen vehicles, including armoured cars and two Soviet rocket-launcher trucks'. 'Late in February,' Condé wrote, 'I saddled my captured enemy mule, called Humhuri ("republican"), and set out for the mountainous royal province of Nahm. Here another young princeling, Seif al Islam Mohamed al Mohsin, held out in a region of naturally impregnable steep gorges at Sawan, a mountain hideout only five miles north-east of Sana. At the time, his were the closest of all the royal forces to Yemen's Egyptian-occupied capital city.'

Condé told of his caring for an Egyptian prisoner, Corporal Bahloul Daoud Gasas, who had a Turkish Mauser bullet in the bone of his left arm. He explained to Gasas that he cared for him because 'it is a debt I owe one of your countrymen in Cairo', and he recalled the way Major Mohamed Ibrahim Sobhi had helped him 'during the three weeks I was stranded at Cairo airport without a passport in 1959'.

In March 1963, Condé moved on to the headquarters of Prince Abdullah bin Hassan, commander of the second army. He explained that, since there was no radio that would work, no journalists and no postal business, he had taken part in military operations. 'At Maswar, between the Egyptian hold-out points of Jihanah and Argoub,' he wrote in his letter, 'I found a convenient rocky hillside overlooking the main enemy lifeline between these two points. At night one of our tribal sheikhs who had an affinity for mine-laying would sow a few anti-tank mines in the sandy road-bed. In the morning we usually noted a few tanks or armoured cars blown up at the spot, with a winch truck from Sana and a tank or two standing by for protection, as the Egyptians worked busily to haul away the disabled armour, reputedly worth £60,000 per tank. We used to shoot at the salvage crews to drive them away from the wrecks, so as to keep the route blocked. Using armour-piercing ammunition in our M-1 rifles we could even drive them from the shelter of the armoured cars, while their tanks would blast away at us with cannon and machine-gun fire without hitting anything.'

Condé described the Egyptians as 'inept, and helpless to cope with guerilla mountain warfare conditions, suffering losses of ten to one in man-to-man infantry engagements'. He said they panicked at the prospect of attacks at close quarters with cold steel and 'whenever our mortar shells landed inside their position. They did not protect their tanks with infantry, so that we could always creep up on the blind side and knock out the tanks with hand grenades.' 'In the belief', Condé continued, 'that they could win the war by penetrating deeply into our country, they lost expedition after expedition. As late as December 1963, their ranking commander, Lieutenant-General Anwar al Qadi, was pulled into a similar trap by Prince Abdullah al Hussein, twenty-four miles north-west of Sana, where he lost hundreds of men and was himself seriously wounded and blinded by a mortar shell.'

Condé said he had been promoted from the rank of major – 'my old World War II rank in the U.S. army until 15 March' – during the fighting at Maswar, where Prince Abdullah 'gave me a battle-field promotion to the rank of lieutenant-colonel'. In April he had escorted Lieutenant-Colonel Neil McLean, then Member of Parliament for Inverness, from Khawlan to British-protected territory at Beihan, with tribal guides in the service of Sheikh Naji al Gadr of Khawlan. He said their route led 'straight through the enemy lines at Marib and Harib'.

As already mentioned, Bruce Condé had renamed himself Abdurrahman Condé. By studying his genealogical background he next satisfied himself that the Condé family were related to the Spanish house of Bourbon, and he therefore became Bourbon-Condé. Through the Moorish influence on the house of Bourbon he claimed also to have Arabic forebears. When I met Condé in Beirut in the summer of 1964, he told me that his full name was now Abdurrahman Bruce Alphonso de Bourbon-Condé and, in a letter to me of 17 May 1965, he added: 'His Majesty the Imam has restored my family's princely rank on the basis that the original title was from the sixteenth-century kingdom of Navarra in Spain and was later recognized and permitted in France when the Bourbons of Navarra succeeded to the French throne. His Majesty therefore now recognizes and permits it in the kingdom of Yemen. In addition, he now permits to me the personal rank of prince, but with the original style of Serene Highness. Thus in Yemen I use Al Agid Abdurrahman Amir al-Kindal, which is Colonel Abdurrahman, the Prince of Condé; and outside, Colonel the Prince of Condé only. On my passport is written: H.S.H. Abdurrahman B.A. de Bourbon, Prince of Condé; and my pen-name is Bruce Condé – as for the past twenty-six years.'

Whether the Imam took all this seriously or not, it seems that he recognized Condé's title and also satisfied his ambition to hold high military rank. At any rate, by the middle of 1965, the former Bruce Condé was signing his letters Major-General Prince Abdurrahman Bourbon-Condé.

When I met him at Prince Abdullah Hussein's headquarters, Condé readily agreed to be my escort and interpreter in Yemen in so far as he could obtain leave from his duties with the prince. While we waited for the prince to awaken and to receive me Condé took me to his tent, where he solemnly performed the ritual of Moslem prayer. He took his conversion absolutely seriously and would tolerate no remarks in lighter vein on this subject. Some young boys from local tribes who had never seen a European before watched me curiously. They asked Abdurrahman: 'Why doesn't he pray?' They listened with round-eyed astonishment to his explanation that I was a Christian.

Condé then got me some breakfast. He introduced me to three boys, aged fourteen, fifteen and sixteen, who had been captured during the recent fighting; the Yemenis, like most living creatures, while willing to kill their adult enemies, preferred to spare the young. Condé had even obtained a rifle for one of the boys, whose name was Sharif Mohsin bin Nasser and who claimed to be of the Ashraf nobility.

A little later Condé and I were admitted to an incredibly hot and stuffy tent to meet Prince Abdullah Hussein. The prince sat cross-legged at the back of the tent, with large burning eyes and rather imperious gestures which set him apart from the mass of humanity packed in front of him. It was the implausibly large number of people attempting to reach the prince that generated so much heat. In fact, the prince conducted his business in this confined space as a kind of self-protection, to limit the number of people who could crowd around him at a single time. The system was that whoever had business with the prince, whoever wanted arms or money from him, or whoever wished to register a complaint, offer his services, or ask his judgment in some dispute would write it on a slip of paper which he would endeavour to hand the prince. The prince would usually make his decision on the spot, either making a note on the paper or issuing an order. If the petitioner – having been told, for instance, that his request for a hundred rifles had been reduced to ten – burst into impassioned speech, the prince would as a rule ignore him. If the petitioner became too insistent the prince's guards would remove him by force.

Speaking easily in English, the prince recalled his political science classes at the American University of Beirut. 'This is a little practical demonstration of public administration,' he joked, 'without offices, files and secretaries.'

I noted that Prince Hussein's tent was pitched under a tree in a large open field. When I asked why he pitched his tent in such an exposed place, he replied that the Egyptians would never imagine that he would dare to put his headquarters so much out in the open and would consequently overlook it. Nonetheless, when a few minutes later several Egyptian aircraft roared over the horizon, he and his headquarters, and I with them, scattered in haste to the high reeds and underbrush of a near-by wadi, where we were completely out of sight.

I contemplated the faces of the tribesmen crowding around us in the wadi. Here were the sheikhs, petitions in their hands, tall, long-headed and long-faced, features which, according to the British scholar Hugh Scott, may represent a Nordic influence. Around them were their tribesmen, not as tall, but darker and more broad-shouldered. The tall sheikhs were for the most part identical with the Sayed, or Ashraf, the descendants of the prophet, some of whose ancestors migrated from Mecca and who now form a religious aristocracy, while the tribesmen are the Qabail, descendants, in part, of the original inhabitants.

The interminable petitioning continued in our hiding-place, while Egyptian planes wheeled in the sky far above us and filled the air with their rumbling engines. At last the prince was ready to talk to me. He addressed me almost fiercely: 'It is your duty,' he declared, 'to tell the American people that we ask for help – not for manpower, but for technicians, guns and ammunition. It is essential that the truth be told in the United Nations. For a month and a half I have been waiting for United Nations action. They are ignoring the situation. Have they lost all sense of conscience and freedom? Are they upholding these unusual actions by the Egyptians? We have heard a lot about this U.N. The whole Yemeni people are asking – where is the U.N.? Where is the peace and self-determination we have been told the U.N. stands for?'

The prince's mountain isolation seemed to have made him eager to talk politics to an American visitor. I tried to steer the conversation back to the fighting and asked him how he had formed the army of which he was now the head.

'When I entered the Yemen about a week after the revolution, accompanied by five or six men, the first village I came to was al Hazm,' he recalled. 'I started calling the chiefs of the tribes and asking them whether they would fight. They gathered around eagerly and all replied that they would fight to the last days of their lives to destroy the enemies of their religion. For, as you know, the system of government we have here is based on religion.'

He said he had urged the tribes to fight a 'jihad' or holy war, and that his army kept growing until he had more men than he did arms. At that time most came from the Dahm tribe, a part of the Bakil tribal confederation who live half in the mountains, half in the desert, and are particularly warlike. The prince sadly observed that the Egyptian bombers had destroyed many villages and that the people had fled to the mountains. 'The crops are going to waste and the cattle are neglected, but because of that men have rallied around me all the more.'

He said he had fought three battles, the first in Wadi Karid, where he had captured one armoured car, two machine-guns and fifteen prisoners; the second in the adjoining Wadi Hirran, where he had now established his camp, and where he had killed more than 100 men and taken twenty-five prisoners. Near the end of Wadi Hirran, about fifteen miles east of the town of Dhibin, he explained, was a castle called Sinwan, which the Egyptians had fortified with four tanks and five or six armoured cars. In his third battle, on 11 November, he had attacked and taken Sinwan, obliging the Egyptians – who fought here for the first time, without any Yemenis in support – to abandon the tanks and armoured cars and to withdraw to Dhibin. The Egyptians left on the hillsides around Sinwan the bodies of about 200 dead, which rotted in the sun and were picked by birds of prey because no one would bury them.

The prince had seen no prospect of using the armoured vehicles and had therefore burned them. After finding the castle too exposed to hold, he had burned that also, and withdrawn to his present position. He said the castle burned for five hours, exploding fuel and ammunition. There had been twenty-five Yemeni women inside, ostensibly scrub-women and cooks. 'I sent them home to their villages after having their names broadcast from our radio station.'

He maintained that, in the three battles he had fought, his forces had killed 245 Egyptians. His next objective was the town of Raydah, fifty miles north of Sana. But before he could approach Raydah he would have to deal with the town of al Harf, which the Egyptians were using as a base from which to strike out and cut royalist communications with Najran. 'Tonight my men will attack al Harf,' he announced. 'When we have taken this place, the Egyptians will be cut off from the whole northern area.' He estimated the force at al Harf to be two tanks, seven armoured cars, 350 Egyptians and 200 Yemeni republicans. At Dhibin, he said, there were 250 Egyptians and 100 Yemenis.

Prince Abdullah Hussein maintained that his great problem was his inability to fight off Egyptian aeroplanes. 'We suffer from the planes,' he said. 'We don't have any anti-aircraft guns, only rifles and some cannon taken at Sinwan.' He said he had written to Prince Mohamed, who was in charge of supplies at Najran, requesting drivers for some trucks he had captured and if possible anti-aircraft guns and bazookas for use against tanks. It took at least two weeks to get supplies from Najran, he said.

He was supposed to be in touch with his commander-in-chief, Prince Hassan, but his radio had broken down and the repair man sent to him from Saudi Arabia had turned out to be a spy. He had sent the man back to Najran in chains. So, for the time being, his communications with other royalist units were entirely by runner.

The prince remarked that his men did not care for the modern American M.1 Garrand rifle, as it was too hard to keep clean. They preferred bolt-action, single-shot weapons of an older model. 'My men are the best shots in the world. Sometimes they can kill the driver through the slots in the sides of armoured cars. If we had 30,000 rifles and 500 rounds of ammunition for each rifle,' he asserted, 'we could take Sana in a week.' Some of his recruits were 'blue warriors' from the Arhabi tribes of the Khowlan, who came carrying spears and battleaxes, their faces discoloured with the indigo dye they used for turbans and clothes.

From my conversation with Prince Abdullah Hussein, it seemed to me that the royalist leaders could not quite make up their minds whether their best chance lay in fighting a purely guerilla war with the simplest arms, mainly rifles, or whether, to be successful, they must learn to use more modern weapons. It is true they captured anti-aircraft guns and other modern equipment, but at this stage of the war they rarely knew how to use them. It took another couple of years for the Yemenis to develop the techniques of guerilla warfare with modern weapons and semi-regular forces. The training camp at Najran (later moved into Yemen at Hanjar) was putting many Yemenis through its courses, but they seemed to forget their skills as soon as they returned to old surroundings. Their reactions to bombing, for instance, seemed to vary between bravado and abject terror. The idea of taking cover never seems to have occurred to them.

A further problem was that the princes had to figure that one-half to two-thirds of their men would be 'on leave', looking after their families and tilling their fields. After all, ordinary life had to go on. If a prince needed men in a hurry he would send couriers through the countryside and the sheikhs and their fighting men would return, carrying their arms with them.

Once a man is issued a gun he considers it his personal property, an important item of individual wealth. The quest for rifles and other weapons may explain some of the vulnerability to bribery of the Yemeni tribesmen. Some would go to Najran to collect weapons, take them back to their villages and then volunteer on the republican side in order to collect another batch of weapons.

Fear was another tribal motivation. At times the princes were incredibly cruel in punishing acts of disloyalty. For instance, the Egyptians once bribed a part of the Dahm tribe called the Dhu Mohamed, who numbered 2,000 men, women and children. Another part of the Dahm, called the Dhu Hussein, stood by the royalists. As a demonstration, meant to teach others a lesson, the princes declared the Dhu Mohamed *kufura*, meaning 'outside Islam'. The royalist forces then proceeded to destroy every house in the Dhu Mohamed villages north-east of al Hazm. They killed all their camels, their sheep, their goats and their donkeys. They beat the women and took one-fifth of the men as hostages to Najran; another fifth they carried off as fighting men. They seized all the tribe's gold, their 'jambiyas' (daggers) and other articles of value.

But neither fear nor venality could explain the success with which the royalists fought on this eastern side of the country between the mountains and the desert. After my visit to Prince Abdullah Hussein

I realized that tradition, religion, dislike of the Egyptians, and the magnetic leadership of the young princes combined with the other factors to keep the recruits flowing into the royalist camp. The balance of loyalty weighed heavily in the royalists' favour.

X

The Queen of Sheba's Capital

Now when the Queen of Sheba heard of the fame of Solomon concerning the name of the Lord, she came to test him with hard questions. She came to Jerusalem with a very great retinue, with camels bearing spices, and very much gold, and precious stones; and when she came to Solomon, she told him that which was on her mind.

And Solomon answered all her questions; there was nothing hidden from the King which he could not explain to her. And when the Queen of Sheba had seen all the wisdom of Solomon, the house that he had built, the food of his table, the seating of his officials, and the attendance of his servants, their clothing, his cupbearers, and his burnt offerings which he offered at the house of the Lord, there was no more spirit in her.

And she said to the King: 'The report was true which I heard in my own land of your affairs and of your wisdom, but I did not believe the reports until I came and my own eyes had seen it; and behold, the half was not told me; your wisdom and prosperity surpass the report which I heard. Happy are your wives. Happy are those your servants, who continually stand before you and hear your wisdom. Blessed be the Lord your God, who had delighted in you and set you on the throne of Israel. Because the Lord loved Israel for ever, he has made you King, that you may execute justice and righteousness.'

Then she gave the King a hundred and twenty talents of gold, and a very great quantity of spices, and precious stones; never again came such abundance of spices as these which the Queen of Sheba gave to King Solomon.

Moreover the fleet of Hiram, which brought gold from Ophir, brought from Ophir a very great amount of almug wood and precious stones. And the King made of the almug wood supports for the house of the Lord, and for the King's house, lyres also and harps for the singers; no such almug wood has come, or been seen, to this day.

And King Solomon gave to the Queen of Sheba all that she desired, whatever she asked besides what was given her by the bounty of King Solomon. So she turned and went back to her own land, with her servants.   I Kings x. 1–29.

Having come so far into this strange land I was determined to visit the city of Marib, where once had been the capital of the Queen of Sheba. To me Marib meant mystery and romance. I knew that because the Imams made access so difficult not more than half a dozen Europeans had ever seen the ruins at Marib. Thomas Joseph Arnaud, the French pharmacist, had been there briefly in 1843; Joseph Halévy, a French rabbi, and Eduard Glaser, an Austrian archaeologist, had managed to get there disguised as bedouin in 1870 and 1889. The only systematic archaeological investigation, led by the American Wendell Phillips in 1951, had ended with the escape of the entire expedition to British protection in South Arabia. Local officials, jealous of the treasure which they imagined the Americans were discovering, had threatened them with arrest, a story Phillips has told delightfully in his book *Qataban and Sheba*.

All these explorations and studies revealed little about the famous Queen of Sheba, or Queen Bilqis, as she is known in Arab legend. She may have been, as the Ethiopians claim, an Abyssinian princess, or she may, as H. St John Philby, the explorer and archaeologist, says, have come from northern Arabia.[1] But it seems much more likely that she came from Saba, from which the name Sheba is derived. In ancient times Marib was called Saba and the name is preserved today in Yemen's Wadi Saba and probably also in Shabwa, a city of the Hadhramaut, 130 miles to the east.

The Queen doubtless ruled over a great trading centre and might reasonably have travelled north to see one of her best customers, King Solomon, known as 'the wisest man in the world', who bought great quantities of incense, spices and silk, and whose

[1] According to the *Matshafa Negast*, an ancient history of Ethiopia, present-day Yemen and Ethiopia were united during the reign from 980 to 950 B.C. of Queen Makeda, who was known as the Queen of Sheba; she ruled over both countries from two capitals, Axum in north-eastern Ethiopia, and Marib.

kingdom lay athwart one of her main lines of communication with the western world. According to one legend, her husband had been killed and her wise men had told her that she, too, would die if she did not bear a son. The story is that after her visit to King Solomon she did in fact become pregnant, and according to Ethiopian historians her son became Menelik I, who was crowned King of Ethiopia. Ethiopians consider the Queen of Sheba and King Solomon to be the ancestors of Haile Selassie I, emperor of Ethiopia, from which claim he derives his title, 'Conquering Lion of Judah'. It is said that King Solomon was worried at first by rumours that his visitor, the beauty of her features notwithstanding, possessed hoofs like a goat. Anxious to avoid embarrassing her the King devised a plan to find out the truth: he ordered the construction of a room with a crystal floor that looked exactly like water. When Queen Bilqis reached the threshold of this room she instinctively lifted her skirts, as though stepping into a pool of water, and the King perceived thankfully that she possessed not hoofs, but the most elegant feet.

Condé, who dreamed that he would some day be the kingdom of Yemen's director of antiquities, seized eagerly on this opportunity to visit Marib. He obtained permission from Prince Abdullah Hussein to accompany me on the rest of my journey. At Marib we hoped to find another of the Yemeni princes, Hassan bin Hassan. It was he who had first raised the Abidah tribe and the tribes of the Khawlan in the first days of the war and with them had occupied Marib and Harib and all but two fortified points at Sirwah. Unfortunately Hassan bin Hassan was unwell. Hours before we arrived at what had been his camp he had departed for Aden and London for medical treatment, while his brother Abdullah Hassan took over from him.

At dusk, as we approached an oasis where we thought Prince Hassan bin Hassan would be, we came suddenly under fire. We heard the crack of several rifles being fired and the unnerving zing of bullets overhead. Our driver lurched forward and doubled his speed so that, clinging to the sides of the truck, we went hurtling through the night and were soon out of range. We never found out who was shooting at us, much less why. But Condé suspected that some of the Murad tribe, who were supporting the republicans, had tried to stop us. This tribe had a long history of trouble with old Imam Ahmed and fell naturally into the service of the republicans, who had, so Condé said, hired a group of twenty of them as raiders.

That night we slept on the ground again, I in my shepherd's cloak, in sight of Marib. The night at the edge of the desert was so cold that we overcame our instinctive desire not to attract attention and built a healthy bonfire. But in the morning my crew of driver and guards showed that they were thoroughly alarmed by the near ambush of the night before. They wanted to spend the day in hiding in one of the wadis. They had never wanted to come so far; they wanted to go back to Najran. But once again we persuaded them to go on.

First we visited some of the villages around Marib that had been bombed in the preceding few weeks. As we approached, the jagged outlines of bombed houses stood out against the skyline; some were blackened by fire. Even trees at the edge of the villages were seared by the heat of fire-bombs. In the fields near by we found the remains of some of these bombs and one of them apparently still intact and unexploded. It consisted of a tin canister about three feet long and ten inches in diameter, presumably packed with some inflammable substance. I had seen exactly the same kind of fire-bomb dropped by the Iraqis on Kurdish villages of northern Iraq.

In the Abidah village of Ghujeila, one of the few people we found among the ruined or abandoned houses was the chief of the village, Sheikh Ali bin Sakeh. He told us that in a raid about ten days previously twenty people had been killed. One of the bombs which fell in the village square had killed twenty camels and five cows; in another attack a few days later, fifty sheep had been killed at the edge of the village by the last stick of ten bombs. In other villages in this vicinity the story was similar: Ramsa, ten dead; al Hathan, seven dead; al Hazan, fifty-six dead. No wonder that most villages around Marib were completely deserted. A single stick of bombs dropped across the village was enough to send its inhabitants running for the mountains, where they would find caves and ravines to hide in.

In a shed at the edge of one of the villages we found an old field-gun, which Condé said the royalists had captured from the republicans in the first days of the war. It could not be used, he said, for lack of ammunition or, for that matter, anyone who knew how to use it.

Condé was soon distracted from observation of bomb damage

by the many stones bearing pre-Islamic inscriptions he found built into the houses of these villages. On the open hillsides between the villages were also thousands of stones bearing inscriptions or carvings – of flowers, leaves, ox-heads, animals, men, women and children – the remains of seventeen temples, with their contents of altars and statues, said to have existed in and around the city of Marib in the days of the Queen of Sheba.

Before we reached Marib we came near the great dam which bears the same name. Called Sudd al Arim in the Koran, it was built by Smoh'Ali ya Nuf, first King of Sheba, who reigned from 850 to 825 B.C. It was 660 yards long and sixty feet high, designed to control the waters of the river Adhanah in the Wadi Shibwan and its tributaries from scores of mountain-sides. It was thanks to this astonishing work of engineering that Dionysius the Greek could write this description of the land of Sheba in his work *Arabia Felix*, dated about A.D. 90:

> You can always smell the sweet perfume of marvellous spices, whether it be incense or wonderful myrrh. Its inhabitants have great flocks of sheep in the meadows and birds fly in from distant isles, bringing leaves of pure cinnamon.

Since those days the bedouin have removed the bronze bolts between huge blocks of granite and sand has drifted high around the base of the dam. Yet large sections are in such good condition still that one can imagine the dam readily restored, to transform the desert once more into perfumed gardens and lush meadows.

The ruins of a similar but smaller dam, about 150 yards long, and built about the same time, may be seen at Hirran, not far from the place where I camped with Prince Abdullah Hussein.

When the Marib dam broke at last, probably around the year A.D. 570, it was undoubtedly because, after centuries of economic decline, the people of Sheba or their successors were no longer able to make the necessary repairs. The collapse of the dam was one of the epoch-making events of the ancient world, for it marked the end of a great civilization built around economic resources derived from the Incense Trail. The Arabs, however, like to attribute the collapse to a giant rat, which is said to have gnawed through the dam's foundations. While it is true that even today the region does abound in gophers of great size, the story of the giant rat is perhaps the ancient equivalent of those favourite modern

Arab stories about the machinations of British Intelligence and the C.I.A., whom they like to make the scapegoats for whatever ills befall them.

Just outside Marib we discovered, of all things, a parked helicopter, incongruous with its long sleek rotor-blades against the near-by skyscraper skyline of the town, which was clustered on a mound like some strange mirage. The helicopter was the one captured by the royalists when it landed there in the first days of the war with a pay-roll sent from Sana and three Russian technicians. The Russians had been sent out to Aden and eventually returned to the Soviet Union via London, leaving behind them on the plane a technical assistance manual and useful maps of Yemen.

At the city gates stood a deserted fort in which the royal governor had established a museum in the 1930s, after the Imam Yahya, grandfather of al Badr, had suppressed the local prince, Abdurrahman Amer, whose family had maintained a certain autonomy for more than three hundred years; later I met the prince's son and several other relatives, all evidently proud of their aristocratic forebears. We found that many of the precious statues and other treasures that had been stored on shelves against the walls of the museum had been shaken to the floor by the impact of bombs dropped near by. Condé was horrified. Lovingly he picked up a beautiful alabaster relief of a bull's head representing the moon god. In the piled-up, dusty confusion of museum exhibits he searched in vain for a particular bronze plaque, three feet by two in size, which showed on one side a boy brandishing a jambiya and riding a griffon (half lion, half eagle), on the other a goddess concealed behind grapes. He was distressed that this particular plaque should have disappeared, for he had some years before selected it, as a noble example of Sheban art, for reproduction on Yemeni postage stamps.

We ventured on foot into the narrow streets of Marib, which is also the home of numerous Ashraf, members of a religious aristocracy which originated in Mecca and which traces its ancestors back to Mohamed. But now the hard-packed earth and stone streets were ghostly and deserted. Every living creature had fled in terror, and the town was a completely empty shell. We did not stay long.

Ignoring the protests of our driver, who kept searching the skies for Egyptian planes, and urging haste, we set off towards midday on a trip into the desert to the site of Marib's greatest monument, the incredible temple of Ilumquh, the moon god. With a great sense of excitement I climbed out of our truck, and under a broiling noonday sun made my way with Condé over hills of soft drifting sand into a maze of monolithic rectangular columns. Grandly and alone, they projected tantalizingly from the billows of sand, begging, so it seemed to me, to be excavated, admired and protected. Beyond the columns we saw a great irregular oval wall, twenty-seven feet high in some places and about a thousand feet in circumference, which surrounded the main temple. Except where repairs had been made no trace of mortar was to be seen, just huge finely-dressed blocks of stone perfectly fitted together.

Dr Frank Albright, the principal scholar of the 1951 Wendell Phillips expedition, believed that, where we could now see nine pillars, thirty-two had once stood, built around an inner court and opening into a forecourt in a great hall at the eastern end of the temple. From the inner court, as Dr Albright described it, broad steps covered with sheets of bronze once led through a portal into the sanctuary of the temple, where stood a marble altar decorated with intricate carvings including creatures whom the Shebans venerated, such as lions, eagles, bulls, horses and serpents. From a fountain in the inner court, water fell fifteen feet to the bottom of the steps that led up into the temple. Dr Albright believed that the water had fallen so long that it had deeply furrowed and finally worn through the sheet of bronze at the foot of the steps.

The walls of the forecourt were hung with bronze votive plaques thanking the gods for some favour, perhaps the completion of a difficult voyage, perhaps the birth of a son. Some also were texts of confessions, for the Shebans believed that offences against the gods could be atoned by public confession. In one a king confessed his sins and declared that he had lacerated his face. Other types of inscriptions were made directly on the stone walls of the fore-court. They included an announcement, decorated with carved snakes down its right side, of a victory won by a Sheban king. Some of the bronze plaques and some of the inscribed stones had been removed to museums, but a great many more of the plaques had been carried off by bedouin to sell or to melt down for use as spearpoints or in a later century as ammunition. And, where the walls had tumbled down, the bedouin, oblivious to art and history, carried off the inscribed stones as building materials. Nonetheless, some parts of the plaques are still in place and many an inscription still remains to be read for knowledge of this remarkable people.

What we saw before us here was above all evidence of Sheban belief in the supernatural. This temple, known to the Arabs today as the temple of Awwam, was dedicated to the greatest of Sheban gods, Ilumquh, the moon god. In addition to Ilumquh, they worshipped a female goddess of the sun called Dat Himyam. The sons of the moon and sun gods were the stars, they believed, and the star god was Athtar. The Shebans loved the moon and the star gods, because they protected the desert at night when they did most of their travelling. They did not like the sun goddess so well, which is understandable, for the sun in this part of Arabia is too often an enemy. They had a personalized conception of their gods, who were said to be owners of flocks and land. The entire state of Qataban was said to belong to the moon god. The gods were served by a hierarchy of priests who, as agents of the gods, collected taxes to administer their properties and maintain the temples.

The seventeen temples of Marib and still others at Sirwah were places of asylum where a man might find safety from his enemies. They contained statues in human and animal form which the Shebans worshipped as symbols of their gods. In the same way they worshipped sacred stones. The faithful might dedicate women and slaves to the service of the gods in the temples or contribute gold, or jewellery, or garments with which to clothe the statues. Or they might make sacrifices of animals or other foods upon altars where fires burned and from which incense rose to heaven. Weapons were brought to the temples to be purified under the patronage of Halfan, the god of oaths. Ritual hunts were carried out to invoke divine favour or to celebrate the building of a new temple. The gods appeared more as spirits to be exorcized and propitiated than as deities to be loved. Prayers, performed privately as well as in temples, were closely associated in the Sheban mind with the power of magic and sorcery. The people carried amulets in leather bags on a cord around the neck to ward off the evil eye, just as modern Yemenis do to this day. Pilgrimages were not only to the temples but to sanctuaries, inhabited by oracles whom the Shebans rewarded with offerings of statues and plaques of bronze, as well as the more useful offerings of food. During pilgrimages sexual relations were prohibited.

In the religious practices of the Shebans one may discern several converging influences. The more superstitious practices are perhaps left over from the Stone Age. The worship of the heavenly bodies may be due to Babylonian influence. Some of their architectural schemes – indeed the circular design of the temple at Marib itself – were Hamitic in origin; others, including rectangular and other geometric designs, were imported by the Semites, who somewhat later penetrated the area from the north. The Semites are believed to have brought with them the custom of worshipping trees and stones as the abodes of spirits. From them also originated the practice of centering religious ritual on a small stone building containing a black stone which became known as the Kaaba.

The archaeologists tell us that the Shebans built tombs into the walls on the eastern side of their great temple, though in other parts of Yemen they were cut into inaccessible cliff faces. At the foot of the temple wall they built rectangular tombs, the fronts of which were carved to look like houses. While they had no windows, the doors, flanked by pillars and surmounted by triangular portals of a vaguely classical character, sometimes opened into rectangular chambers that had been hewn out of the natural rock of the cliff.

In the autumn of 1964, with my son Dana, then ten years old, I visited a most remarkable example of these tombs at Meda'in Saleh, in Saudi Arabia, which was a major station on the Incense Trail at its intersection with the caravan route between Mesopotamia and the Nile valley. We had been invited to accompany the American ambassador, Parker T. Hart, on his overland expedition from Jeddah to Meda'in Saleh. But, because I could not arrive in time to join the ambassador's convoy of diplomats, the Saudi authorities arranged to fly us to Meda'in Saleh aboard a Saudi Arabian Airlines Dakota. The American pilot, called Bob Glover, was an expert in desert landings. Twice he flew over a great salt flat dropping down just far enough to thump one wheel at full power on the ground and test its hardness. Then, as casually as though he were landing on a concrete strip, he brought us in. Before us lay a scene which Ambassador Hart, in the article he wrote later, described as follows:

The sheer grandeur of this valley is comparable to the American south-west. Its colour is tawny like a lion's skin, the shades moving from light yellow to dark brown. We made our camp under a great oval sandstone outcropping, cut with tombs on

146

all sides. The valley north and south was cut in sandstone walls, columns and pinnacles in an architectural style almost identical to the tomb front of Petra, the 'rose-red city – half as old as Time'. Although there is nothing equal to the Graeco-Roman styles of the great Petra tomb fronts and public buildings, and the rock colour is less striking, these tomb fronts were better preserved, perhaps because here there is almost no rain.

One formation, known as the Jabal Ethlib, consists of a collection of sandstone pinnacles covered with inscriptions and featuring a large square room, perhaps once used as a ceremonial hall very similar to the one which faces the monastery at Petra. This is known by the Arabs as the Diwan, or 'council chamber'. But most of the cliff carvings were clearly intended as tombs.

Up and down the valley rock columns, cliffs and ranges rise like islands in a sea of white sand forty miles from north to south and twenty-five miles from east to west.

We slept that night inside one of the tombs, the floor of which was littered with bones. It was said that these bones were the remains of meals eaten by generations of earlier travellers, although why they should have thrown their refuse into the cave rather than out of it is puzzling. While they clearly were not human bones, we might have found some had we dug down into the floor. We might then have found cups, plates, jewellery, perfume bottles and many other things which the Shebans and the inhabitants of the other pre-Islamic kingdoms believed the dead would require in the after-life. These were among the things that Wendell Phillips and his team of archaeologists found in their deep excavations at Timna, capital of Qataban, and at Marib. We chose these ghoulish surroundings because the air in the tombs, if slightly fetid, was warm. Outside where we built our camp fire the temperature plummeted immediately after sundown.

While sheikhs and other notables of the region arrived at the diplomats' camp site with invitations to dine on rice and roasted sheep, the villagers came to tell stories and to sell artifacts which we presumed to be of Nabataean origin. The Nabataeans were the people who controlled the Mediterranean end of the Incense Trail from their capital at Petra, which is now in the kingdom of Jordan; at times during the millennium their rule extended far into what is now Saudi Arabia, where it undoubtedly met the sphere of the Sabeans. The artifacts included much-oxidized copper coins bearing traces of eagles, rosettes and other inscriptions similar to those on the façades of the tombs. They also included bits of pottery, of a type that litters sections of this valley. One member of the diplomatic party purchased an undamaged urn and some slightly damaged bowls and jars. Another member, burrowing in the floor of a tomb, turned up bits of textile that he took to be the remains of Nabataean burial clothing.

The villagers might have had more to sell had they not been so afraid of entering the tombs. According to their stories, drawn from the Koran, a messenger of God named Salih once tried to convert the people of this place to a belief in God. To convince them he performed a miracle, bringing a camel out of a rock. The camel gave so much milk that she could supply the whole town and still not go dry. But the villagers would not believe. Then Salih told the people to go to their homes, for they would know God's wrath. An earthquake overturned their city: all that remained was the sites of their graves on the mountain-sides. According to local superstition, anyone who cultivates the earth in this valley will perish. The tombs, it is said, are haunted. Yet nothing disturbed our sleep that night.

Like the tombs at Marib the façades of the tombs here, ten to sixty feet in height, are characterized by portals flanked by Corinthian-type columns closely attached to the side of the cliff and surmounted by classical decorative motifs, such as eagles, griffons, rosettes and urns. Over the portals are also carved tablets, with or without epitaphs, and pyramidal zigzag designs of Semitic character. In the low-ceilinged interiors are sunken grave pits and curious shelves hewn out of the walls. Marks made by iron stone-cutting instruments 2,000 or more years ago still show white in the dim interior of the caves, as though they had been made yesterday.

The site was first explored eighty years ago by Charles M. Doughty, the British author and traveller. The names Doughty used for the principal monuments in his account of his explorations are still familiar to today's villagers. They include one monument called Kasr al Bint, 'the maiden's bower', high up on a ledge and almost inaccessible; also Beit es Sany, 'the smith's house', where according to local legend a sheikh fought to the death with a smith who had dishonoured his daughter. Other monuments mentioned by Doughty were the Mahal al Majlis, or 'senate-house', which is exceptionally large but unfinished; and the Diwan. The Diwan is the only monument hewn in a mountain called Ethlib, and the only one of the monuments presumably intended for the living rather than the dead. Instead of the usual small door, its front is wide open, its interior large and high as in a council chamber. Indeed, the Diwan looks as though it might have served as a public building.

All that we saw at Marib and at this station on the Incense Trail reflected the lives of a people who were handsome, skilled and prosperous. Their delicately shaped features, short straight noses and relatively fair complexions were much like those of today's Yemenis. Their kilted dress, too, was similar. Their accomplishments, on the other hand, undoubtedly exceeded those of their descendants.[1] They were expert workers in stone and metal, who knew how to cut translucent alabaster for windows and how to fashion exquisite jewellery. They were engineers who could plan and build temples, dams, wells, tunnels and multi-storeyed houses unrivalled in the ancient world. They were administrators whose realm extended at certain times nearly as far as Mecca in the north to Aden in the south, and from the Red Sea in the west to the Indian Ocean in the east. Their merchants ranged much farther still, for this was above all a kingdom built on trade. By sea they travelled down the coast of East Africa, as far as the Cape, around the periphery of Arabia to Persia and across the Indian Ocean; by caravan they moved across North Africa to Carthage, south to the headquarters of the Nile, north to Nineveh. Above all they travelled up and down the Incense Trail, the network of caravan

---

[1] But Harold Ingrams in his book *Arabia and the Isles* offered this comment on the artistic abilities of the ancient and modern Arabs: 'The pre-Islamic Arabs of the south had no more artistic ability than their Moslem descendants today. They were far behind some African and Indonesian tribes in these matters. To this one must except only their architecture. The ancient South Arabians built well in stone, shaping their blocks better and carrying their cumbersome monumental scripts with greater skill than could the Hadhramis of today. But these latter are superb architects in mud, and in this medium are no whit inferior to their ancestors, working in stone. Taking it all in all the Hadhramis of today seem neither better nor worse than their ancestors in their way of life and the things they make.'

routes that linked the four corners of the ancient world, and the key to their wealth and civilization.[1]

In March 1967 Wendell Phillips made a sentimental return visit to Marib under somewhat harrowing circumstances.

In trucks supplied by the Sharif of Beihan he and his party made a one-day dash from Beihan to Marib, where he discovered to his dismay that most of the archaeological treasures which he had left in the fort there had disappeared. The sheikhs of the Abidah tribes who welcomed Phillips maintained that the treasures had been removed by the Egyptians when they withdrew from Marib. But I believe it is just as likely that the tribesmen themselves, thoroughly aware of the value of these archaeological specimens, had carried them off. Upon his return to Aden Phillips issued an appeal to President Nasser to ensure the safety of the missing treasures.

[1] The information in this chapter is derived from *Arabia Before Mohamed* by Dr Lacy O'Leary, 1927; *The Religious Beliefs and Practices of the Arabians* by W. E. N. Kensdale, 1953; *Manners and Customs and Various Religions of the Pre-Islamic Arabs*, published by the Mohamedan Tract and Book Depot, Lahore, Punjab, 1891; and *Journey through Yemen* by W. B. Harris, 1893.

XI

The Qadi in Harib

✦✦

AT Marib, ancient and modern times were telescoped. Bombs had fallen among monuments of the past; today's warriors clambered wondering among the ruins: an intriguing, nostalgic situation, tempting to linger over. Yet we must turn back to today's reality.

Our journey out of the past back into today's war turned out to be an easy jaunt of a few hours in our red Ford truck across the desert from Marib to Harib. For part of our journey we travelled over an extraordinary road of large, roughly-hewn blocks of stone, each perhaps a foot or two square, fitted artfully together to form a hard and almost indestructible surface, in surprisingly good repair in some places, washed out or covered deep in sand in others. No one seemed to know by whom the road had been built. Clearly it was very old. It may well have been part of one of the famous roads constructed in the eleventh century by Queen Sayida.

Harib, where we arrived late on the afternoon of 6 December 1962, proved to be a nerve centre of the war. Here the long supply line from Najran, in Saudi Arabia, and the much shorter one from Beihan, in South Arabia, came together in a considerable population centre, where there were storage facilities and workshops. This was the natural base of operations for Prince Abdullah Hassan, commander of the royalist force in the Khawlan mountains east of Sana. His strategy was to threaten the capital directly, while others, such as his cousin, Prince Abdullah Hussein, his father, the Prime Minister, and the forces under the Imam's direction farther west, effected more indirect pressure. In the centre of Harib, guiding operations in the southern sector generally, was a man called Qadi Ahmed al Sayaghi.

We found Qadi al Sayaghi deep within the labyrinth of the governor's fort. Reclining against cushions on the well-carpeted floor of a large, cool and pleasant reception-room, a window at his back, he talked long about his own career and ambitions, about Sallal and the Imam, about the strategy of the war, and about political policy. Condé acted as his interpreter, for, surprisingly in such an intelligent and highly placed man, he spoke no language except Arabic. Yet he showed himself to be the most sophisticated, politically and intellectually, of all the Yemeni leaders.

Somewhat older than the princely army commanders, except for the Prime Minister, Prince Hassan, Qadi al Sayaghi was the man whom Ambassador Wadsworth, formerly the United States envoy to both Saudi Arabia and Yemen, had called 'the key man in Yemen'. He was a large, well-built man from whom emanated an aura of authority. He spoke forcefully and with, I sometimes thought, just a touch of arrogance. He told us that during the last years of the Imam Ahmed's rule he had been in exile in the town of Lahej, a few miles outside Aden in South Arabia, because he had disapproved of the Imam's autocratic rule. 'The Imam sent his brother Prince Hassan to get me to return,' he recalled. 'But I refused, even though I hated the separation from my family and the town of Ibb, where for many years I had been the Imam's viceroy and provincial governor. I said I would return only as a private citizen outside the government. The Imam was not satisfied; but he took care of my family. He did not force my decision.'

The astonishing toleration which Imam Ahmed showed for this unusual and strong-minded Yemeni commoner, who never hesitated to speak his mind, was continued under the rule of the young Imam, Mohamed al Badr. When Imam Ahmed died his son al Badr offered Sayaghi the post of deputy Prime Minister; but al Sayaghi refused, because he knew al Badr planned to be his own Prime Minister. 'I did not agree,' he said. 'If al Badr became Prime Minister I was sure that – his pretensions to Nasserism notwithstanding – in the end there would be no real change in Yemen. For instance, he proposed a consultative assembly with thirty-five elected and thirty-five appointed members. This composition would have neutralized its usefulness.'

But when elderly Prince Hassan bin Yahya, the Imam Ahmed's brother, appeared on the scene, first as the new Imam at a moment when al Badr was believed dead, and then as al Badr's Prime Minister, Qadi al Sayaghi became more co-operative. He said that he hoped that under the stress of the *coup d'état* young al Badr would 'change his attitude', and would prove 'better than his father'. He said al Badr had incorporated in the list of reforms he announced upon accession to the throne five points proposed by Prince Hassan. The qadi had therefore accepted the post of deputy Prime Minister and Minister of the Interior. He and the princes were now willing to rally round the Imam as a symbol of unity 'so long as he does not interfere in the real affairs of the government'. Although he avoided saying so, he left me with no doubt that he held the Imam's abilities in low esteem.

'The one blessing in the present situation, which is darkened by revolution, is that Sallal has united the people against him,' he said. He recalled that at the time of the *coup d'état* 'Sallal had an agreement with some of the Zeidis who wanted to make a small revolution'. I did not understand at the time what he meant by a 'small revolution', but I realize now that he was alluding to Sallal's scheme to use the conservative, religious sheikhs, who supported Prince Hassan, for a *coup* against the Imam.

Sayaghi believed that Sallal's hopes of gaining widespread support among the tribes had been dashed because he formed a government without tribal representatives and without personalities of note, indeed a kind of socialist 'people's democracy' in the eastern European sense. 'After that,' he said, 'there was no more possibility of tribal support. He had to make a government of military people. It would be unseemly for us to follow such a man as Sallal, who is not of the religious element and who has neither influence, nor background, nor following, nor respect.' Sallal had alienated the Yemeni people by trying to change the whole structure of Yemen at once, by ruthlessly killing many people in order to attain his ends and then by bringing in the Egyptians. 'After all,' he said, 'we would rather have bad Yemeni rule than any kind of foreign rule. The Yemeni people are very much attached to the imamate, for it represents the religious law to which they are accustomed.'

He believed that it was quite impossible for Sallal or any other republican leader to get the support of the whole Yemeni people: 'The tribes who can fight are already doing so and others are quiet only until they can get enough arms to make it worth their while to fight. Were it not for the Egyptians, Sana would already be in our hands. The only Yemenis who support Sallal are those in Aden, tribes of the south and west, such as those of the Hugeriya province, and a few people in Taiz and Ibb who are in contact with expatriate merchants.'

The qadi considered attempts to capture outlying centres, such as Sadah in the north, as wasted energy. 'We don't want campaigns for isolated posts,' he asserted. He insisted most emphatically that 'we should concentrate our people and weapons on the main object, which should culminate in a one-day assault of Sana. Thus,' he declared, 'we must crush the head of the snake.'

Sayaghi was busy, as he put it, 'contacting all the tribes, particularly those around Sana'. He offered the following notes on the situation of various key tribes:

The royalist tribes around Sana were the Bani Harith and the Arhab in the north, the Hamdan and the Bani Matar in the west.

Somewhat farther from the capital, south of the Bani Harith, were the Bani Hushaysh and the Sanhan, to the north-east the Nahm, and in the region of Marib in the east the Abidah tribe.

To be stressed was the military importance of the Khawlan and the Nahm, some twenty-five kilometres from Sana. Only one of the seven tribes of the Nahm was with Sallal.

The paramount chief of the Bani Hushaysh was in Najran, and two sub-chiefs in Harib were with him. Others in this group of tribes were keeping their attitudes quiet because they did not want reprisals.

The paramount sheikh of the Arhab was in prison and the tribe were bitterly resentful.

The paramount sheikh of the Bani Harith was in Najran and also the son of the paramount sheikh of Hamdan.

The chief of half of the Bani Matar, west of Sana, was now in Najran and three of their other sheikhs were in Harib.

South-east of Sana were the al Haddah, whose important sheikhs, Gausi and al Bohaiti, had been enticed into going to Egypt. One of them had sent his son on a mission to Moscow.

The Dhamar tribe, situated half-way between Sana and Taiz, its territory extending as far as Ibb, had made an independent raid on Ibb.

Sayaghi reported that the republicans were getting some manpower from the large Yafai tribe, whom he estimated to have 100,000 men, in the British-protected South Arabian Federation. He said this tribe had been in revolt against the British for years and that its sultan, Mohamed bin Aidrus al Afifi, felt that the Imam had not given him sufficient support. Now, he said, Sallal had sent the sultan money, and as a result Yafai tribesmen were turning up on the fighting front.

For similar reasons, the Awalek tribe was also supplying manpower to the republic.

Like every other royalist (then and now) Qadi al Sayaghi devoted much of his time to insisting on the friendship he felt for the United States and the folly of American policy in not supporting the royalists. He had been disgusted with young Mohamed al Badr's attachment to Nasser and his involvement with the communist régimes of eastern Europe, but hoped that he had now learned his lesson. 'All the Americans get out of supporting the Egyptians,' he observed, 'is neutralizing Ahmed Sayid, the Egyptian propagandist. Is it worth it?' He proposed that the Egyptians and Russians should withdraw from republican Yemen and that the Saudis withdraw all their assistance from the royalists. 'Then,' he said, repeating the plea I had already heard from Prince Hassan, 'let the United Nations come to Sana and hold a plebiscite free of any outside influence.'

As he talked, the qadi chewed and with a sly smile handed me particularly succulent sprigs of *qat*, with a suggestion that I try it. I did, persistently, but got no effect out of it. The qadi advised me that I must really keep it up for half a day, until my whole system was impregnated with *qat*, before it would do any good. He obviously refused to regard his *qat* as anything but the most harmless and amusing of vices. *Qat* leaves lay strewn all over the floor.

At the end of our talk, Sayaghi informed us that he had four Egyptian prisoners and would like us to see them. He said he told the sheikhs at every opportunity that it was as foolish to kill prisoners as it was to set them free; instead they should be kept, cared for and exchanged at some time for royalist prisoners, or at any rate for an advantage of some sort. We were shown four men quite comfortably installed on cots in a surprisingly clean and airy room at the fort. But I cut the visit short, because I have always felt that, since prisoners of war are under such a variety of pressures, interviews with them are undesirable.

A year and a half later I met Qadi al Sayaghi in different circumstances – though he was still chewing *qat*. Harib had by then been occupied by the Egyptians and republicans, and Sayaghi was living under British protection – with a uniformed guard at his door – in an upper room of a house in Lahej. Politically he had by this time moved into a curious limbo between the royalists and republicans, in search of a third force. He had promoted a meeting on the border with one of the leading moderate republicans, Abdurrahman al Iryani, then a minister in President Sallal's government. While this meeting was undoubtedly connected with an effort by Sayaghi to make arrangements to protect his property interests at Ibb, it was also an attempt to find common ground between conservative republicans and moderate royalists.

But Sayaghi was before his time. The 'third force' movement had not yet started inside the republic, and nothing came of the meeting. Soon afterwards, towards the end of 1963, he was assassinated while travelling through the Jawf in the territory of the Dhu Mohamed, the tribe upon whom the royalists had inflicted such brutal vengeance for their defection. While this would suggest that he was killed by the republicans, the point is actually uncertain. Both sides had reason to resent him.

At our meeting in Lahej, Qadi al Sayaghi seemed embittered and spoke even more harshly of Imam al Badr than before. In his personal demeanour he seemed far more gentle and modest than when I first met him.

Before and after my first talk with Sayaghi I walked around the fascinating old town of Harib. Here again was the skyscraper architecture, though not so grand as in Sana, Sadah or Najran.

But what interested me most were the faces of the tribesmen. The two tribes inhabiting Harib and its surroundings are the Bani Garuyi and the Bani Abd, both of whom are said to have kept themselves relatively free of marriage outside their tribes since the days of the pre-Islamic kingdoms. The Garuyi are very dark, sometimes with a blackness that seems almost blue. They fix their curly hair in a way not seen anywhere else in Arabia, entirely shaven except for two small locks, one on the forehead and the other on the neck, with a small tuft in between. The Bani Abd are also unusual. They are not so dark and their hair is straighter; some might be taken for Indians. The women of both tribes wear their hair in a dark blue cloth tied with a red ribbon. Their robes are long and dark blue, and they wear heavy silver jewellery, rings on fingers and toes, hooks on arms and ankles and pendants at their throats.

At this time, of course, men and women of many other tribes were also in Harib, creating a kaleidoscopic confusion of colourful head-dresses and robes. I joined such a crowd moving out to an open area at the edge of the town, where the Imam's forces held a kind of military demonstration with the imamate flag — red, with a white sword and five stars — and the usual war-dances. The young men in the crowd kept playing a kind of ritualistic game in which they would pretend that one of them was Sallal; the others would hurl themselves upon him, screaming and brandishing their jambiyas.

A young man who observed my camera came to me with several rolls of film and begged me in broken English to get them developed for him. I took the film, and later sent him the prints from Beirut; but I doubt whether he ever got them, for they showed a joyous demonstration of victorious royalists, and I mailed them just a day before learning that Harib had been taken by the Egyptians.

In and out of this crowd hopped a lad of eleven or twelve whose legs were chained together, so that instead of running he had to jump. He seemed quite cheerful about his predicament which, I was told, was the usual form of punishment for a Yemeni boy for whatever it was that Yemeni boys did wrong, like not studying their Koran.

While we were in Harib we were joined by James Mossman, a BBC reporter who was doing a documentary for 'Panorama'. He had come across the border from British-protected Beihan, in the South Arabian Federation, and had visited Prince Abdullah Hassan, who was then leading a campaign against the Egyptian position at Sirwah (not to be confused with Sinwan). Sirwah had been occupied in the very first days of the war by Prince Hassan bin Hassan but had then been lost to the Egyptians. In November the Egyptians had attempted to reinforce this outlying position by staging the first big paratrooper drop of the war, and this had turned into a real disaster for them. The first three groups of sixty paratroopers were dropped too high, and were picked off by Yemeni sharpshooters before they reached the ground. Very few of them survived. The fourth group of sixty established a defensive position at the northern end of the town. So now there were two Egyptian strongpoints in the town, one in the castle and one to the north, with a garrison between them of about 100 men. The Egyptians supplied these positions by air and maintained communications between them by means of several tanks.

As on many other occasions, there was talk among the royalists about staging a massive assault and eliminating these two Egyptian strongpoints. But in the end, as was usual with them, they wisely avoided heavy casualties and by-passed both strongpoints. The Egyptians were left with forts of doubtful value which they could maintain only at great cost in air transport.

Prince Abdullah Hassan moved on to concentrate on the more rewarding targets closer to Sana. From their positions in the lower valleys close to the desert, where they depended on the Jawf and the Dahm tribes, Princes Abdullah Hassan and Abdullah Hussein had leap-frogged forward by-passing non-essential Egyptian strongpoints. They had armed the tribes of Arhab, Ayyal Surreya, Nahm, Hamdan and al Jabal in the areas north, north-east and north-west of Sana. From these forward positions they could hope to ambush Egyptian supply columns trying to get through to Dhibin, Rawdah and Beit Marran, in the Arhabi tribal area about twenty miles north of Sana. One consequence was that the Egyptians were obliged more and more to supply distant outposts such as Sadah, al Harf, Sirwah, Hajjah, Barat and Marib by air.

It is a reflection of the Egyptians' difficulties in overland transport that they were reported at this time to be using helicopters to sow mines on royalist supply routes. In an attempt to interfere with royalist use of these routes by night they also attempted night bombing with flares.

Abdurrahman Condé, who after he left me had transferred from Prince Abdullah Hussein's to Abdullah Hassan's headquarters in Arhab, wrote me on 21 February what he called a 'little picture' of the situation. 'We are much more isolated than when you were with us,' wrote Condé. 'We have moved headquarters forward to a series of strong and well-connected caves one and a quarter miles' walking distance from Sinwan and near the source of abundant waters, including a fairly large (and deep) pool (eight feet or more deep, beneath enormous overhanging trees where we could swim! But we had no fishing tackle with which to catch the enormous fish near the spring).

'Our communications situation is terrible,' he continued. 'Our radio telegraph has been out of order most of the time. We have found that the former operator was in Nasser's pay and was deliberately sabotaging it, and have sent him north in irons for King Saud to deal with (a Saudi, not a Yemeni).' Condé went on to complain that his 'postal sendings' were supposed to be going out via Harib to Beihan and Aden, and via Najran to Jeddah and Riyadh, 'but we never get any replies'. For this he blamed a 'bogging-down or a Nasserite link somewhere. . . . The way Nasser buys treason throughout the Arab world is phenomenal'.

Nor was Prince Abdullah Hassan's supply situation easy. Condé reported that a camel-borne ammunition train which his cousin, Prince Abdullah Hussein, had tried to send him at this time had been ambushed *en route* and there was some doubt as to when, if at all, alternative supplies could get through. In spite of these difficulties Condé indicated a somewhat euphoric attitude among the royalist fighting men.

He said he had gone to a place called al Hayfeh, twenty-three miles north of Sana, and had found some tribesmen who were 'spearmen' and 'some with battle-axes', who had gathered to ask for guns with which to fight the Egyptians. He said that at al Hayfeh, which was on the Egyptian military route through Arhab, the Egyptians had lost eighteen vehicles, including two huge Soviet rocket launchers with all the rockets in place, and 205 of their men were killed. This battle, according to Condé, marked the high-water mark of the Egyptian invasion of the province of Arhab. After that, the Egyptians were unable to send any wheeled vehicles over the road they had built with so much effort.

Condé described another battle in which 'our Arhabis over-turned twelve tanks with tree-trunk levers, poured oil on them and burned them up'. He told a story about one tribal sharp-shooter who had 'picked off fifty Egyptians with fifty rationed bullets in a single day'. Whether this was literally true or not the tribesmen were indeed great marksmen.

The closest royalist approach to Sana had been made, Condé reported, by the Bani Hushaysh tribe, who lived between the Nahm tribal territory and the capital. They had taken Sawan, five miles north-east of Sana, and had occupied Jabal Barash, only two hours' walking distance behind Jabal Nuqum, the 'guardian mountain' two miles east of Sana, which dominates the capital with its great height and thousand-year-old fort. At two points the royalists had used commanding heights overlooking Sana to bombard Egyptian airfields. The Nahm tribesmen, firing from the al Firs heights, had brought direct artillery fire to bear on the main Egyptian northern airport of Ar Rahabah, eight miles to the north of Sana. In addition forces in the Bani Bahlul country, south and south-east of Sana, had succeeded in bombarding the military airport south of Sana, thereby obliging the Egyptians to shift their MiGs and Ilyushins to a safer base at Hodeidah. The old north airport outside Sana at Jiraf could, according to Condé's information, handle only Yaks and Dakotas and the helicopters supplying the outlying Egyptian strongpoints.

The grand strategy of the war at the beginning of 1963 seemed to me as follows. The Egyptians, with their republican auxiliaries, could be regarded as occupying a kind of ridge-back extending from Sana through such strongpoints as Raydah and Amran northwards to Sadah, through the rugged heart of Zeidi tribal territory. The Egyptians maintained their hold of this vital ridge-back from two rear positions: one at Hodeidah, the port, through which flowed their supplies, and the other at Taiz, the diplomatic capital of Yemen, situated in the part of the country which adheres to the Shaffei sect and from which the republicans drew the bulk of their strength. From this Sana-Sadah ridge-back, the valleys lead off eastwards towards the desert and westwards through a mass of mountains and plateaus towards the sea.

One could distinguish four main fighting fronts. The Imam, from his headquarters at Qara, an inaccessible mountain position in the north-western corner of the country, challenged the Egyptians more or less ineffectually from the west. From there royalist control, exercised by a succession of princely commanders, extended loosely in a southerly direction to the vicinity of the town and castle of Hajjah, which was occupied by a republican garrison of 100 men, without Egyptians – the only important republican stronghold in the western mountains. The word 'loosely' must be used of the royalist line because the Egyptians could always penetrate it with their tanks and armoured cars. On the other hand the royalists could move freely most of the time since the Egyptians used their precious armour sparingly. If the royalists could have taken the castle at Hajjah it would have opened the way for effective operations against the main Egyptian supply line over the road between Hodeidah and Sana. But this they did not manage to do, and in consequence later attempts to close the Sana-Hodeidah road proved ineffective.

From the Imam's headquarters the area of his control extended northwards in an arc between the Egyptian strongpoints at Haradh

A rifle and a prayer. *Dr. Ulrich Middendorp*

Arriving for the press conference at the Imam's camp, October 1962. It was here that the Imam proclaimed that he had survived the *coup*.

The Imam al Badr (*right*) outside his cave on Jabal Sheda. With him is his cousin, Prince Hassan bin Hussein.

The Prime Minister, Prince Hassan, talking to tribesmen outside his cave in Wadi Amlah, December 1962.

Prince Abdullah Hussein (*below, center*) with his men soon after the Egyptian air attack in Wadi Hirran, December 1962.

A group of sheikhs waiting to petition Prince Abdullah Hussein. On the left is Abdurrahman Condé, the American-born adviser to the Imam.

The camp used by royalist mercenaries at Hanjar, in north-eastern Yemen.

A Russian-manufactured armored car, captured by royalist guerillas from the Egyptians near Haradh

One of the old Turkish engines from the Pilgrim Railway, the line sabotaged by Lawrence of Arabia in the First World War. The railway follows the original route of the Incense Trail.

The entrance to the Temple of the Moon God at Marib.

The marketplace at Najran.

The village of Amlah, in the Jawf, which the author visited on his trip through royalist territory in December 1962.

A republican helicopter, captured early in the war by the royalists outside Marib. The republicans had not yet painted out the imamic flag on the fuselage.

Egyptian bomb damage in a village near Marib.

Yemeni Jewish family, resettled in camp near Tel Aviv. *United States Technical Aid Mission*

A view of Sadah, showing Yemeni "skyscraper" architecture.

Colonel Hassan Ali Kamal, Egyptian chief of operations, at his desk in Sana.

Two Yemeni girls at Sana's first girls' school, run by Egyptian teachers.

An Egyptian instructor at the Sana military academy shows a Yemeni how to use a bayonet.

Sheikhs of the Sanhan tribe line up to petition the Egyptian commander at Sudah.

These bags of wheat, intended as gifts from the American government,
were being illegally sold in Sana.

A *qat* party in Sana.

n Egyptian soldier accompanies a demonstration in Sana to raise funds for FLOSY, March 1967.

The author with President Sallal, March 1967.

King Faisal at Jeddah

The Imam on Jabal Sheda, December 1964. His health
had begun to suffer from the strain of war and cave life.

The International Red Cross hospital at Uqd.

Pre-Islamic, probably Minaean, rock paintings near Uqd. *Dr. Ulrich Middendorp*

Prince Abdurrahman bin Yahya, youngest brother of the Imam Ahmed, with a veteran of the imamic army, at Uqd.

In the labyrinth of caves at Amara, the royalist supply base south of Uqd, with Prince Abdullah al Kipsy the camp commandant.

With Abdullah al Asnag, one of the leaders of FLOSY, at his headquarters in Taiz, March 1967.

Prince Mohamed bin Hussein, deputy to Imam al Badr, in command of the royalist forces besieging Sana, December 1967. He is a likely candidate to succeed al Badr. *Mark Lennox-Boyd*

and Sadah, through the Razih mountains on the Yemen-Saudi Arabian border, and from there eastwards towards the headquarters of the Prime Minister, Prince Hassan, near Wadi Amlah. On the eastern side of the mountains Prince Hassan was nominally in overall command as well as political chief at this time. But the defective nature of his radio links prevented him from exercising anything like real control over the other princes and most of the time he was preoccupied with operations around Sadah and Harf. Later, in 1964 and 1965, when communications improved, Prince Mohamed Hussein replaced him as Commander-in-Chief in the east.

Prince Hassan's military area overlapped that of the Imam in the Razih mountains; in a southerly direction it met the military area of Prince Abdullah Hussein, the next commander, in the region of Harf. This third front was centred in the mountainous region south-west of the Jawf basin. In three battles just before I visited him Prince Abdullah Hussein had opened the way to Sinwan. While I was with him he was co-operating with Prince Hassan at Harf in an attempt to eliminate Egyptian interference with his lines of communications so that he could turn his attention towards Sana, the fourth fighting front.

Already in the immediate vicinity of Sana, as described earlier, was Prince Abdullah Hassan, who had worked his way from the general area of Harib past Sirwah into the high ground overlooking the capital. His main objective was to occupy strategical points in the mountains as close as possible to the capital. Small wonder, then, that Qadi al Sayaghi should think in terms of 'crushing the head of the snake' and that Condé should have written me from Prince Abdullah Hassan's camp a few weeks later, on 21 February 1963, of the 'definitive assault' upon the capital.

These first months of the war were indeed a season of hope for the royalists; but the pattern was rudely shattered by an Egyptian offensive at the end of February and the beginning of March, by which the Egyptians thrust their armoured forces deeply into the Jawf, occupied the towns of Marib and Harib and made it inevitable that the war would drag on for years.

I personally moved on, in the company of James Mossman, to the comforts of Beihan in the British-protected South Arabian Federation. There I was able to spend a few days in the clean and pleasant guest-house of the Sharif of Beihan, typing up my notes and sending my stories off to the *New York Times*.

Much intrigued, the British officers of the South Arabian Federation army post at Beihan offered to have their signals officer transmit my stories by morse code to the cable and wireless office at Aden. Of course this also gave them an opportunity, which I was delighted to afford them, of reading my stories even before they reached the *New York Times*. They were all understandably antagonistic towards Nasser and the Yemen republic, and enthusiastic about the exploits of the royalists. Had they not been restrained by higher authority I have no doubt that they would have provided the royalists with all the help at their command. At the time, however, their natural instincts appeared to be frustrated, and as far as I could find out such help as went across the border from South Arabia appears to have been channelled through the Sharif of Beihan without any direct assistance from British officers.

I personally knew only about a small fleet of perhaps a dozen Land-rovers which the Sharif of Beihan was said to have contributed personally to the royalists. But there may well have been many things going on that I did not know about. Certainly I learned in the ensuing months and years of regular camel caravans bearing ammunition and arms, making their way from South Arabia to royalist Yemen. Richard Anderegg, a Swiss journalist employed by Radio Suisse, told me late in 1963 that he had seen one of these convoys of camels with cases of ammunition and weapons, some of which he believed had been contributed by the Shah of Persia. And at the beginning of 1964 I was offered passage with a similar convoy from Beihan to Prince Abdullah Hassan's headquarters in the mountains.

XII

The Fighting Fronts

I T has seemed at times during the long struggle in Yemen as though the protagonists were frozen in changeless attitudes – the Imam, smiling boyishly, forever posing, surrounded by his doughty warriors, at the entrance to his cave; the royalist tribesmen forever ten miles outside the gates of Sana; President Sallal, blue-chinned and glowering, forever embarking aboard an aeroplane for medical treatment in Cairo; the Egyptian army forever being reinforced, forever annihilating infiltrators on the borders of Saudi Arabia and South Arabia.

Broadly speaking, the two sides have in fact been locked in a stalemate, in the sense that neither has been able to defeat the other. The Egyptians have never succeeded in their central military aim of isolating and destroying the royalist opposition; they have not even been able to take the first step of sealing the frontiers and cutting the royalists' lines of communication with Saudi Arabia and the British-protected Federation of South Arabia. Nor have the royalists ever been able to achieve their central military aim, to 'crush the head of the snake' by capturing Sana, the capital of the republic and the main Egyptian headquarters and garrison. They have not even achieved their subsidiary aim of cutting the Egyptian lines of communication on the road between Sana and Hodeidah.

Nonetheless, when we examine this four-year period closely, we discover that the convulsive efforts of both sides to break the stalemate have at four distinct stages indeed changed the shape of the conflict. The first of these great efforts was made by the Egyptians in February and March 1963, in what has become known as the 'Ramadan offensive', which carried them into the Jawf in north-eastern Yemen and to the occupation of Marib and Harib on the eastern side of the country. The second effort, made by the royalists, followed a period of disengagement initiated by the United States.

In January and February of 1964 the royalists succeeded for several weeks in closing the Egyptians' main artery, the road from Sana to Hodeidah, and interfering seriously with traffic on the Taiz and Sadah road. This was a highpoint in the royalist war effort.

The third effort, Egyptian again, began that summer with a concentration of men in the north-west, and came to fruition in August and September in the largest of all the Egyptian offensives, in the region of Haradh, aimed at closing the border with Saudi Arabia and capturing or killing the Imam. In both of these objectives they failed. Meanwhile the royalists were building up in the north and north-east for their own biggest offensive, making the fourth notable effort in a period of more than four years. Following the complete breakdown of the Alexandria agreement between King Faisal and President Nasser, this stinging reverse for the republicans led to the Jeddah agreement of August 1965 and the withdrawal of the Egyptians from northern and eastern Yemen.

Let us now look back at the details. The 'Ramadan offensive' began with the arrival in Sana in February 1963 of Marshal Abdul Hakim Amer, deputy president of the U.A.R. and deputy supreme commander of its armed forces, and Lieutenant-General Anwar Sadat, member of the U.A.R. presidency council in charge of Yemeni affairs. The marshal had asked Cairo to double the 20,000 men then in Yemen, and in early February the first 5,000 of his reinforcements arrived.

On 18 February 1963 a task force of fifteen tanks, twenty armoured cars, eighteen trucks and numerous jeeps took off from Sana moving northwards; it headed for Sadah, the principal town of the north. More numerous garrison troops followed in its tracks. A few days later a further task force, spear-headed by 350 men in tanks and armoured cars, struck out from Sadah south-eastwards in the direction of Marib. This was probably the Egyptians' most brilliant operation. They manoeuvred into the Rub al Khali desert – probably well into Saudi territory, although it is hard to say where the border runs in the ocean of the desert. In the desert their forces were built up by an airlift. Then suddenly they headed westwards. On 25 February they occupied Marib and on 7 March, Harib.

When the Egyptians struck out from Sadah (into the Jawf) the royalists attempted unsuccessfully to head them off with a force of 1,500 men. This force was ordered down from Najran, where the men had been training under the command of Prince Mohamed bin

Hussein. But their training had just begun, and it was too soon for them to cope with the Egyptian tanks and armoured cars. Nor were the royalists in any way able to defend Marib and Harib. While Marib had been nearly empty, having been almost entirely evacuated after previous Egyptian bombing, Harib had been a lively town, full of repair shops and supplies. The royalist commander at Harib, Abdul Qarim al Wazir, who succeeded Qadi al Sayaghi, did not resist but departed prudently to Beihan, on the British-protected side of the border. It should be pointed out in explanation that his forces had been sent to assist Abdullah Hassan in the mountains east of Sana, ten days before the Egyptians attacked, and owing to the breakdown of Abdullah Hassan's radio contacts they were beyond recall when the attack came. The sharif of Beihan received al Wazir with little sympathy, but provided him with transportation northwards through the Saudi desert so that he might rejoin the battle.

The Egyptian thrust into the Jawf and the occupation of Marib and Harib were very serious blows to the royalists. The Egyptians were now in positions from which they could hope to interdict the movement of supplies to the royalists in the high mountains north and east of Sana. They could also make communications with the Federation of South Arabia very difficult.

In an attempt to cope with the military consequences of this disaster the royalists held a conference with King Faisal in Riyadh at the beginning of April 1963. Those present included Prince Sultan (a brother of Faisal), a special Saudi committee headed by Colonel Mohamed Juweini and, on the Yemeni side, Qadi al Sayaghi and the Princes Mohamed and Abdullah Hussein. They decided they must adopt new tactics. These included attempts to get supplies around the positions now held by the Egyptians by using camels instead of trucks: the camels would thread their way over high mountain trails in the west and centre of Yemen and would cross over the Sana-Sadah road to reach royalist positions east of Sana. Camel caravans from Beihan, which previously had moved through the desert between Harib and Marib, would swing far out into the Rub al Khali desert and come into Yemen north of Marib. It was also decided that since the Egyptians were now so well established in the east the royalists must strengthen their operations on the western side of the mountains. On this side three so-called 'armies' under the nominal command of the Imam were co-ordinated by Prince Mohamed bin Ismail. These were Prince Mohamed's own army, known as the fourth, a fifth under Prince Abdurrahman bin Yahya and a sixth under Qadi al Sayaghi.

Before he was overrun by the Egyptians Sayaghi, operating from Harib, had developed a kind of flying column technique for operations into the Shaffei-populated parts of the country to the south and west. He had gathered a force of about 200 men with jeeps, mounting light guns, which could go almost anywhere. But the idea was really too advanced for the Yemen and did not succeed; it had not been possible to maintain the necessary vehicles or keep together enough qualified men at this stage of the war. The royalists were therefore obliged to postpone their dream of assaulting Sana. They had to limit themselves to using the simpler forms of guerilla warfare of which they were capable at this time, to interfere with Egyptian communications and isolate their distant strongpoints.

Both sides during the early months of 1963 devoted their attention to building up their forces. One reason for making haste was that the United States had entered the scene by throwing its influence behind disengagement of the opposing forces in Yemen. This will be fully dealt with in Chapter Thirteen. Suffice it to say here that the U.S. began with the recognition of the republic on 19 December on two basic conditions: one was that the republic pledge itself to respect Yemen's existing international obligations, by which was meant in particular the 1934 treaty with Britain, guaranteeing the *status quo* on the border between Yemen and South Arabia; the other was that the Egyptians make a parallel undertaking to withdraw troops from the Yemen. Simultaneously the U.S. was backing the mission of Ambassador Ellsworth Bunker, who succeeded in persuading King Faisal and President Nasser to subscribe to a disengagement agreement beginning on 29 April. The Saudis were to end their supply operations; the Egyptians were to leave the country.

To Saudi and Jordanian supplies were added at this time a trickle of arms from Pakistan – mostly old British rifles – routed through Saudi Arabia. There was talk also of arms from Iran, and a few may have arrived via Aden as well as through Saudi Arabia. But Saudi Arabia remained the main source of royalist support. There was talk of hiring mercenaries to fly fighter aircraft as defence against Egyptian bombers. But even if the Saudis had been willing to provide the necessary money there seemed no solution to the problem of where to base a royalist air force. Inside Yemen they would be bombed out of existence by the Egyptians before they ever got started and the Saudis were not prepared to involve themselves to the extent of allowing the Yemenis to fly from their territory.

The Egyptians meanwhile committed more and more men and material. As they came to grasp the cost and danger of maintaining overland contact with their outlying strongpoints they resorted to the use of helicopters and air transport. They did more and more bombing, using relatively slow Russian Yaks for tactical purposes, and long-range Ilyushins which flew all the way from Aswan in upper Egypt to bomb strategic targets.

The republicans, assisted by five hundred Soviet technicians, were hard at work on the construction of an airfield capable of handling four-engined Soviet jet aircraft at Rahaba, a few miles north of Sana. When completed in September 1963, Rahaba offered the Egyptians a base inside Yemen from which heavy bombers could operate against the royalists; and, probably more important, it offered the Soviet Union a stepping-stone over which it might at some future date maintain air connections with Africa. The importance of access to Africa and of African air routes was brought home to western strategists in August 1964 when a pro-communist force took control of Stanleyville, in the eastern part of the Congo, but withered because neither Nasser nor the communists were able to supply them by air.

Knowing that the royalists' existence, their military growth or decline, depended mainly on what they got from or through Saudi Arabia, the Egyptians were tempted from the very beginning of the war to bomb Saudi Arabia. They felt perhaps a little like General McArthur in 1951, when he wanted to bomb the Chinese in their 'privileged sanctuary' of Manchuria. As early as November 1962, the Egyptians were bombing villages near Jizan, in the south-western Asir province of Saudi Arabia. (These were the raids whose rather ineffectual results I went to look at on my way to my first meeting with the Imam in November.) Shortly thereafter the Egyptians also raided the towns of Jizan and Najran, each of them funnels through which supplies were being routed to the royalists.

This was the period when the Egyptians imagined that they could stir up a revolution in Saudi Arabia by a combination of subversion and military threats. They even went as far, in November 1962, as to parachute military supplies by night on the Jeddah–Medina road to a revolutionary group which, however, never materialized. Sana radio for a few days even began talking about a 'republic of the Arabian peninsula', until silenced by Cairo, for whom this seemed, perhaps, a little too rash and provocative to various established governments in the peninsula.

The Saudis reacted vigorously. In addition to installing anti-aircraft guns around Jizan and Najran they alerted their armed forces and announced the formation of five new recruiting and training centres. Of even more significance to the defence of Saudi Arabia, perhaps, was the fact that they succeeded, on 14 November 1962, and again in the first week of January 1963, in persuading the United States to stage a show of force with jet fighter aircraft which flew over Riyadh and Jeddah. A sequel to the show of force was 'Operation Hard-surface', when, as already seen, a squadron of American fighter aircraft was stationed at Jeddah for several months in 1963.

But the Egyptians were not deterred and on 7 June they bombed Najran, Khamis, Mushait, and Jizan. In the raid on Jizan thirty people were killed and nineteen wounded by bombs which fell in the centre of the town and damaged the town's hospital. The Egyptian air force, like the American air force in Vietnam, undoubtedly sought military targets then and during all the subsequent years of bombing. But such targets were hard to find. The Yemeni armed forces were scattered and they possessed almost nothing in the way of surface installations. Their supplies, such as they were, were stored in caves and their transport moved mostly at night. For this reason the Egyptian air force, for lack of more military targets, systematically destroyed scores of Yemeni villages and small towns. The inhabitants fled, the women and children to the caves and the men to the armies.

In 1963 and 1964 the Egyptians had five squadrons of aircraft in Yemen at airfields near Sana and Hodeidah. They were using Yakovlev 11 piston-engined fighters, MiG 16 and 17 jet fighters, Ilyushin 28 twin-engined bombers, Ilyushin 14 twin-engined transports and MiG M.14 transport helicopters. In addition they were flying four-engined Tupolev bombers from bases in Egypt, such as Aswan. All the air crews were Egyptian, though the Tupolev bombers from Egypt were thought to have mixed Egyptian and Russian personnel. The Ilyushin transports flying between Egypt and Hodeidah did have Russian crews. The royalists claimed to have shot down fifty of these planes, but twenty seems a more likely figure.

Egyptian control of the air did not deter the royalist armies. Terrified in the first four weeks, they soon became accustomed to air attacks, confident that high explosives and napalm would be dropped mainly on the villages and that the fighting men on the mountain-sides would escape. Bravado soon replaced terror, and in the end many unnecessary casualties resulted from the unwillingness of tribesmen to take cover during air-raids. They would stand up boldly on a height, shouting at the attacking planes or firing their rifles, wild, hirsute fellows in the dirty white nightshirts of the desert tribes, or the shorter khaki kilts of the semi-regulars, with great, loosely-wound turbans on their heads and waists festooned with cartridge belts and daggers.

Almost every Yemeni, even the very poor tribesman, possessed a rifle of some kind which, in the manner peculiar to the South Arabians, he would carry by the muzzle and which, when he saw an Egyptian plane, he would fire at the sky. After the plane had passed the tribesman's eye might be attracted by a shiny thing on the ground, an inch-long miniature pipe, shaped like a bomb. If he picked it up and played with it, twisting the ends, it would explode. This was just one of a variety of booby traps which the Egyptians scattered from the air in territory which they could not control. Another type consisted of cigarettes which exploded when they were lit. When the tribesmen were hurt by an Egyptian strafing or bombing attack, or by one of the booby traps, they reacted stoically. Except for a handful of men trained by the International Red Cross and in some forms of native medicine (to be described in a later chapter on the International Red Cross), the royalists had no medical services and the men did not expect any. Much as they were given to shouting for every other reason, they accepted physical affliction with little protest. If there was a truck going in the direction of the International Red Cross hospital at Uqd, a wounded man would be loaded aboard and his wounds crudely bandaged, all covered with flies. But if there was none he would be left groaning in the shade of a rock.

By the end of April, a date which coincided with the beginning of the disengagement agreement between Egypt and Saudi Arabia on 29 April, the royalists had recovered considerably from the shock of the Egyptian Ramadan offensive. They claimed to have regained some of the positions the Egyptians had occupied in the Jawf. In particular they said they had occupied the small but strategic town of Barat and the smaller locality of as Safra, both in the rugged mountains between Sadah and the Jawf, and were able to move freely in the whole eastern desert known as the Khabt. In the Jawf itself they claimed to have cleaned up all Egyptian strong-points except the town of al Hazm. In the west they said they had occupied the town of al Batanah, in an area commanded by Prince Hassan bin Hassan, who had returned from medical treatment in London.

After the beginning of May both sides lapsed into a certain passivity. The principal Egyptian stronghold facing the royalists in the west was Hajjah, but no major engagements took place until the period of 'disengagement' ended in September. Similar torpor prevailed in the east in the area of the Prime Minister, Prince Hassan, facing Sadah, and that of Prince Mohamed Hussein in the north-east, where he was training a force variously known as 'ranger' and the 'northern frontier defence force'. Prince Abdullah Hussein was in contact with the Egyptian stronghold at al Hazm, but launched no major attacks. On the most critical of the fronts, spread in a kind of horseshoe around Sana, as close as five miles at one point, and ten, twenty-five and thirty-five miles from the capital at others, Prince Abdullah Hassan entered into a local truce in April, even before the disengagement agreement. With localized interruptions, this lasted well into September. The truce on this front suited both sides: the Egyptians would be safe from ambushes and the Prince would be able to maintain his supply line.

Truces here and in many other places were arranged by Naji bin Ali al Gadr, the remarkable paramount sheikh of the Baqil con-federation. Although he himself was chief of only a small tribe possessing 120 rifles, he had risen to this eminence by sheer wisdom and force of personality. He is described as having a small, hard bedouin face with sunken cheeks and black hair, a strong black beard, and dark eyes. He has been called 'the bedouin's Imam'. A mysterious, morose man, noted for his forbidding silences, he was able for long periods to convince both the republicans and the royalists that he was really on their side, so that he was able to move freely between Sana and the royalist headquarters. Once he brought back from Egyptian headquarters 500 rifles and 300 gold sovereigns, which the Egyptians undoubtedly regarded as a bribe in return for which al Gadr would bring the Khawlan into the republic. Yet on another occasion it was al Gadr who did the bribing. In return for al Gadr's favours, the Egyptian commanders permitted royalist supply columns to move freely into the mountains of the Khawlan. The Arabs called him a fox among foxes. Early in 1964 he was elected paramount sheikh of the Bakil at a conference at Qaramish, a village which lies between the Jawf and the Khawlan. He theoretically controls about 190,000 men, including about 50,000 belonging to the Hamdan and Hajur tribes, who had withdrawn from the Hashid confederation. While the tribal confederations were probably a declining factor in the lives of the tribesmen, they are likely to prove a useful political base for al Gadr on the future political stage of Yemen.

In September 1963, when I visited the republicans in Sana, I found the war still at a low ebb. Prince Abdullah Hassan's truce extended to the tribal areas north as well as east of Sana. But I heard of some tribal raids against Egyptian convoys in the Jawf and in the Hajjah area. Just south of Sadah an Egyptian column was reported to have been ambushed in the last week of August and 100 Egyptians slain. (The royalist tribesmen were said to have resumed the mutilation of prisoners – cutting off ears and noses – that was common at the beginning of the war, until discouraged by the Imam.)

Later that month Prince Sharaf bin Mutahar, a teenage prince who before the war had been in a German sanatorium with some kind of blood sickness, conducted a series of successful operations against an Egyptian enclave called Beit Murran, in the Arhab region north-east of the capital. The royalists claimed that this was a very costly Egyptian outpost in terms of lives and that they lost 1,500 men in dead and wounded in its defence and supply. While this figure is almost certainly imaginative, Prince bin Mutahar is undoubtedly an effective guerilla commander.

In the Jawf an Egyptian armoured force from a camp at Lebena, where a garrison of some 4,000 men was based, attempted a thrust in early September towards the royalist lines of communication from Najran. This had always been their objective, ever since the Ramadan offensive. But the royalists, here under Prince Mohamed Hussein, were ready. They had already captured a number of armoured cars, along with enough prisoners to keep them in repair.

They had also captured a big Egyptian gun said to be capable of firing ten miles. Altogether, with some heavy guns contributed by the Saudis, the royalists, although they had very little ammunition, were able to lay down such a barrage that the Egyptians were quickly discouraged from further attempts to approach the Saudi border in this area.

Towards the end of the year, after the U.N. observers had entirely withdrawn and the pretence of 'disengagement' had been abandoned by both sides, military operations began to step up again. The Egyptian commander, General Anwar al Qadi, launched an attack under his personal command upon Prince Abdullah Hussein's positions west of Sana. He fell into a trap set by the prince, was seriously wounded and was rushed to Switzerland for specialist treatment of injuries to his eyes. He was replaced by Lieutenant-General Abdul Majeed Kamal Murtaji.

On 2 January 1964 Prince Abdullah Hassan's men succeeded in occupying the town of Jihanah, south-east of Sana, for a few days. Of course, the royalists could not hope to keep it against Egyptian air and armoured strength. But the raid was nonetheless significant as a diversion in support of a much more important operation, the second military stage mentioned at the beginning of this chapter which was taking shape to the west of Sana.

During the first days of the month tribal warriors under the command of Prince Abdullah Hussein set up road blocks on the road between Sana and Hodeidah at Boam and Suq al Khamis, and succeeded in keeping the road closed to Egyptian traffic for almost a month. Boam and Suq al Khamis are situated about twenty miles south-west of the capital, at one of the most dramatic sections of the winding road that connects Sana to the port of Hodeidah. Boam is a small market town that is populated only during market days twice a week. In between market days its primitive stone houses, constructed almost as part of the mountainside, stand deserted. Suq al Khamis, which means 'market of the sun', consists of a small number of stone and mud huts, whose inhabitants are noted for their long fleece-lined sheepskins. Such warm attire is desirable, for the road here crosses a peak 8,500 feet above sea level, and the cold is intense at night and in the early mornings, even during the warm seasons. The village stands at the top of a cliff which drops away for thousands of feet to the steamy, almost tropical jungle far below. One looks across a wide valley to Manakha, the largest and highest town, 9,000 feet above sea level, from which the road finally descends to the malarial plains of the Tihama and the sea coast. Around Manakha live about 3,000 adherents of the Ismaili sect, remnants of the once powerful and numerous group founded by Queen Sayida, whose religious allegiance is to the Aga Khan in Pakistan. Traditionally opposed to the Imam on religious grounds, they have maintained a neutral attitude during the struggle between royalists and republicans.

As was to be expected, Egyptian armoured strength prevailed and smashed through the royalist road blocks, while the Egyptian air force wreaked terrible vengeance on the nearest royalist tribes, in particular the Haymatain and Bani Matar, who had taken the initiative to close the road and who had been bold enough at certain times to collect tolls from those vehicles which they chose to allow through their road blocks. Before these tribes were finally subdued at the beginning of February they raided the town of al Haddah, five miles south-west of Sana and an Egyptian camp only a mile west of Sana. American diplomatic representatives in Sana could hear the sounds of battle on the outskirts of the capital.

During and after the operation against the Sana-Hodeidah road the royalists also succeeded in cutting Egyptian communications on the roads between Sana and Sadah to the north and between Sana and Taiz to the south. North of Sana young Prince Sharaf bin Mutahar occupied a mountain called Jabal Sama, from which he was able to inflict painful losses on Egyptian convoys attempting to reach garrisons in Arhab and beyond. He also was able to plant numerous mines on the road used by the Egyptians. Prince Mohamed bin Mohsin, another of the youthful commanders, whose province was the Nahm tribal territory, at the beginning of February captured the provincial capital of Beit al Sayed and the town of Rijm, holding them until Egyptian reinforcements arrived. Then, following the pattern established at Jihana, he withdrew to surrounding heights. Five truckloads of republican troops, numbering about 300, who were sent to re-establish republican control, deserted to the prince at this time.

To the south of Sana, Prince Abdullah Hassan's men captured a republican pay convoy with 180,000 silver Maria Theresa thalers near the Naqil Islah pass, which, together with 80,000 thalers previously captured on the Sadah road, transferred to royalist hands a large part of three months' pay owing to outlying republican and Egyptian garrisons. Prince Abdullah Hassan followed up this *coup* by setting up a road block in the Naqil Islah pass and succeeded in maintaining it throughout February. For a while he was in direct contact with the al Haymatain and the Bani Matar tribes under Prince Abdullah Hussein who had cut the Hodeidah road.

From mid-February until 10 June 1964, when the Egyptians began the third of the military stages with a new offensive towards the north-west, fighting consisted of more or less isolated incidents. An account of some of these will show how much was going on in Yemen even during a quiet period – and almost none of it was ever reported in the world's press.

In the area between Harib and Marib, Sheikh Naji Mansur Nemran of the Murad tribe raided the Egyptian base camp at al Juba, north of Harib in the eastern desert, in the last week of February and again in early March. He claimed to have killed twenty Egyptians and wounded thirty out of a garrison of only about 100. After that the Egyptians rarely emerged from behind a dense minefield surrounding their camp, depending on air supply and leaving the countryside in royalist hands.

In the Jawf the so-called Jawf rangers, the mixed tribal reserve force which Prince Mohamed Hussein had been training, raided an Egyptian outpost at Dukaimah in March and inflicted losses of eleven dead. The Egyptians abandoned the post and withdrew to their base camp at Lebena, where they were commanded by Brigadier Mahmoud Qasim. Later the same month the Jawf rangers raided the Egyptian communications centre at al Afka, sixteen miles north-east of al Hazm, and claimed to have destroyed a tank, to have killed twenty-five Egyptians, and to have taken one prisoner.

Farther south, between Marib and Harib, a sub-section of the Abidah tribe called Fuje turned against the Egyptians, with whom they had been collaborating fitfully since the beginning of the war. On 14 April, unable to resist deeply ingrained habit, they ambushed an Egyptian truck convoy, killed about twenty Egyptians and made away with the loot. The Egyptians were furious at this sign of their crumbling support among the tribes. They sent an armoured column whose assignment, according to the royalists, was to destroy all Fuje villages, kill all livestock, destroy all wells, and kill all male inhabitants. They killed five Fuje men, the royalists reported, and dragged their bodies behind tanks and armoured cars through all the other Abidah villages. Many of the Fuje women and children fled across the border to Beihan, while their men went north to join the royalist forces.

Towards the end of March Prince Abdullah Hussein, who had been operating in the west since the attempts to close the Hodeidah road in January, tried to capture Hajjah. The Egyptians met this pressure by despatching to Hajjah the largest republican force assembled up to that time. It consisted, according to Sana radio, of 2,000 men under the command of Sheikh Abdullah al Ahmar, the paramount sheikh of those parts of the Hashid confederation who supported the republic. Sheikh Abdullah was appointed Governor of Hajjah. This appeared to be an attempt to make the best possible military use of pro-republican elements among the tribes, after most of the Hashid had either rallied to the Imam, or lapsed into a sullen neutrality.

The royalists claimed to have shot down four Egyptian aircraft during March; they used 12.7-millimetre Soviet Degtyarev Shpagin heavy machine-guns, which they found superior to the 15-calibre American machine-guns previously used. Two of the aircraft shot down were bombers attacking royalist positions around Sadah and in the Nahm tribal territory, and two were MiGs operating over the Jawf and to the north-west of Sana.

During the spring of 1964 a number of tribes previously quiescent either declared their support for the Imam or promised to take to arms and begin fighting as soon as the royalists could get them the necessary weapons and money. Those who gave promise of future military services included the tribes of Rida, south-west of Marib and Harib, the tribe of Rasasi, of al Baydah, in the south-eastern corner of Yemen, and also the Mumurais at Qataba, near the South Arabian Federation border, where there has been constant trouble between the British and the republicans.

Sheikh Abdullah al Ahmar's hold on the Hashid confederation began to break up in the early spring, when the traditional system of hostages by which he, in ancient imamic tradition, ensured the loyalty of other tribal sheikhs, suddenly broke up. The story is that he held more than thirty of the minor sons of his Hashid sheikhs as hostages at an Egyptian-occupied town, al Qaflah, about sixty miles north-east of Sana. Emissaries of Prince Hassan bin Hassan made a deal with the guards in charge of these children which undoubtedly involved a substantial payment of gold sovereigns. Then one night the guards looked the other way and the hostages were abducted to the headquarters of Prince Hassan bin Hassan who, so far as was possible, returned them to their fathers.

Meanwhile the Egyptians had released from captivity a number of women and children of the royal family who had been held in Sana or taken to Cairo since the beginning of the war. Their release took place thanks to the mediation of André Rochat of the International Red Cross, who visited Sana and Cairo early in the year. It was thanks also to Crown Prince Faisal's direct appeal to the Egyptian Marshal Abdul Hakim Amer during meetings in February. On 19 May their royal highnesses the Princes Abdullah, aged fourteen, and al Abbas, aged twelve, youngest sons of the late Imam Ahmed, and their nephew Prince Ahmed Abdullah Abdul Qarim, grandson of the late Imam, paid a visit to their brother the Imam al Badr at his mountain headquarters at Jabal Qara. They were joined at Qara by one of the Imam's young nephews, Prince Hassan Ahmed bin Zabarah. The young princes were returned after a few weeks to school in Jeddah, and the Imam sent Prince Hassan Zabarah to the American University of Beirut.

On 25 May the Dhu Mohamed, the sub-section of the Dahm tribe who were working with the Egyptians, raided Prime Minister Prince Hassan's headquarters near a village called al Burqah. The raiders were driven off without much trouble, and in reprisal Prince Ahmed al Hussein sent his men through the Dhu Mohamed villages, destroying them and driving out their inhabitants. It would seem that royalist reprisals were very similar to those earlier carried out by the Egyptians against the Fuje.

May 1964 was marked by an especially heavy Egyptian air attack upon the historic city of Shaharah, about eight miles north-west of Sana, a centre of religious learning for many centuries, filled with imposing historic buildings. It was in Shaharah, in 1904, that the last Turkish attempt to conquer Yemen had ended in disaster; the Turkish army, 15,000 strong with artillery and cavalry, had been decimated by the Hashid and Bakil tribesmen led by the Imam Yahya. The Egyptian attack may have been a reprisal for a congress of the ulema held in the Jawf in April. The religious elders and teachers were engaged in drafting a new constitution, and held their meeting in the Jawf under the chairmanship of Prince Mohamed Hussein, as deputy of the Imam. Combined protector, host and secretary-general of the congress, Prince Mohamed directed his ranger units, organized by him into something like regular army style, in an impressive ceremony within a hollow square of troops drawn up on the open plain. While heavy weapons pointed outwards on the periphery of the square, electric lights maintained by portable generators illuminated the protected area within. Prince Mohamed's welcoming speech, which was broadcast on loudspeakers, launched the religious leaders, who were drawn about equally from republican and royalist, Shaffei and Zeidi areas, on a path of political reform well-explored during the preceding year by the royalist Foreign Minister, Ahmed al Shami. The prince declared that the religious teachers could look forward to playing an important part in a future imamic council which would collaborate with an elected parliament broadly representing the tribes and the people.

By the end of the congress, on 26 April, a British-style constitutional document had been drawn up. Its principal points were that Yemen was to have an elected Imam with a cabinet system, an independent judiciary and an elected legislative assembly; there were to be far-reaching allowances for local autonomy and regional differences of administration. Succeeding passages included the declarations that imamic constitutional government was based on 'love, hope, charity, human rights and evolutionary progress', that Islamic principles were 'reconcilable with progressive and evolutionary change', that the Shaffei and Zeidi sects were equal, and that the Imam was bound by the pursuit of 'social justice and evolutionary reform', according to the standards of progressive countries but in keeping with Islamic principles.

This congress and its constitutional proposals must be regarded as a significant effort by the royalists to carry on war by other means. Their effort was in part an answer to the provisional republican constitution, which Prince Mohamed had stigmatized as mere 'dust in the eyes'.

This was the time when President Nasser was visiting Sana. Prince Abdullah Hassan, from his eyrie in the Khawlan highlands, sent him a message of defiance. He had the royalist radio station broadcast an invitation to the Egyptian President to come and negotiate with him. 'I offer you safe conduct to my headquarters,' he said. 'I am only an hour's drive away.' As though to underline his words, Prince Abdullah Hassan sent his men to raid Jihana. He claimed in a communiqué, read over the royalist radio, that his men had killed 100 Egyptians and captured two armoured cars, several machine-guns and a 120-millimetre mortar.

Another royalist conference of political import brought together the sheikhs of Khawlan, Nahm and Arhab at the end of May. More than 700 sheikhs from this most densely populated and staunchly royalist part of central Yemen gathered together under the protection of Prince Abdullah Hassan and the two younger princes who operated under his direction, Mohamed al Mohsin and Sharaf bin Mutahar. Prince Abdullah Hassan led the sheikhs in a renewal of their oath of loyalty, called the *bia'ia*. He lectured them on guerilla tactics. They were to avoid frontal assault of fortified positions, to harass Egyptian enclaves and lines of communication, to conduct their raids preferably by night and to mobilize tribesmen for the tricky and burdensome task of placing mines on those roads most used by the Egyptians.

The Egyptians' offensive in the north-west of Yemen, the largest of all their military operations, and the third of the stages mentioned at the beginning of this chapter, began on 12 June, probably with the intention of scoring a major shift in the balance of power in Yemen before the Arab summit conference, which was to include meetings between President Nasser and King Faisal and which was scheduled for September 1964 in Cairo. Egyptian infantry numbering 4,000, reinforced by the republican army and by mercenaries from Radfan, Yaffa and Dathina in the Aden Protectorate, overran the little town of Beit Adaqah, about thirty miles west of Sana, where Prince Abdullah Hussein at that time held his headquarters for a front extending from the Hodeidah road, through Kawkaban province, to the southern uplands of Hajjah. In two days the attacking forces advanced about twelve miles, until the royalists launched a counter-attack which carried the Egyptians back on to the heights overlooking Hajjah and Maswar and re-established Prince Abdullah Hussein's front. The Radfan mercenaries whom the Egyptians used to spearhead their attack fought well, and the royalists admitted exceptionally heavy losses, about 250 men killed.

The royalists reported a particularly grievous loss on 15 June, when Prince Ali bin Hussein, commanding a force harassing the Sana-Sadah road, was killed by enemy rifle fire. He was the first of Yemen's royal family to be killed in action. With his brother Ahmed Prince Ali had hidden in the home of a loyal palace guard in Sana during the week of terror after the *coup d'état*. Escaping then to the mountains, he had raised and armed the Arhabis for a revolt after which the Egyptians were expelled from most of the Arhabi territory, early in 1963.

The next precursor of the big Egyptian push in the north-west was a thrust in the region of as Sudah, some 100 miles north-west of Sana. On this occasion the Egyptians exploited the unpopularity of a local royalist commander to bribe a number of sheikhs around as Sudah. This enabled them to move forward unopposed and to occupy the town. After a month of Egyptian occupation the as Sudah sheikhs, having so easily allowed the Egyptians to take over their territory, sent delegations to the Imam soliciting royal pardons, asking for money and guns with which to expel the occupier; this is the sort of double-dealing that goes on constantly in Yemen, back and forth between royalists and republicans, with the sheikhs filling their purses on both sides. In this case the Imam sent in new forces under a popular commander named Hassan bin Ismail, who managed to regain the surroundings of as Sudah but had to leave the town itself in Egyptian hands.

The Egyptian build-up in the north-west reached its climax on 15 August with an offensive launched from their major north-western base, the town of Haradh. There were 1,000 Egyptian troops and about 2,000 republicans under two sheikhs, Abdullah al Ahmar of the Hashid confederation with 1,400 men, and Ali Mohsin Pasha of the al Udain, with 600 men. The Egyptian plan, as subsequently interpreted by British intelligence, appears to have been as follows: to cut the thirty-mile track that winds southward, through extremely rough mountain terrain, from the Saudi border at al Khoubah to the Imam's headquarters in the Qara mountains near Washa; then to split into two task forces, one moving eastwards through Washa to the Imam's headquarters, the other north-eastwards along the track to the point where it turns into Saudi Arabia just below the Razih mountains.

Early on a Saturday morning the Egyptians and their tribal supporters moved from Haradh through two ravines, Haradh and Tashar. On Saturday and Sunday afternoons heavy rain fell and the attacking vehicles, including twenty tanks and about forty armoured cars, began to sink axle deep into mud. The defenders left them alone until Monday at dawn. Then the Imam, who had left his headquarters at three that morning with 1,000 men of his personal bodyguard, the Ugfa, directed a counter-attack in the Tashar ravine, while Prince Abdullah Hussein simultaneously counter-attacked in the Haradh ravine.

Meanwhile both the Egyptians and the royalists had begun supporting movements from other directions. The Egyptians had planned a co-ordinated drive from Sadah to the south-west, below the Razih mountains, with the idea of linking up with the force coming from Haradh. For this supporting movement the Egyptians counted on tribal forces led by a dissident chieftain, Sheikh ibn Hassan of a branch of the Juma tribe, who was also supposed to join up with 250 Egyptian parachutists who were dropped in the Razih mountains. Finding no tribal support the parachutists made their way back towards Sadah, suffering sharp losses from snipers on the way. The Imam had sent radio messages and urgent summonses by runner in all directions calling for reinforcements and diversionary action. He asked reserve forces who were training in the Jawf to rush in trucks mounting 55- and 57-millimetre cannon and 81 millimetre mortars and heavy machine guns. Normally it would have taken them four days to negotiate the primitive tracks that led through the mountains skirting the Egyptian base at Sadah. But they made it in forty-eight hours, in time to contain the attacking forces. The two Egyptian columns, still deeply sunk in mud in the Haradh and Tashar valleys, were outflanked and attacked from all sides. The royalists were able to announce a few days later that anti-tank cannon and mines had knocked out ten of the Egyptian tanks and about half of their armoured cars. They also claimed to have shot down an Ilyushin bomber.

The Imam's appeal for support resulted in two more supporting movements, both carried out under the direction of Prince Abdullah Hassan from his headquarters in the Khowlan mountains east of Sana. One was a raid on the already much-raided town of Jihana, in the course of which several staff officers were killed. The other was an attempt to bombard Sana from a near-by mountain peak.

This second extraordinary operation is a story in itself; it also raises the question of mercenaries. It was directed by a group of British advisers and friends of Prince Abdullah Hassan. One was Major John Cooper, who had been a member of the Special Air Service, the regiment which fought behind enemy lines during the Second World War and against communist guerillas in Malaya from 1951 to 1959. After that he had been in the service of the Sultan of

Muscat and Oman against the rebellious Imam of Oman, a service to which he returned after his period in the Yemeni mountains. Another occasional visitor to Yemen was Anthony Alexander Boyle, son of Marshal of the Royal Air Force Sir Dermot Boyle, who until October 1963 served as aide-de-camp to the British High Commissioner in Aden. A third was Bernard Mills, a tough and resourceful soldier of fortune who has contributed much expert knowledge to the royalist cause. These men, in addition to the group of ten or twelve, were European mercenaries — a few British, but mostly French and Belgian — whom the royalists recruited late in 1963, not so much to do the fighting for them as to operate the radio communications system, teach the tribesmen how to fire and maintain mortars, machine-guns and anti-tank weapons, and perhaps to advise on tactics. Some were French and Belgian mercenaries who fought for Moise Tshombe in Katanga province in 1961 and 1962. When that cause was lost they had joined the Yemeni royalists. While a few were attached to Prince Abdullah at this time, most were later stationed at Amran and Hanjar, the two main royalist supply and training bases in the north-eastern Jawf. A larger group of fifty French mercenaries waited in Saudi Arabia for about a year but were never used except for minor repair jobs and advice. Their contracts ended in the autumn of 1967 and they dispersed.

In this operation, the British advisers took ten men and three camels with a 75-millimetre recoil-less cannon to a mountain-top within range of Sana. They could clearly see the lights of the town and the square outlines of the old fort on Jabal Nuqum above it. On their way to the mountain-top Prince Abdullah's men could not resist the temptation, as they passed through friendly villages, to celebrate the occasion by firing a few rounds from their wonderful new toy. Sanche de Gramont of the *New York Herald Tribune*, who was visiting Prince Abdullah at the time, wrote that the British were angered at this waste of ammunition. 'I am fed up,' one of them cried. 'Do you realise these shells cost £70 each? Do you realize the trouble we have getting them?' Prince Abdullah, who had a better understanding of his people's psychology, calmed them down by replying that the firing was not meaningless. 'They want to show that we are strong. But I have told them not to waste any more shells,' he said.

In yet other diversionary operations, similar royalist raiding parties managed to fire bazookas at Egyptian aircraft and tanks at the south airport of Sana and a mortar at the al Urdhi suburb of Taiz, where Egyptian and republican staff are housed. But none of these somewhat romantically conceived raids seemed to have made much impression, and I heard nothing about them when I visited Sana and Taiz in October 1964. Perhaps the only ones of Prince Abdullah's shells that were not wasted were those fired in joyful demonstration.

Although the Egyptians proclaimed in the press and on the radio that they had scored a great victory in their Haradh offensive, and that the Imam had been driven out of the country, there seems little doubt that the operation was in fact an almost unmitigated *débâcle*. As the attacking force withdrew in confusion the Egyptians even machine-gunned some of their tribal allies, who were fleeing along the roads to Maidi and Abs, Egyptian strongholds well removed from the fighting. While the Egyptians and their tribal allies never reached Qara, it is true, however, that the Imam was obliged to leave his headquarters and moved to a cave on Jabal Shedah, a few hundred yards from the Saudi border, where I visited him in December 1964, and where he remained for more than a year.

If it was President Nasser's intention to create a *fait accompli* by closing the Saudi border and driving out the Imam by this offensive before he met Prince Faisal at the summit conference in Cairo, then he failed most dismally. On the contrary, he was obliged at the Cairo meeting to agree to a cease-fire, which was signed at Erkwit in the Sudan on 2 November. This conference, attended by royalist and republican delegates and Egyptian and Saudi observers, was in effect a triumph for the royalists. The Egyptians and republicans were obliged to abandon the pretence that the royalists did not exist, and to treat them as equals; the conference was a form of recognition. The cease-fire was supposed to be followed by an 'all-Yemen conference', which would set up an interim régime of royalists and republicans and prepare a plebiscite to determine the ultimate government of the country.

Thus the Haradh *débâcle* and the Erkwit conference marked the end of a period in the Yemeni war. In the ensuing period settlement of the war began to be seen as a serious possibility. Militarily, it was the period in which the royalists scored their greatest successes.

PART
THREE

✦✦

The Struggle for
Peace

XIII

U.S. and U.N.

••

UNITED STATES policy in the Middle East has always had a
schizophrenic quality. This has long been the case in the Arab-
Israeli conflict, in which the U.S. has been torn by its ties to both
sides. It is also the case in the conflict between Nasser and Faisal.

In the Yemen, however, the United States has, perhaps un-
intentionally, in the guise of an even-handed policy of mutual
disengagement, committed a fraud at the expense of the royalists.
In effect, until quite recently the U.S. has played into Nasser's
hands. It was only in 1967, not long before the June war between
Arabs and Israelis, that the United States came around to a different
view of Nasser's objectives, of the values represented by the opposition to him, and of U.S. interest in the matter. There appeared
from that time to be a more realistic recognition of Nasser's neo-
imperialism, a recognition of the positive features of King Faisal's
evolutionary reformism (which was obscured, it is true, as long as
Saud was king). The practical reflection of this new approach has
been the cutting off of wheat shipments to Nasser and of aid to the
Yemen republic.

The purpose of this chapter is to look back at the sequence of
events in an effort to anticipate and understand the way in which
United States and United Nations policy has been changing.

In the 1950s some consideration was given by the State Department
and other branches of the American government to the possible
value to the U.S. of the corner of the Arabian peninsula known as
the kingdom of Yemen. The conclusion was that Yemen was of
very little value indeed. As a result, the United States government
was satisfied to conduct its relations with Yemen through its
consulate in Aden, until 1959, when a legation was opened at Taiz.
After Soviet and Chinese communist aid programmes had got

under way, however, the United States agreed in 1960 to build a water system for the town of Taiz.

The Yemen *coup d'état* of 26 September 1962 took place when the Kennedy administration was eight months old. This was a time when the 'new frontiersmen' were anxious to escape from the stigma of American association with reactionary, feudalistic and sometimes anachronistic régimes in various parts of the world. They were eager also to break out of a certain impasse into which American policy had drifted in the Middle East as a result of American association with Israel and of John Foster Dulles' opposition to Nasser on the Aswan Dam project.

Under the circumstances, recognition of the new republic was probably a foregone conclusion. It was inconceivable in a part of the world to which the American government attached so little importance that the U.S. would stand by the old imamic régime with its repressive, pre-medieval, isolationist tradition. Recognition of the new republic, which under the protection of President Nasser laid claim to liberal ideals, seemed an easy way to help restore mobility to American policy in the Middle East and identify the U.S. with progressive and popular forces. There was concern also about active Soviet and Chinese involvement in this area. Their estimation of Yemen's value seemed markedly at variance with that of the American government: before the revolution the Russians had already built the deep sea port at Hodeidah, and the Chinese the asphalt road from the port to Sana, and both seemed eager to expand their post-revolutionary presence. If the U.S. did not recognize the régime, there would be no major western presence to offset the activities of the communist blocs.

The fact that the move towards recognition was nonetheless delayed for nearly three months was due to several considerations. Some State Department officials were impressed by very real doubts as to whether the situation in the Yemen could be reconciled with usual State Department criteria for diplomatic recognition. Although Robert W. Stookey, the U.S. chargé d'affaires in Taiz, reported the republican régime in full control of the country, except in some border areas, there were reasons for questioning his report. One of these was that the British government was insisting on the strength of the tribal support of the Imam's opposition to the republic. The State Department may also have read the despatches which I wrote, as correspondent for the *New York Times*, following my visit to the Imam in November and my trip from Najran through royalist Yemen to Beihan. In them I reported that the royalist opposition was active, popularly based and growing, and concluded that while one could not confidently predict a victory for the Imam one must certainly concede that the royalists had a chance.

The American government's hesitation was reflected in a series of steps it took to appease and reassure the rulers of Saudi Arabia before recognition was finally announced on 19 December 1962. First and most significant was the letter written by President Kennedy to Crown Prince Faisal (as Premier), dated 25 October, just a month after the *coup d'état* in Sana, which had meanwhile been followed by an influx of Egyptian troops, Egyptian bombing of Saudi Arabian border towns and propaganda talk over Sana radio about the coming 'republic of the Arabian peninsula'. This letter, the most positive assurance of American support, was kept confidential even in Saudi Arabia at the time, but it was published with American consent in January 1963 after further Egyptian air-raids had taken place. In it the President said: 'You may be assured of full U.S. support for the maintenance of Saudi Arabian integrity.'

Meanwhile the State Department had begun to sound out all those concerned – all except the Imam al Badr – in its search for a settlement. Following up this activity, President Kennedy sent letters towards the end of November proposing steps towards a settlement to Crown Prince Faisal, King Hussein and President Nasser; once again the Imam, although still officially recognized by the American government, was left out. The President proposed, as a first step towards the restoration of peace, that Egyptian troops withdraw from the republican side and that Saudi Arabia and Jordan halt their material support of the royalist cause.

During the two weeks before President Kennedy's move, American jet aircraft twice staged shows of force in Saudi Arabia. On the first occasion, six F-100 jets staged stunt-flying demonstrations over Riyadh and Jeddah, and on the second, two jet bombers and a giant jet transport, while returning to their base near Paris after a visit to Karachi, in Pakistan, put on a demonstration over Riyadh. The demonstrations, in conjunction with the President's assurance, suggested that the U.S. might use force to prevent Nasser from expanding beyond the Yemen.

On 19 December the U.S. finally recognized the Yemen republic. Recognition was accompanied by statements which the U.S. had elicited from both the republic and the Egyptian government. In the first, the Yemenis undertook explicitly to honour their 'international obligations, including all treaties concluded by previous governments, and abide by the charters of the United Nations and the Arab League'. The Yemen republic, the statement continued, wished to live in peace 'with all our neighbours' and called upon Yemenis in adjacent areas 'to be law-abiding citizens'. It also said that 'we shall concentrate our efforts on our internal affairs'. As explained in an accompanying American statement, the State Department took this as a reaffirmation of the 1934 Treaty of Sana between the British and the Imamic government which 'provided for reciprocal guarantees that neither party should intervene in the affairs of the other across the existing international frontier dividing the Yemen from territory under British protection'. It was clearly intended to reassure the British and to encourage them to follow the American example.

The second statement, by the Egyptian government, consisted of a formal declaration of intention to withdraw from Yemen, which is worth quoting in full:

Issued by U.A.R. Ministry of Information
on 18 December 1962

The United Arab Republic confirms and supports the full contents of the communiqué released by the government of the Yemen Arab Republic. The United Arab Republic is proud of having extended full support to the Yemen revolution since the early hours of its outbreak, a support in consonance with existing agreements. Now that the Yemen Arab Republic has firmly established itself as the government of Yemen and inasmuch as we deplore the continuation of bloodshed, the United Arab Republic hereby signifies its willingness to undertake a reciprocal expeditious disengagement and phased removal of its troops from Yemen as Saudi and Jordanian forces engaged in support of the dethroned King are removed from the frontier areas and as external support, including Saudi and Jordanian support of the Yemen royalists, is terminated, whenever the government of the Yemen Arab Republic should make such a request. To this we pledge ourselves provided the foregoing conditions are met.

These documents were accompanied by a State Department statement which, in the light of what has happened since then, appears most extraordinary. The State Department had decided to recognize the Yemen republic, it said, 'in believing that these declarations provide a basis for terminating the conflict over Yemen and in expressing the hope that all the parties involved in the conflict would co-operate to the end that the Yemeni people themselves would be permitted to decide their own future'.[1]

Rarely has the American government been so completely deluded. The Egyptian and Yemeni statements were plainly drafted with a view to supplying the words the Americans wanted to hear and without the slightest intention of abiding by the pledges made. A few days later I wrote the following story for the *New York Times*:

Beirut, 24 December 1963.

United States recognition of the republican insurgents in Yemen is one of the most controversial moves the U.S. has made in the Middle East since it came to Gamal Abdul Nasser's rescue in 1956. The difference is that then Nasser was fighting a defensive war against British-French-Israeli aggression and the entire Arab world supported him, while today he is engaged in an offensive war against other Arabs and a considerable proportion of the Arab world is against him.

The British and French operation at Suez can be regarded as the last gasp of British and French imperialism in the Middle East. Nasser's operation in Yemen can be regarded as the first military move in a campaign whose objectives reach far beyond Yemen; to overthrow the monarchy of neighbouring Saudi Arabia and win control of that country's and other Arabian peninsula oil. It can be regarded as Nasser's biggest gamble.

Among Jordanian and Saudi Arabian officials who take this view of Nasser's operation, one of the mildest comments heard during the past few days was attributed to Premier Wasfi Tel of Jordan, who is said to have claimed that the U.S. move was 'a grave mistake'. Jordanians, who are conscious that their country is the only one in the Arab Middle East that has given the West a hundred per cent support, were especially bitter. The Saudis sputtered about the disadvantage of being too closely

[1] The full text of the American statement on the recognition of Yemen may be found in Appendix 1 at the end of this book.

tied up with the U.S. They predicted an early resumption of
diplomatic relations with Britain, with whom they broke off
in the early fifties when the dispute over the Buraimi Oasis began.

U.S. recognition of President Sallal's republican régime was
seized upon by both the monarchist and the leftist wings of the
anti-Nasserites in the Arab world, as conclusive proof of what
they have been alleging for months – that the U.S. is committed
to support Nasser. Why the U.S. should be so committed was
explained according to the political slant of the various groups.
Monarchists put emphasis on the theory that Nasser had promised
in exchange for economic and political support, to lay off anti-
American and anti-Israel propaganda. Leftists conjured up
visions of a joint U.S.-Nasserite imperialism in the Middle East.
No one thought it would end the Yemen war. Among diplomats
tuned in to Washington, the explanation was that, after a long
wrangle inside the State Department over recognition, the day
was carried by the 'New Frontier' element, who were anxious
to prove that the U.S. is not necessarily committed to reactionary
anachronistic régimes and is, on the contrary, anxious to help
progressive young elements who are the wave of the future.

After similar debate, the British Foreign Office decided to
delay recognition of the Sallal régime. Experts on the area are
understood to have persistently argued as follows:

Yemen differs from all other Middle Eastern countries in the
degree of preponderance of religious, conservative, xenophobic
and warlike Zeidi tribesmen. The Shaffei element, which populated the coastal plain and the south-west, is completely unwar-
like, is not accustomed to bearing arms and scarcely weighs on
the military scales. The republic and Egyptians will never defeat
the Zeidi tribesmen in their mountains. On the other hand, the
Zeidi tribesmen might defeat the republicans and the Egyptians
in their towns and strongpoints. They surely can drag the war
out at least as long as an Algeria-type war. And if the Egyptians
withdraw, the royalist tribesmen will surely win.

As these British experts see it, U.S. recognition is not going
to halt the war in Yemen, nor is it going to set the U.S. on any
wave of the future. Jordanians and Saudis have told the British
they will continue to supply royalists with arms, ammunition
and money as best they can. They have no troops in Yemen, and
do not plan to send any.

The Egyptians will have to decide either to go on fighting a war they cannot afford, or withdraw and face the probability of defeat for their friends. In either case, as British experts see it, results for Nasser will be disastrous, and the U.S., like a surf rider who leaps too soon, may find a wave of the future breaking over its head.

United Nations recognition followed that of the United States by a day. Thereafter the U.N. acted as though the republic were the only authority in the land and as though the royalists did not exist – an attitude which proved legalistic, unrealistic and inefficacious.

Meanwhile in London a debate as heated as the one in Washington had been in progress, as to whether Britain should recognize or not. For the United States the intrusion of the Egyptians into Yemen may have created a dilemma. But for the British, with their profound commitment to South Arabia and their base at Aden, the arrival of an Egyptian army on the Arabian peninsula as protector of a puppet republic was a real threat, not at all counterbalanced by reassuring Yemeni and Egyptian statements. Or, at least, so it seemed at the beginning of 1963, when the Conservative government was still in office. Certainly recognition was anathema to the ruling sheikhs and sultans of the South Arabian Federation, to whom Britain was bound by a complex web of treaties. In years past they had disliked the Imam's pretensions as head of the Zeidi sect and had resented his claims to 'Southern Yemen'; now all that was forgotten in their greater fear of the republic and the Egyptians. South Arabia's ruling caste identified themselves totally with the royalists in Yemen and with Saudi Arabia, and they urged the British to do likewise.

Strange to say, there is evidence that the Foreign Office would have liked to recognize the republic. Like the State Department, the Foreign Office had, and has still, its pro-Nasser school, and those who agreed that sooner or later Britain must come to terms with him. Some believed Britain could buy security for Aden by recognizing the republic in Yemen. But the government, then headed by Harold Macmillan, was not impressed. The decisive influences against recognition were Duncan Sandys, Secretary of State for Commonwealth Relations; Peter Thorneycroft, Minister of Defence; Hugh Fraser, Secretary of State for Air; and Julian

Amery, who as Minister of Aviation was not a member of the cabinet but was nonetheless influential. And one should also mention Neil McLean, known to his friends as 'Billy', the M.P. for Inverness and veteran of the Middle East who, in articles for *The Times* or the *Daily Telegraph*, repeatedly made the case for the royalists and against the republic. This he did on the basis of his travels the length and breadth of the royalist area in October and November and again in January and February 1963. On these journeys Neil McLean won the admiration of the Yemeni royalists, sharing their food and hardships, and accompanying them to their most advanced positions on the outskirts of Sana and Sadah. He won the friendship of all the royalist leaders. In London he became their unofficial ambassador, a close associate of Foreign Minister Ahmed al Shami, who makes his home in London. Whatever help has trickled through to the royalists from British sources in subsequent years has been largely due to his efforts.

The British government did not, therefore, fall in line with the United States. It decided not to recognize. The republican government, having waited almost two months, on 13 February 1963 asked C. T. Gandy, the British Minister in Taiz, to close the legation within seven days.

Others who withheld recognition of the republican government of Yemen were of course the Saudis, the Jordanians and the government of Iran. Alongside them were Turkey and most of the governments of western Europe, with the two exceptions of West Germany, which moved in quickly in order to forestall the East Germans, and Italy, whose policy seems to have been motivated by the fact that she had for many years enjoyed special ties with Yemen, and hoped to protect this relationship. The others who recognized were Canada and Australia, who, however, maintained no mission in Yemen, the remaining Arab governments, Ethiopia and the entire communist bloc.

The U.S. therefore found that its only western colleagues in the Yemen diplomatic corps were the West Germans and the Italians, of whom the former were soon deleted as a result of a quarrel with the Arabs over arms sales to Israel. It is a peculiar aspect of the British relationship with the Yemen, however, that although Britain continues to recognize the Imam on paper, and a Yemeni legation continues to operate in London, the British government has not acted as though it regarded the Imam as the sovereign of his country. It has not tried to send official representatives to the Imam's headquarters in the mountains and has seemingly submitted to the American view that, while there is nothing wrong with military and civil support given the republic by various countries, similar support of the royalists by countries who still recognize the Imam is quite improper.

Only a week after American recognition of the republic President Sallal made a mockery of the assurances given the Americans by boasting at a military parade that the republic possessed rockets capable of striking the 'palaces of Saudi Arabia'. And while this was doubtless exaggeration, in the first weeks of January the Egyptians did again bomb and strafe the region of Najran. The United States replied with yet another 'show of force', an aerial demonstration over Jeddah and a courtesy call by an American destroyer at Jeddah on 15 January. This was the time, in addition, which President Kennedy chose to publish the letter he had written to Crown Prince Faisal on 25 October, assuring him of 'full U.S. support for the maintenance of Saudi Arabian integrity'. This and other American shows of force in Saudi Arabia were undoubtedly meant to say to Nasser: 'Thus far and no further.' They may, indeed, have succeeded in preventing deeper penetrations of Saudi territory by the Egyptian air force.

The negative, military side of American policy was balanced by positive endeavour, based on two missions, one by Ralph Bunche, and the other by Ellsworth Bunker. After consultation with the State Department, U Thant, the U.N. Secretary-General, sent to Yemen Dr Bunche, the U.N. Under-Secretary for Special Political Affairs who had so distinguished himself in helping end the Arab-Israel war in 1949. He arrived at Taiz on 1 March, about the time when the Egyptian army's most successful military operation into northern and eastern Yemen was in full swing, and his progress for the next few days became the focus of a considerable political demonstration. According to Sana radio he was welcomed not only by Yemeni officials but by large crowds carrying banners inscribed: 'Down with British imperialism. Death to the British. Death to Kings Saud and Hussein,' and so on. Greeted as a 'messenger of peace', while balloons with pictures of Sallal and Nasser were launched in the air, it took Dr Bunche more than two hours to travel from the airport to town. The demonstrations were repeated the next day when Dr Bunche arrived at Sana, where he had talks

with President Sallal. The third day he asked to fly to Marib, which
it so happened had just been occupied, or liberated, depending
on the point of view, by the Egyptian army. Here again an excited
crowd of regional sheikhs noisily demonstrated their affection for
the republic. After five hours in Marib Dr Bunche was returned
to Sana by helicopter for a meeting with Field Marshal Abdul
Hakim Amer, the deputy supreme commander of the U.A.R.
armed forces.

To those who met him privately in Aden next day Dr Bunche
gave the impression that he had been much impressed by President
Sallal's unemotional, factual presentation of his republic's problems.
He said he thought that the republican régime was in effective
control of the country. On 6 March Dr Bunche was in Cairo, where
President Nasser, according to reports through diplomatic channels,
assured him that he would gladly withdraw his troops from Yemen
if the Saudis would end their support of the royalist tribes.

About the time Dr Bunche was returning to New York to
report all this to U Thant, the State Department asked Ambassador
Ellsworth Bunker, a veteran of the American foreign service who
has repeatedly been drafted for especially difficult missions, to
take a hand. His mission was based on one of the last policy decisions
made by the National Security Council, namely National Security
Action Memo 227, dated 27 February 1963. This memorandum
was the product not so much of State Department policy but of
bolder thinking in McGeorge Bundy's 'little State Department' at
the White House, in particular by Robert Komer, a special counsel
at the White House, who made himself the advocate of what
became known as 'Operation Hard-surface'. The idea was to trade
American protection, or the appearance of American protection,
for a Saudi commitment to halt aid to the royalists, on the basis
of which the Americans hoped to get Nasser to withdraw his troops
and so to put an end to the Yemen war. 'Operation Hard-surface'
was to consist, as Mr Komer put it, of 'eight little planes' which
would be, if not the substance, at least the symbol of American
power. Ellsworth Bunker was selected to make the deal.

Mr Bunker arrived in Riyadh on 6 March 1963 and, according
to the record I have from Saudi and American sources, some
remarkably tough talk between him and Prince Faisal ensued.
Faisal's first response to the American proposition was: 'If U.S.
government help and support is forthcoming only as a result of a

condition imposed on me, then all I can say is, "We cannot have it that way".' The Crown Prince was especially indignant, it seems, because Ambassador Bunker had, with an astonishing lack of diplomacy, attempted to hitch the American offer also to pledges of reform and development.

To anyone who knows Faisal's character and what he was doing in Saudi Arabia, such crude intrusion into Saudi internal affairs must come as a shock. But better was to come. On his second trip to Riyadh Bunker 'raised the ante'; he brought along a promise of aid to Saudi Arabia in the form of American television experts. He is said to have observed to Prince Faisal that President Kennedy thought disengagement would enable the Crown Prince to attend to 'unrest and rebellion' in his own country.

Prince Faisal's retort was quite angry. He would never remain in the seat of authority, he declared, if ever he thought his people did not want him. The real problem, he declared, was that 'we have been subjected to attacks and attempts to crush us'; yet all he had received from the U.S. was a 'stream of good wishes and noble sentiment'. These were 'fine, but not a deterrent'. 'We suffered several attacks,' said the prince. 'We folded our arms in deference to your advice. How far will you go in defending us?'

Mr Bunker must have been hard put to answer this question. The original instructions for 'Operation Hard-surface' were that American planes would 'attack and destroy' any intruders over Saudi air space. But this was later watered down to read that they would simply defend themselves if attacked. The evidence from Saudi sources is that Mr Bunker stuck to the original formula and did not tell Prince Faisal of the change. He emphasized to Prince Faisal that if only the Saudis would halt their aid to the royalists the U.S. would be able to put the heat on Nasser to withdraw his troops.

In the end Prince Faisal accepted the television experts and the 'eight little planes' and the implied commitment to defend Saudi Arabia by force, although I believe he had little confidence in the latter. Ambassador Bunker departed and, after ten days cooling his heels in Beirut waiting for an appointment, was received by Nasser, appropriately on April Fool's Day. The Egyptian President repeated the assurances he had given Dr Bunche.

Out of the Bunche and Bunker missions was born the idea of the U.N. Yemen observer mission to observe the 'disengagement' from Yemen. Major-General Carl Von Horn, the Swedish

chief of the United Nations Mission in Yemen in 1963, has stated
the terms of the disengagement agreement in his book *Soldiering
for Peace*. General Von Horn served as Chief of Staff of the United
Nations Truce Supervision Organization in Palestine and Commander of U.N. troops in the Congo before his Yemen episode.
He wrote that the disengagement agreement called for the following:

1. Establishment of a demilitarized zone extending twenty
kilometres on either side of a demarcated Saudi Arabian Yemen
border, from which all military equipment was to be excluded.
2. Stationing of U.N. observers within this zone on both sides
of the border to observe, report and prevent any continued
attempt by the Saudis to supply royalist forces.

In addition, he wrote: 'The Egyptians gave reluctant lip service
to an arrangement that they were to stop fighting and bombing
the royalists as soon as the disengagement agreement came into
force. They also agreed to the stationing of observers to ensure
that their troops kept out of the buffer zone, and to supervise
withdrawal of their units, when and if this took place, from the
whole country.'

On 30 April 1963, General Von Horn was sent on an exploratory
mission to discover what kind of observer force was required. A
few days later, at his first meeting with Field Marshal Amer in
Cairo, the general was told that Egypt had no intention of withdrawing all her troops from the Yemen. 'Whatever international
agreements might be reached,' the Field Marshal told Von Horn,
'a security force would always have to be left to ensure the continuation of Sallal's régime.' A few more days, and he was told
equally emphatically by the Saudi deputy Minister for Foreign
Affairs, Omar Saqqaff, that the Saudis were 'not prepared to accept
any attempt by the Egyptians to leave security forces in the country
when eventually their army withdrew'. The tough old Swedish
general got the message from the start. 'I doubt,' he wrote, 'the
Egyptians or the Saudis had any intention of seriously observing
the terms of disengagement.'

Beginning with this inauspicious impression, Von Horn's
mission was jinxed still further by continuous squabbles over
administration and supply. His Swedish, Irish, American, Guate-
malan, British and Canadian staff was supplemented on 4 July by
a mobile reconnaissance unit of 122 Yugoslavs, whose handicap

was that their every move was controlled by a political commissar who got his instructions through a secret radio in the Yugoslav embassy. For weeks the mission had no medical officer and its troops were delayed. It lacked food, it lacked transport on the ground and in the air. It became the victim of the U.N.'s financial difficulties.

There were things to delight General Von Horn, such as the use of a magnificent automobile which had once been a present to the late Imam Ahmed from King Ibn Saud – a vast Daimler, as the general puts it in his book, 'on whose chassis a famous Paris coach-builder had erected a magnificent body, with sumptuous (but now somewhat faded) upholstery, armoured windows and windscreen, and a wealth of opulent fittings which included a huge mahogany cabinet with a positive plethora of drawers'. Another delight for the general was the Imam's white stallion, on which he went riding in the early mornings outside the walls of the city of Sana, un-embarrassed by the royal crown stamped on his mount's saddle blanket as he counted the heads of the executed royalists stuck on poles outside the city gate.

But these were small compensation for what he considered the impossibility of his task, only part of which was to oversee the so-called demilitarized zone of 6,000 square miles. Gazing balefully from the air at his parish he wondered 'which was worse, the desert and broken rocky country, or the savage, jagged peaks which rose as high as 11,300 feet'. He looked down upon a broken and scarred piece of ground 'that looked as though the earth had been hacked up with some titanic prehistoric rake . . . the least inviting terrain for observer teams I had ever encountered'. He noted that even air patrols would be hampered by the cloud formations that built up around the mountains every afternoon during the summer. He mourned that 'this was territory no U.N. jeep would be capable of penetrating . . . where mountain villages recognized no authority, Saudi, Yemeni, royalist or republican . . . where convoys moved at night, and air observation would not find much to observe'.

Nor did residence in the quarters that had once belonged to the harem favourite, in the somewhat damaged former palace of the Imam, bring much joy to General Von Horn. 'We soon discovered,' he said, 'that the Imam's palace must have been built exclusively for dwarfs. The lintels were so low that one might have imagined a tribe of Swedish trolls inhabiting the dark, winding stairways, and every corner had niches which must have once concealed a crouching Yemeni guard.' To live in this palace he had to acquire 'the Yemen stoop, a sort of shuffling defensive crouch, particularly repulsive to an old guardsman like myself'.

Von Horn thought that disengagement might have worked had there been 'a swift and impressive assembly of an international force whose appearance would have made an impact'. But the chance had been missed; now, he found, both sides had had time for second thoughts. Another handicap of which he complained was that his instructions approved by U Thant were 'under no circumstances to enter into contact with the royalist authorities'. This remained the rule, in spite of repeated approaches from the royalists, until the Egyptians were accused of using gas against the royalists. At that time Von Horn was asked to make his inquiries wherever it might be necessary. Although he did not indicate that he took advantage of this relaxation of the ban, he noted that it was 'clear to me that the Imam held large sectors of the southern buffer zone where we were proposing to operate. . . . The royalists were a force to be reckoned with and Egyptian armour and planes had been able to achieve little results.' The Egyptian garrison at Sadah, he wrote, 'sat in lonely little groups, patently disillusioned and homesick for the gentler atmosphere of the Nile delta'.

On 16 June the commander of the Egyptian troops in Yemen, General Anwar al Qadi, told Von Horn that there was still no overall plan for a phased withdrawal. As the days went by, Von Horn grew more and more bitter. He lacked the means to deal with the royalist raids, ambushes and small-scale attacks on Egyptian and republican garrisons, let alone the continuing Egyptian air-raids of which he heard. He was appalled also by the 'complete lack of interest by the U.N. towards any royalist complaint about bombing and massacres in royalist-held territory by the Egyptians'. He concluded that 'in real terms the whole story of the mission was one of calculated deceit. I, its commanding officer, had been misled, the general public had been deluded and the Egyptians and Saudi Arabians had been taken straight up the garden path.'

At last, on 20 August. General Von Horn resigned. But it was not yet the end of the U.N. story. Temporarily replaced, first by his Yugoslav deputy and then by the commander of the U.N. emergency force, he was succeeded on 5 November by Signor

Pier Spinelli, head of the U.N. European office at Geneva. The appointment of a civilian as head of the observer mission coincided with U Thant's decision to withdraw the military components of the mission, partly because they had not succeeded in bringing about disengagement and partly because the Saudi government had baulked at paying another two-monthly instalment of the mission's expenses. When the Saudis at the last minute changed their mind, he extended the military mission's life. Its Yugoslav reconnaissance unit was nonetheless withdrawn soon thereafter and a new staff of military observers brought in from Denmark, Ghana, India, Italy, the Netherlands, Norway, Pakistan, Sweden and Yugoslavia. The new staff, according to the January report by U Thant to the Security Council, was deployed as follows: Sana, headquarters staff and three observers; Najran, ten observers; Jizan, five observers; Sadah, two observers; Hodeidah, one observer; Jeddah, one liaison officer.

U Thant's report said that 'the functions of the observers at Najran and Jizan are to maintain permanent check-points at the main border crossings into Yemen, temporary check-points on an irregular basis at the more difficult crossings, as well as patrols, in order to observe the nature of the traffic across the border. Most United Nations patrols and check-points are accompanied by Saudi Arabian liaison officials, who check cargoes as requested by the observers. Occasionally observers visit royalist areas on the Yemeni side of the border, in order to check on the extent to which arms and ammunition may be reaching them from abroad, and the degree of fighting occurring between them and the U.A.R. forces in Yemen. The observers in Sadah, Sana and Hodeidah observe the extent to which the U.A.R. forces are being disengaged from Yemen.' The description of functions in royalist areas represented a distinct change from General Von Horn's original directives. U Thant reported that Pier Spinelli's discussions with the Saudi, Egyptian and Yemeni republican governments had sought 'areas of agreement between the parties which might, through bilateral discussions or otherwise, lead to further progress towards disengagement and towards a peaceful situation'. He thought the discussions encouraging.

The United Nations mission struggled on in this way in two-monthly spurts till at last, in September 1964, the Saudis refused to go on. Although the U.N. found that some unofficial traffic in arms was going on from Saudi into Yemeni territory, the Saudis maintained that they had 'faithfully and honestly' halted their official support of the royalists ever since 29 April 1963, when they had signed the original Bunker agreement. But, the Saudis charged, with some reason, there were no signs that Egypt was carrying out its side of the bargain. The number of Egyptian troops in Yemen had not declined. On the contrary it had increased from an estimated 20,000 in April 1963 to no less than 60,000 in the autumn of 1964. Thus, at forty-eight hours notice, on 4 September 1964, the United Nations admitted failure and withdrew its mission from Yemen.

Throughout this period American policy continued to show signs of bias, as indicated by a reply written by the Assistant Secretary of State, Phillips Talbot, to an inquiry by Senator Bourke Hickenlooper in a letter of 16 July 1963, as to whether, in view of 'the growing discredit of the republican government', American recognition should be withdrawn. Mr Talbot revealed that the United States had never insisted on withdrawal of Egyptian troops after Saudi Arabia had begun to observe the terms of the disengagement agreement, but merely expected the Egyptians 'to withdraw in a phased and expeditious fashion'. He said that American recognition of the republican government was based on 'its control of the apparatus of government and most of the country, apparent popular support and ability to honour international obligations'. The letter continued:

> During the regrettable delays in putting the disengagement agreement into effect there was no net reduction in Egyptian forces in Yemen, nor did Saudi Arabia fully terminate its aid to the royalists. However, we are satisfied that the Saudis have terminated their assistance since the date the disengagement went fully into effect, and we are hopeful the U.A.R. will fulfil its part of the agreement.
>
> Peace has been established in the country. Egyptian troops are still tied down coping with guerilla warfare mounted by the tribes who are traditionally opposed to any central government. But it is our view that the intensity of tribal resistance will abate once the drying up of the Saudi supply line takes full effect and a stabilizing of the situation permits reconciliation of the tribal factions. We are not aware that the Egyptian troops have enlarged the area of attack in recent days.

Mr Talbot explained that the Egyptians were not prohibited by the disengagement agreement from fighting tribes who continued to operate against the central government although the agreement did prohibit punitive attacks. He concluded with the statement that 'restoration of the notoriously despotic imamate would not be supported by the people at large and it is generally acknowledged to be out of the question'.

The letter indicates that the American government at this time did not admit that the forces opposing the republic and the Egyptians were an organized royalist army. Rather it chose to regard them as 'tribes who are traditionally opposed to any central government'. Mr Talbot's total rejection of the imamate notwithstanding, there were indications at this time that, in addition to seeking military disengagement, the United States was trying to promote a political solution in the form of some kind of compromise between Yemeni republicans and Yemeni royalists. The British, who remained in direct contact with the royalists, worked along similar lines. The Saudi Arabians, partly through contacts established in Beirut by Kamel Adham, Crown Prince Faisal's brother-in-law, explored the same kind of possibilities. There was talk about the possibility of a 'coalition government' from which both the Imam and President Sallal would have to withdraw. The Imam would be reduced from the status of ruler to that of purely spiritual religious head. The phrase 'third force', meaning those who were opposed both to the U.A.R. presence and to the Imam, also became current at this time.

The strain of the United States' attempt to bring about disengagement in this conflict was reflected in U.S. relations with Saudi Arabia and Egypt. The 'Hard-surface' squadron was withdrawn at the end of January 1964 after a wrangle with Prince Faisal over the extension of the disengagement agreement.

Towards the end of the period of 'disengagement', the complacent attitude indicated by Mr Talbot changed and the State Department tried very hard to obtain Egyptian compliance. When in mid-October Dr Abdul Moneim al Kaissouny, the Egyptian Minister of the Treasury and Economic Planning, asked the United States for help to meet Egypt's mounting foreign exchange difficulties, the State Department replied with a reminder that the war in Yemen was draining Egyptian finances. The U.S. could not be expected to continue, much less increase, its aid unless the Egyptians began carrying out their obligations under the disengagement agreement.

Nor was this the only form of pressure on the Egyptians. In Washington a young American named Bushrod Howard was playing a role on behalf of the Yemeni royalists very similar to that played by Billy McLean in London. This remarkable young American came to his task by way of the oil business, which he learned first as the employee of some of the big American companies and finally as their opponent, in the employ, variously, of the British, the French and the Iraqis. He learned his business from a variety of angles, including working as a lobbyist for the National Maritime Union, which wanted fifty per cent of American oil shipped in American-flag tankers, and for the National Coalminers' Union, which was anxious to protect coal against the competition of imported oil. At various times he worked also on questions related to oil in the Middle East for Senators Fulbright and Hubert Humphrey.

The son of the director of Standard Oil of New Jersey, Howard first worked in the legal department of the Iraq Petroleum Company in 1948. From there he went on to handle 'concessionary, political and social matters for Socony' in 1952. For Socony and Standard Oil of New Jersey he was an observer at the first Suez Conference in 1956. But in 1957, finding that 'when certain people retired from Socony no one would be particularly interested in my views', he quit. By this time he knew every country in the Middle East, along with its politicians, and he was ready for his education in lobbying tactics, which he supplemented with a steady flow of anti-oil company articles for the new republic in *Reporter Magazine* and the *National Mineworkers' Journal*. It was natural at this point that Howard should strike up a friendship with Hasseb Chuwab, the Iraqi delegate to the United Nations, who was one of the very many Arab diplomats and politicians he had entertained in the late fifties under the auspices of the oil company-subsidized Council on Islamic Affairs in New York.

In the winter of 1963 Howard went to Baghdad to get a job as adviser on oil affairs to Premier Kassim. But this time his timing was wrong; he arrived just before the Baathist *coup d'état* that overthrew Kassim. Late in December 1963, he was back in Beirut, wondering what to do next, and came to see me and my wife Tania.

I had just returned from my trip through royalist territory from Najran to Beihan, and suggested that Howard should have a look at the royalists of Yemen. He jumped at the idea. He remembered that he had been especially friendly in his Islamic Council days with the Yemeni delegate, Prince Hassan bin Yahya, who then seemed particularly in need of help and guidance in the turmoil of New York and the U.N.; he was now the royalist Prime Minister. And so, a few days later, in the guise of a writer for the *Reporter Magazine*, Howard arrived in Aden, managed to get himself a lift with the R.A.F. to Beihan, and hitch-hiked, in spite of some mild British misgivings, across the border to Harib. Sharing a truck with sixty Khawlani sheikhs, he arrived in Najran just in time to be bombed by the Egyptians on 13 February 1963. From Najran he went on to the headquarters of the Prime Minister.

Howard himself described the visit as follows. 'I came up to Hassan's cave in the Wadi Hishwah about dawn. Of course he had worked all night as usual and was praying and the guards kept me away until he stopped praying. Then he turned round and said: "Oh, it's you. What are you doing here?" I said: "I came to visit you. Isn't it normal?" He agreed this was normal and gave me what turned out to be his bed in his cave. We talked for two or three days, and he told me that he wanted me to work for him, and I agreed'.

What Hassan wanted most was arms, but Howard did not feel that he knew the arms business. So he concentrated on the second thing the Prime Minister wanted, namely propaganda and political work in the U.S. With a first objective of cutting United States aid to Nasser, Howard was surprised to discover that the field of anti-Nasserite propaganda was wide open. The oil companies, who had been active against Nasser in 1955–56 and in 1957, had withdrawn from the struggle since 1958 and allowed it to become a purely Zionist operation. The opportunity now, he found, lay in getting republicans and southern democrats interested. He was amazed at the response he found. One of those who supported his objectives was Senator Ernest Gruening, a brilliant veteran of the Senate with an extraordinary past as doctor, newspaperman, President Roosevelt's man in South America, and governor of Alaska; in addition, he was Jewish and a strong opponent of Nasser. Another ally proved to be L. G. Fountain, the representative for North Carolina, who was head of the Near Eastern Sub-committee.

Howard's first achievement was to get the so-called 'anti-aggressor amendment' through the Senate and the House of Representatives over the opposition of the Kennedy administration.

This amendment would enable a president to cut off aid to any country if he found that aggression was being committed. His next project was to cut aid to Nasser by attaching a rider to a supplementary agricultural Bill in 1964. This failed by three votes, but it was effective in the sense that the anti-Nasserites got a pledge from President Johnson that he would sign no new aid agreement while Congress was out of session.

It was after this, on 23 December 1964, that Nasser made the famous speech in which he told the Americans to go and 'drink up the Red Sea', meaning that if they did not want to help him he could not care less.

When Congress reconvened in January another amendment opposing aid to Nasser passed the House and was only narrowly defeated in the Appropriations Committee of the Senate – only after very substantial commitments had been made by the administration about any new aid to Nasser. In fact it would seem that Howard's efforts had gone far to set the stage for finally cutting off American grain shipments to Egypt in 1966, and perhaps for a major turn in American foreign policy.

On the propaganda side Howard succeeded in getting an N.B.C. television crew, headed by Frank Burckholtzer, into northern Yemen in the spring of 1964. In January 1967 he was on hand to organize international press coverage of the effects of Egyptian gas bombing at Kitaf. To help the Saudis make up their minds that it was worth while trying to draw world attention to this affair, he went to Kitaf two days after the bombing, dug up some of the animals which had been killed by the gas and brought them back by truck into Saudi Arabia for examination by medical specialists. In the spring of 1967 Howard was planning a new lobbying campaign. His aim this time was to get Yemen discredited as a member of the United Nations. But military events forestalled him.

After the final failure of the United States and United Nations policy of disengagement in Yemen, the U.S. and the U.N. retired from the scene, and a period of direct diplomatic confrontation between Egypt and Saudi Arabia ensued. Military engagements in Yemen were followed by a prolonged and tacit truce. United States involvement was limited to a certain amount of diplomatic hand-wringing, mainly in order to persuade the Saudis not to 'unleash' the royalists. The most important development was that the United States' relations with Egypt deteriorated.

After Britain, in the Defence Review of February 1966, announced her intention to withdraw from Aden 'by 1968', the main focus of attention shifted to South Arabia and Aden, where U.S. policy still remains notably undefined. As in other parts of the periphery of the Arabian peninsula, from Yemen round to Kuwait, the United States has for many years modestly conceded British primacy in South Arabia and Aden. In the entire area the United States was represented only by consulates-general in Dahran and Aden. Not even in Muscat (with which the U.S. concluded its first foreign treaty in the year 1833) has the U.S. maintained a consulate, let alone fully-fledged diplomatic representation. (All this was conceded to be an area of exclusive British influence.)

If it is assumed that it is still American policy to give 'full U.S. support for the maintenance of Saudi Arabian integrity', as President Kennedy said on 25 October 1963, then South Arabia and the rest of the periphery are as important to the U.S. as Yemen. That is, it is important that these places should develop political independence and should be neither occupied nor dominated by unfriendly powers.

As a consequence of the June war between Arabs and Israelis, the Egyptians have at last withdrawn from Yemen, thereby removing the Egyptian military threat from South Arabia and, indeed, from the whole Arabian peninsula. In this more hopeful situation Britain has withdrawn from South Arabia but is still clinging to bases on the island of Bahrein and in the sheikhdom of Sharga in the Persian Gulf; the United States has still to evolve a policy to meet the demands of the changing circumstances of this region.

XIV

Peace Talks

BONFIRES burned in the mountains of Yemen every night from 2 November until 8 November, 1964. Tribesmen on both royalist and republican sides of the war were celebrating the decision, taken on 2 November at a secret conference of royalists and republicans at Erkwit, a resort on the Sudanese coast, to declare a cease-fire effective at 1 p.m. on Monday 8 November.

For two days after the cease-fire went into effect republicans and royalists fraternized in many places. At as Safrah, in the Barat mountains south-east of Sadah, a royalist caravan boldly approached Egyptian positions and proposed a feast. The royalists slaughtered sheep, the Egyptians brought tinned goods. But after a few hours, it is said, a high-ranking Egyptian officer arrived on the scene and indignantly put a stop to the festivities.

At the end of the two days the Egyptians resumed their bombing of royalist positions. In at least one instance the bombing may have been motivated by the royalist refusal to put the cease-fire into effect in the broadest possible sense. Thus the longing of the Yemeni people for peace was frustrated once again. Instead of the national conference of 168 tribal leaders, which the Erkwit conference had planned for 23 November, another bloody round of the war was begun.

The Erkwit cease-fire was nevertheless a notable event, for it was the first of three conferences which attempted to end the war in Yemen; it was followed by the Jeddah agreement between King Faisal and President Nasser, in August 1965, and by the Haradh conference of royalist and republican Yemenis in November 1965. Each of them was in vain, it seemed, but each was a contribution towards the settlement which had inevitably to take place.

The shift to the conference table was a direct result of the failure of United States and United Nations attempts to bring about disengagement; the United Nations observers had finally departed in September 1964. While some moralists might argue that the Arabs got along better when outside attempts to influence them were withdrawn, it seems realistic, however, to assume that the ground-work for Erkwit was in fact laid during the intense round of visits between Riyadh, Cairo and Sana made in the first part of 1964 by Pier Pasquali Spinelli, personal representative of United Nations Secretary-General U Thant, and last head of the United Nations observer mission. The mediatory efforts of a joint Iraqi-Algerian delegation, which came to Riyadh at this time, may also have helped.

But the most significant thing to note is that these conferences took place in each case after the Egyptians had suffered sharp military reverses. Erkwit (and the preceding Alexandria meeting between Faisal and Nasser) followed the *débâcle* of the Haradh offensive of August 1964. The Jeddah agreement was signed by Faisal and Nasser (and the Haradh conference, which was its sequel, took place) after the Egyptians had been defeated in the north-east and were obliged to begin to withdraw from that part of the country.

Some Cairo diplomats believed that Nasser's desire to get out of Yemen dated all the way back to the incomplete success of his armies' first major offensive in February and March 1963. A sequel to this frustration was the removal of Abdurrahman Baidani, deputy Premier of republican Yemen, who was married to the sister of Anwar Sadat, President Nasser's expert on Yemen. But the Egyptians were trapped: though reason might call for withdrawal, prestige and ambition prevented it.

King Faisal (then still Crown Prince) personally attaches special importance in the evolution of the Yemen question to his meeting with President Nasser at Alexandria, the summit conference of Arab kings and presidents which took place at the beginning of September. Certainly both he and President Nasser seemed anxious to build up their bargaining positions before that conference. Five days before their meeting and four days before the U.N. observers were due to wind up their mission in Yemen, the Saudi leader gave a most unusually outspoken interview to the Beirut newspaper *al Nahar*. He made a veiled threat to escalate Saudi support of the royalists from the level of arms and money to that of armed force. He observed that under the Treaty of Mutual Assistance of 1956 between Saudi Arabia, Yemen and Egypt, help given Yemen by the Saudi armed forces, at the request of the Imam, 'would not constitute interference on our part, as this assistance would be in accordance with an agreement existing between us and the Yemeni government'. American diplomats in the area heard in August and September that the Saudis had reacted to the winding up of the United Nations observer mission by sending a rush of fresh military supplies to the royalists.

President Nasser meanwhile made a determined effort to achieve a *fait accompli* in northern Yemen before the summit meeting. In August the Egyptians made their big push from Haradh and Sadah, in which it was intended to kill, capture or expel the Imam and end royalist resistance in the north. The Egyptians did in fact oblige the Imam to flee from his headquarters at Mount Qara to a new set of caves on Mount Sheda, near the Saudi border. But they failed in their main objectives, and the cost in casualties and material was so great as to amount to a serious reverse.

The story was put about in Beirut at the time that the Egyptians had offered the Imam al Badr £5 million if he would abdicate and withdraw, say, to the French riviera. Although the Imam denied, when I saw him in December 1964, that he had ever received such an offer, I should not be suprised if the Egyptians did try it. They were desperate for some way out of their Yemeni impasse and would gladly have paid ten times the figure suggested for a solution. At the time of the Alexandria conference there was talk among diplomats about 'swopping Badr for Sallal', meaning a deal in which both sides would sacrifice their topmost figure in order to make it easier to come to terms. Diplomats in Cairo heard for the first time that the Egyptians might be willing to agree to a solution which would preserve the imamate but reduce the Imam from the status of a temporal ruler to that of a purely spiritual figure. The Egyptians seemed more than ever anxious to impress foreign observers with the idea that they really wanted to find an honourable way to withdraw from Yemen.

The most notable result of the Alexandria summit meeting may have been the communiqué in which the two men spoke of the need to bring about peace between the 'two parties' in Yemen. This was the first time that the Egyptians had officially acknowledged the existence of 'two parties'. Previously they had always insisted that the republican government was in full control and that the opposition consisted merely of isolated bands of infiltrators. They had pretended that the royalists no longer existed. Both sides now grudgingly acknowledged the legitimacy of the other's interests and agreed to begin to look for ways of coming to terms.

When I visited republican Yemen between the meetings in Alexandria and Erkwit, as described in more detail in Chapter V, I was impressed by the efforts the Egyptians were making to win their war in Yemen by other than military means. Although their military efforts were in fact constantly frustrated the Egyptians persistently ignored all reverses and claimed victories with so much conviction that they convinced themselves and probably some of the Yemenis. I was amazed, for instance, by the easy conviction with which Colonel Hassan Ali Kamal, the Chief of Operations, made statements to me which I knew to be untrue. The statements included the following: that the tribes in the region of Qara had turned against the Imam and had driven him out; that the Egyptian forces could freely travel to the Saudi Arabian border by camel; that the Egyptians had lost only three men during their August offensive from Haradh; and that Prince Abdullah Hassan in the Khawlan had been 'knocked out' by the tribes' unwillingness to work with him.

I was impressed also by the extent of the Egyptians' 'hearts and minds' campaign among the Yemenis. The army had a section entirely devoted to civilian activities, including such things as installing water pumps, school-teaching and providing all kinds of professional services and advice – agricultural, engineering and medical. These were all ways of introducing the Yemenis to modern life, ways in which the Egyptians could do things for the Yemeni people which their traditional leaders could not. The Egyptians had also brought 100 Egyptian ulema into the country, in the hopes of persuading the Yemenis that there were really no important differences between the Sunnis and the Shia in general, and the Shaffei and Zeidi sects in particular. They may even have tried to persuade the Zeidis that they did not really need an Imam.

On 2 and 3 November at Erkwit, nine royalists and nine republicans, with a Saudi and an Egyptian observer, worked out the terms of the cease-fire. The first formal meeting of royalists and republicans since the *coup d'état* was a moment of great emotion for the men who participated. They fell into each other's arms and kissed each other, and tears rolled down their cheeks. According to the Imam, whom I met little more than a month later, many of the republicans had sent him greetings through the royalist delegates. They agreed that after the cease-fire, which was to begin on 8 November, a national conference of royalists and republicans should gather on 23 November.

As the royalists understood it, the conference was to become an embryo national assembly which would name a provisional national executive of two royalists, two republicans and one neutral, to administer the country provisionally and to plan a national plebiscite. The plebiscite, to be held following an Egyptian withdrawal, would decide whether Yemen was to be a monarchy or a republic. While the provisional executive was in power the governments on both sides, including the chiefs of state, President Sallal and the Imam Mohamed al Badr, were to step aside.

Eager to bring about the success of the conference, the royalists made a remarkable concession. Apparently convinced that sheikhs and ulema from the republican side would see things much as they did, they agreed to accept only one-third of the seats in a conference of 168 delegates. Three-eighths of the seats were allocated to the ulema as the religious leaders, three-eighths to the sheikhs as the secular leaders, and two-eighths to other notables. But the royalists refused the republican demand that they agree in advance to retain the republican form of government and to exclude members of the Hamid Eddin dynasty from participating in the conference. The Foreign Minister, Ahmed al Shami, said that the royalists would be willing to accept as one member of the provisional executive the current Prime Minister of republican Yemen, Hamoud al Jaifi. He said the royalists had in mind a constitution that would make a future Imam a mere figurehead with religious and ceremonial political functions. The real power would be vested in a legislature elected by universal suffrage.

Physical arrangements for the conference were left to be worked out by a joint Saudi-Egyptian commission of ambassadors which met in Jeddah. This commission postponed the conference first for a few days, and then until 30 November, and at last indefinitely. The republicans blamed the non-arrival of royalist delegates; the royalists maintained that Egyptian bombing made their coming impossible. The only thing the commission did decide was that the conference should be held near Haradh, in north-western Yemen.

YEMEN: THE UNKNOWN WAR

There was no agreement on what the conference should do or whether the members of the ruling Hamid Eddin family could participate.

There are reasons to believe that the Egyptians and republicans lost interest in Erkwit and its proposed political sequel because they were politically and militarily embarrassed at that time. The first embarrassment was that in attempting to form the republican delegation the Egyptians discovered that most leading Yemenis were reluctant to become official representatives of the republic or to commit themselves to following Egyptian directives. The Egyptians began to realize that the sheikhs and notables who were qualified to attend the Haradh conference would probably line up with the royalists at the conference even if they were sent as republican delegates. The Egyptians reacted to this situation by arresting a number of sheikhs and ulema, and many of the intended victims took flight; some headed for republican territory, others for Aden. The so-called 'third force' movement, which played a prominent role at this time, will be discussed in more detail in Chapter XX. The disintegration of President Sallal's government began at about the same time. Some of Sallal's ministers resigned; others he dismissed for suspected disloyalty.

The second embarrassment was that the military situation in the Razih mountains near the Imam's new headquarters made a cease-fire highly inconvenient to the Egyptians. Since the costly Haradh offensive in August had obliged the Imam to flee from Qara to Sheda, the Egyptians had mounted a series of thrusts – always aimed at killing or capturing the Imam – into the Razih mountains. After one of these thrusts in the first days of November, some 400 of the republican army had defected and left half a dozen Egyptian staff officers, together with the republican Minister of Defence, Hussein al Dafai, stranded in a castle on one of the highest peaks of the Razih mountains. A group of Yemeni officers were left in the castle of Hurm on another peak a mile away. After the cease-fire the Egyptians asked that a mixed Egyptian-Saudi cease-fire team be allowed to take food, water and medicine to the two isolated castles. But the royalist commander refused. He also refused the besieged officers a safe conduct back to Sadah; he was bent on destroying the Egyptians in these mountains.

If this attitude seemed unnecessarily arbitrary there was also very little evidence that the Egyptians themselves were seriously ready to compromise. When I arrived at Jeddah at the beginning of December 1964, less than a month after the cease-fire, I found the Saudis alarmed by a concentration of 7,000 Egyptian and 3,000 republican Yemeni troops at Haradh and at Maidi, the sea port just south of the Saudi frontier. This was by all comparisons the largest Egyptian striking force ever assembled close to the Saudi frontier. The Saudis were nervous about the possibility that the Egyptians might use this force for a sudden thrust across the border into Saudi Arabia, across the plain of the Tihama and the desert, and around to envelop Mount Sheda from behind, thus finally capturing the Imam.

I travelled on this occasion with Joe Alex Morris, who was then with *Newsweek*. From the Saudi governor we obtained a truck – remarkable for its uncertain lights, uncertain brakes, unresponsive springs and temperamental driver – for a ride almost all night long to the Imam's headquarters. We travelled inside Saudi territory eastwards from Jizan. As we moved inland, the terrain to our right changed from semi-desert, populated by a half-naked negroid people living in circular straw huts and wearing conical flower-pot hats, to rocky hill country, where the hilltops were crowned by the stone houses and forts of the Zeidi tribesmen.

When the truck had gone as far as it could it was only a thirty-minute climb through the boulders and up the hillside to the Imam's headquarters. The time was just past dawn and guards showed us to a cave where we rested and waited for the Imam to wake up. Since he usually talked and worked most of the night the Imam did not wake up till about noon, and it was mid-afternoon before we were allowed to see him. In the meantime we roamed about the headquarters and the surrounding countryside. In the distance we could hear the boom of guns, or was it falling bombs? We were told that there had been a number of attacks on the Imam's headquarters in the preceding few weeks, but no planes approached that day. The great depth of his cave and the elaborately cemented stones and boulders around the entrance made the Imam secure as long as he stayed underground. Three armed men sat night and day on a rocky ledge facing the entrance to this cave. They were part of a group of 200 guards scattered across the surrounding mountain-side. Beyond that there was little to see except the royal privy, artfully contrived between the rocks for the Imam's use, and an open-air kitchen, over which a cheerful Egyptian prisoner presided as chef.

The Imam, now thirty-seven years old, had spent more than two years living in caves of this kind. The one at Qara was far more inaccessible; it took seven hours of climbing by mule and on foot to reach it. It was more spacious and more comfortable than his cave at Sheda. Probably it was also healthier, because the height made it cooler; at Sheda the heat was oppressive, mosquitoes abounded and flies thrived on the faecal waste of an army stationed too long on one mountain-side.

The Imam did not look well; we were told that recently, as he slept in his cave, he had been stung in the hand by a scorpion. His skin was grey and rings had formed beneath his large eyes, which seemed to rove nervously between his visitor and the entrance to his cave. After some urging he came out of his cave for pictures. He was slightly stooped until he remembered to straighten up. He wore khaki uniform, a long scarf which he wound round his head in the form of a loose turban, with a long end hanging down over his left shoulder. It was the only external mark which said: 'I am different from other men – I am the Imam.'

After two years of cave life al Badr had hardened physically, but he was also weary. The flabby figure in dark glasses, known for his indulgence in a wide variety of pleasures during the last days of the rule of his tyrannical father, now seemed a distant memory. Today he had no indulgences. The ebullient boastfulness he displayed in November 1962 when he first met correspondents in northern Yemen, following his escape from his palace in Sana, had now disappeared. He had boasted then that within two weeks he would meet the newsmen again in Sana. Intoxicated by the faith of his tribesmen, he had perhaps dreamed of leading his men militarily in the manner of the great Imam Qarsim, of his grandfather Yahya and his father Ahmed. Now he was more realistic. He knew the limitations of his guerilla forces in the face of an army equipped with tanks and aircraft and he knew his own limitations. Those forces had held out and held together. They had obliged the Egyptians to seek a cease-fire in which they were obliged to treat with the royalists as equals. It was not in fact he who had achieved this, militarily speaking, but the young princes, his nephews and cousins; the will and ability to make decisions was theirs. After two years in the mountains he received a constant stream of visitors, messengers, ministers, petitioners, emissaries, journalists. His strength lay less in day-to-day leadership than in the aura of religion, mystery and remembrance of power of the imamate.

When the photographs were over, the Imam said to his visitors that he hoped and believed that the often-postponed peace conference with the republicans would take place. 'I hope King Faisal can arrange it with Nasser,' he said. 'But the world should know that we cannot negotiate with an Egyptian pistol at our heads and Ilyushins in our sky.' The royalist delegation, he said, was still ready for the proposed conference, but the Egyptians, sensing the implications of the process begun at Erkwit, were now afraid that republican delegates would support their Imam once the meeting began. This had caused disagreement among Egyptians and between Egyptians and republicans. While denying that he had agreed to exclude members of the royal family from the conference, the Imam said he preferred to 'keep the family away, lest anyone should say they exerted undue influence'. As locale for the meeting, he said, the royalists would prefer Sadah, the capital of the north, or Hajjah, in the west, but were willing to accept the Egyptians' choice of Haradh, which lies close to the Saudi border in the north-west. He remarked that the meeting would in any case have to be outside a town – 'somewhere between the Egyptian and the royalist lines'.

As far as he was concerned the conference had only two important aims: firstly, to halt the shooting completely, all over the country, for it had resumed with growing ferocity since the Erkwit cease-fire; and secondly, to demand that the Egyptians leave the country as soon as possible. Meanwhile there could be an interim settlement of the war with a five-man council acting in place of a head of state. Both he and President Sallal would have to step aside while the council was sitting. After the Egyptians were all out of the country, the Yemenis would hold yet another, much bigger conference to determine the country's future. This body could draw up a constitution which would be submitted to the country in a plebiscite.

XV

Royalist Offensive

••

THE thrust through Saudi territory by the Egyptians massed at Haradh and Maidi, about which the Saudis were worrying in December, did not in fact take place. Instead they expended their energies in the ensuing months in ineffectual attempts to drive directly into the Razih mountains. In three months from December 1964 to February 1965 the royalists discerned four such thrusts, of gradually diminishing intensity, and estimated that the Egyptians lost 1,000 men killed, wounded and taken prisoner.

There may have been local tactical reasons why the Egyptians gave up their bold plans in the north. Their top commanders may also have boggled at the international implications of a strike through Saudi territory. But the real reason, I believe, was that in the largest sense the Egyptians were losing the initiative while the royalists were gaining in equipment, in training and in organization. This had become evident in a long period of localized encounters, but beyond that there were signs, which cannot have escaped the attention of Egyptian intelligence, that the royalists were engaged in an offensive build-up in the north-eastern corner of the country. There Prince Mohamed bin Hussein was in command of the recently-developed force of semi-regulars. Prince Mohamed was also emerging as the commander-in-chief of all the forces in eastern Yemen, having taken over from the elderly Prime Minister, Prince Hassan bin Yahya. He had devoted his attention not only to training but to communications and liaison among different elements among the royalists, so that a co-ordinated effort of widely dispersed royalists elements was becoming possible.

Then, between 10 and 14 March, the royalists got some unplanned but epoch-making assistance from the tribesmen in the vicinity of Harib, opposite the South Arabian sheikhdom of Beihan. Tempted by the fact that the Egyptians in the town were few and by defections among the republicans, the powerful Murad and Abida tribes swarmed in and took over. They were no royalists; they merely wanted to be rid of the republicans. But by the time the Egyptians were able to send troops the royalists themselves had succeeded in getting a force of 400 of a new command of semi-regulars into the town. When the tribesmen took to their heels at the appearance of Egyptian tanks, these semi-regulars stood their ground, turning the Egyptians back at a place called al Juba. This was one of the turning-points of the war. For the first time the Egyptians had been deprived of one of the important towns of Yemen and had not been able to take it back.

The origins of the new semi-regular force went back to the early days when Prince Mohamed bin Hussein was in charge of a training camp at Najran, where Saudi and Jordanian officers had first taught Yemenis how to use modern weapons. At the beginning of 1963, after Najran had been subjected to a series of raids by Egyptian aircraft – twice on 29 December and 31 January, once on 1 January and three times on 7 January – the Saudis firmly suggested that their Yemeni friends move southwards. As a result a remarkable supply base was born, in a labyrinth of caves known as Amara, about three or four hours' fast driving across the desert south of Najran, well into Yemeni territory. A royalist training camp grew up in another area of caves, called Hanjar, four or five hours farther south. Ordinary maps do not show these places. I visited them in the company of John Rigos, then of the *Christian Science Monitor*, at the beginning of May 1965.

At Amara the caves within caves extend over six levels. They are lighted by a central power plant. Some are air-conditioned, comfortably furnished in the oriental manner, with carpets and cushions, for long-term occupancy. The surrounding desert is interspersed with jagged, black basaltic rocks. Between the rocks are stretches of true sand desert, semi-desert with sparse grass, and occasional oases of palm-trees. This terrain affords the royalists almost perfect protection from air attack. The Egyptian bombers come regularly, but they rarely do any harm, for the caves are secure and surface activity takes place almost exclusively at night. Nor are these places as vulnerable to Egyptian land attack as one might think. While there are places where the desert is like an open sea and armoured forces can choose their route at will, the jutting rocks in this part of the Jawf oblige vehicles to follow fairly well-defined routes that can be easily observed and mined.

The wilder the terrain, the more favourable to the royalists' tribal forces, for this is their home. And it was tribal forces that were trained and equipped for the most part at Najran and later at Amara and Hanjar. Very early in the war, however, Prince Mohamed realized that tribal forces, limited by their loyalty to a particular sheikh in a particular part of the country, have distinct disadvantages. To meet a particular challenge, as one of the princes put it to me, such forces can rise 'like a flame to great heights of intensity. But only for a short time. Then it fades again. If the flame is not used it loses its ability to flare up.'

Prince Mohamed's scheme was to move away from the tribe as the basis of the royalists' force and to organize something more permanent, more disciplined and more flexible. These were the semi-regulars. He recruited and organized them into formal units called *sariya*, with forty-five men which were broken down into *arifa* of five to ten men. Each *sariya* had two officers. A chief of two *arifa* was called a *mulazem*. Semi-regulars were supposed to serve for at least a year without returning to their homes. The informal, unrecorded drifting back and forth that was taken for granted in other parts of the royalist forces was not permitted here. If a man wanted leave to attend to his harvest or some family matter he must ask his officer for permission. They received fifteen silver Maria Theresa thalers a month (about £5 5s.), their rations and a khaki uniform. In contrast to the tribal forces, colourful in multi-hued turbans and richly ornamented bandoliers, the new semi-regulars were more businesslike in khaki. But they stuck to the knee-length Yemeni kilt instead of trousers.

Some of the training was carried out by foreign mercenaries. At the beginning of May 1965, when John Rigos and I visited Hanjar, four Frenchmen and five Belgians were using a camp called 'Le Petit Bidon', an area surrounded and partly covered by huge boulders. One man had recently been killed and two wounded, we were told, by a bomb dropped in the entrance. Their chief was a former French colonel who had been cashiered after participating in the abortive 1961 O.A.S. coup in Algiers. Some of his men were French and Belgian mercenaries who had served with Moise Tshombe in Katanga in 1961 and 1962; when that cause collapsed fifteen of them joined the royalists, that number arrived during the next twelve months. Several Englishmen served in the mountainous Khawlan province under Prince Abdullah Hassan. A dozen German, French, Belgian and British technicians, with a few Yemenis whom they had trained, operated a radio station and a radio communications network for the whole royalist area, centred on the royalist broadcasting station near Amara. Although headed by a German, they used English as their international language. Their pay averaged $900 (£321) per month.

At Hanjar Rigos and I found that the mercenaries were either on leave or nearer the front line, backing up Prince Mohamed who was leading his troops in combat farther south.

The twenty-eight-year-old Prince Mohamed, the man mainly responsible for the progressive evolution of the royalist armed forces, was one of the formidable clan of six Hussein brothers. Three among them, including Mohamed, had a mother of Persian origin. Humorous, sometimes even gay, Mohamed also possessed a most un-Arab quality; he was imperturbable. At his headquarters voices were rarely raised, and good-humoured discipline was always maintained.

Unashamedly chewing his *qat*, his lips parted in an ironical smile, Prince Mohamed usually wore a turban of yellow cashmere. He had gone to school in Egypt, where he had acquired from the Nasserites a strong sense of the equality of man, political liberty and democracy, along with an embittered conviction that these virtues were not practised by Nasser's men. After secondary school in Cairo he had wanted to study at a university but was instead sent by old Imam Ahmed to head the Yemen legation in Germany. He succeeded Abdurrahman Baidani as minister in Bonn.

When the revolution took place in Sana, Prince Mohamed asked himself: 'Have I the right to resist this revolution?' He decided that he did, 'because they are only puppets of Nasser'. The prince recalled these conflicts of conscience in a conversation with me late one night in December 1963 at the Jeddah Palace Hotel in Jeddah, where he was completing his convalescence after being seriously wounded at the front. He had been ripped from ankle to shoulder by Egyptian bomb fragments. 'I may become a republican myself some day,' he declared, 'but not yet. To be a republican now would be like getting a son before you get a wife.'

To illustrate his political thinking Prince Mohamed recalled some of his encounters with the Egyptians. One had occurred

217

earlier that year while he was fighting an Egyptian armoured unit in the Jawf. The Egyptian commander proposed to meet Prince Mohamed under a flag of truce, to discuss an exchange of prisoners. But Mohamed declined, because, he said, 'I would rather not meet you personally while your country occupies mine with a strong force'. He remembered, too, that in the summer of 1963, when he went to a conference with the Egyptians at Harrlesh in order to negotiate a local truce, he challenged the Egyptian commander: 'Why are you here?' The Egyptian replied: 'Just to make sure that the republic is protected, and for the sake of justice.' Mohamed said he had insisted that the Egyptians must withdraw from Yemen and leave the Yemenis to choose their own government after they had left, to which the Egyptian rejoined: 'Our task is first to get rid of the Hamid Eddin family, including all the princes who are leading the fighting. Secondly we must protect the republic from any external or internal aggression.' Prince Mohamed said that the sheikhs representing the Bakil confederation and some of the Hashid refused to accept any such terms, but that nonetheless they made a 'small agreement' with the Egyptians to stop shooting for one month, during which the royalists would enjoy freedom of movement in the use of heavy weapons. Mischievously, he added: 'This proved to be a good chance to send ammunition to my cousin Abdullah Hassan on the Sana front in the Khawlan. And indeed we sent him everything that he needed.'

A third encounter between Mohamed and the Egyptians occurred as a result of an Egyptian request for contact with a Colonel Hassan Effet, whom the royalists had captured. The reasons for this unusual proposal by the Egyptians was not clear to me, but I got the impression that they wished to assure themselves that this high-ranking prisoner was being well treated. 'We agreed to a meeting-place north-east of Samat Beit Assayed,' he said, 'and two high-ranking officers came there from Cairo. We sent our prisoner to the meeting-place guarded by 100 of our men.' The significance of the ensuing conversation was somewhat diminished by Prince Mohamed's admission that he took care never to allow the colonel to be alone with his Egyptian visitors. He quoted the Egyptian colonel as follows: 'My friends, don't believe that the Yemenis will in time become republicans. I have had much contact with them and have talked to many sheikhs of the Bakil and to many high-ranking personalities from Sana. I have been a prisoner for five months and I know their ideology and their beliefs.' According to Prince Mohamed the Egyptian officers were shocked to hear such testimony from one of their own kind.

The prince said these things in English, which he spoke better than any of the other princes except Abdurrahman. He spoke at length about his family. 'We think of families,' he said, 'the way you did two hundred years ago.' What he had in mind, I think, was that the Yemenis were at a stage of development in which war and affairs of state were very personal family matters. He once remarked to a friend of mine: 'I like you because you like my family.'

Prince Mohamed spoke warmly and with respect about his grandfather, the Imam Yahya, 'although he tried to stop everything until he died'. His aversion to change notwithstanding, old Imam Yahya was loved by his people and kept his country independent – one of the few Arab countries in the Middle East that were independent. The prince's uncle, the Imam Ahmed, whom he in some ways resembles, came in for reproach because 'he did not keep the line of his father. He fell between two stools, he was very nervous.' What he meant by the Imam Ahmed's 'nervousness' soon emerged: the prince reflected sombrely that he had had thirteen uncles of whom only two, Prince Abdurrahman and the elderly Prince Hassan who was now Prime Minister, had survived the reign of Ahmed. Most of them had died violently by the will of the Imam. His own father had been killed in the attempted *coup d'état* of 1948 in which he had supported the revolutionaries who wanted to prevent Ahmed from inheriting the throne.

In spite of this macabre background Prince Mohamed obviously remained convinced of the value of the Hamid Eddin family and loyal to Mohamed al Badr as Imam. 'He has suffered much,' he said of al Badr. 'It has given him wisdom. So now we fight for him as we did for his grandfather. He is more popular than was his grandfather.' The prince's evaluation of al Badr was one of the most generous I have heard from a member of the Hamid Eddin family. It was especially remarkable coming from Mohamed who was sometimes known as 'the prince with a future', his evident ability leading to speculation that he might some day replace the Imam, or that he might prefer in a future constitutional monarchy to occupy the post of Prime Minister. On the future of Yemen, he said to me: 'We will try to build a new people, to get rid of ignorance, economic weakness and spiritual weakness. We will build a new Yemen.'

The man we found in charge at Hanjar was Prince Abdullah Hussein, the brother of Mohamed, whom I had first met in Wadi Hirran in December 1962. The prince was in bad physical shape, suffering from a blood disease, as he had been throughout the war. We arrived about midnight and found him asleep at the back of his cave on a slightly elevated ledge. His servants tried to wake him but could not; it was as though he were in a coma. Without his direction his men seemed uncertain what to do with us. We stood there in the dark for ten or fifteen minutes, hoping someone who spoke English would turn up. No one did, and somewhat desperately I finally took the initiative. Trading on our previous acquaintance I moved our kit into the front part of the cave and spread out our sleeping bags. The prince slept on until about noon the next day. When he awoke he showed no surprise at our presence. I discovered him much more emaciated than before; his eyes seemed unusually large and glowing. But he managed to keep going, and towards evening, when the sun was not quite so fierce, he supervised exercises with the royalist armies' new artillery. He seemed fully informed about the technicalities of the different types of guns, and quite accustomed to the eardrum-shattering explosions as his men engaged in target practice.

The purpose of creating semi-regular units was not only to teach a body of men to use complex modern weapons, but to instil in them a sense of discipline much firmer than is usual in tribal forces. Yet in this, according to my experience, the royalists scored only a relative success. More than one incident suggested to me that their discipline was not what it should be.

Rigos and I had been allocated a driver and three guards who were to accompany us as far as Hanjar. When, late one evening, we were ready to leave, we found our jeep full of men who had heard that we were returning to Amara and who wanted a ride. We told them there was no room as we had to load our own luggage as well as the three guards. But they refused to budge. Angrily I trudged back up the hill to Prince Abdullah's cave and informed him. He told one of his askaris (soldiers) to go down and order the men out of the jeep. I went down with him, thinking that our problems were over. Not at all: our squatters paid no attention at all to the soldier, and after some expostulation I went up the hill again, stumbling in the dark over the boulders, cursing, and finally rather rudely bursting in on a conference the prince was holding. He did not seem particularly surprised and sent a somewhat higher ranking man with me for another try. But this too failed. It was now late at night; we were tired and anxious to be on our way, and so we finally piled our things in as best we could, let our guards climb in on top of the squatters, and angrily drove off.

I was reminded of another incident, which, however, I cannot attribute to the semi-regulars; it had occurred during my previous visit to the Imam. Joe Alex Morris and I had asked the Imam for permission to visit one of the forward positions of the royalist army under the command of Prince Hassan bin Hussein. This was another of the remarkable Hussein brothers, a family known to carry its share of the royalist military burden with considerable nerve – a young, tough and thoroughly delightful character, who managed to combine charm with a swaggering 'Yer wanna start something?' manner. The Imam assigned a man to accompany us to the prince's headquarters, and off we went in a truck which was supposed to take us a quarter of a mile down the mountain-side to our own erratic vehicle. We were in the cab of the truck while our guide had mounted in the back. When we reached our own truck we discovered that the guide had jumped out somewhere in the dark and had disappeared. Apparently he had decided he did not want to accompany us on this mission. We never saw him again; in fact, we were obliged that night to abandon our plans.

As has been seen, Rigos and I were present at Hanjar and Amara at a climactic moment. For the first time in the war the entire royalist force in the eastern desert under the general command of Prince Mohamed bin Hussein, having prepared themselves from the point of view of training, equipment, communications and planning, were on the offensive. Prince Mohamed's object in the key region was to cut the Egyptians' line of communications into north-eastern Yemen and to force them to withdraw. This the royalists hoped to do by overpowering the garrisons along this line and establishing positions from which royalist guns might interdict Egyptian movement.

The Egyptian line of supply went from Sana to Amran, then to a place called al Khairath, where it branched off north-eastwards to al Harf. After al Harf it turned sharply due south to Farah, and then south-eastwards to Humaidat, Mutamah and Hazm. From

Hazm the line led south-eastwards to Marib and Harib. A military convoy went over this route twice a month. There was no other way, for the royalists had long since, in the early days of the war, closed the direct route across the mountains from Sana down towards Marib.

The royalists had prepared their attack with the help of the Nahm tribe, who tricked the Egyptians into believing that they need not station their own or republican troops in the mountains overlooking the pass, known as Wadi Humaidat, on the grounds that the tribesmen themselves would take care of it. The royalist deal was that the Nahm would be entitled to the loot taken from whatever Egyptians were ambushed in the wadi. Nonetheless, the Egyptians seemed to have suspected that something was up, for the day before the attack they sent reconnaissance aircraft over the Humaidat area. The Nahm tribe's trick enabled the royalists to occupy two mountains, the Black mountain (Asfar) and the Red mountain (Ahmar), and to install 75-millimetre guns and mortars overlooking the critical wadi.

The day after the last Egyptian convoy went through, on 15 April, the royalists had launched a surprise attack. First, their guns opened up from concealed positions on the Red and Black mountains; then the Nahm tribesmen came out from behind the rocks; finally, Prince Mohamed's regulars followed up. Over-whelmed, some of the Egyptians at Humaidat surrendered without resistance; others fled to the camp at Farah, only 800 yards to the north. As both sides brought up reinforcements the battle shifted back and forth between Harf and Hazm, gradually moving north-wards towards Harf. The forces engaged in this battle were not very large – a couple of thousand Egyptians and about the same number of royalists, both regulars and tribesmen. Nevertheless in its wider context the battle was crucial.

For once, the royalists' operation had been fully co-ordinated by radio. While Prince Mohamed bin Hussein was overrunning Humaidat and Egyptians were distracted by attacks elsewhere, Mohamed's cousin, Prince Abdullah bin Hassan, began to raid Egyptian positions north-east of Sana at al Urush. Prince Mohamed bin Mohsin, at eighteen years the youngest of the royalist com-manders, was harassing the Egyptians with a force of 500 a few miles west of Humaidat, in the mountains near Dhibin. Prince Hassan, the Prime Minister, struck out from his mountain stronghold near Sadah; and in the west Prince Hassan bin Hussein, Mohamed's brother, moved from his headquarters at Jumaat, west of Sadah, to within mortar-firing distance of the Egyptian airfield west of Sadah.

One of the first results of this battle was the conditional surrender of fifty Egyptians at Mutamah, near Humaidat. Through tribal leaders, and against the will of Mohamed, who wanted a total surrender, they struck a bargain under which they were allowed to evacuate to Sana with their arms. Other republican commanders tried to arrange similar terms. They may have been encouraged by word that the royalist leaders were attempting to prevent the tribesmen from following their normal instincts and beheading prisoners. The policy Prince Mohamed recommended was to keep officers as prisoners, to treat them decently until they could be exchanged, and to allow soldiers to go unscathed in return for their arms.

Prince Mohamed said that if he could keep the Egyptians' line of communications closed for two months he would be satisfied. In fact, his aides said he was convinced he could keep it closed permanently, and they proved right. Three to five thousand Egyptian troops, in garrisons on the eastern slopes of the mountains and in the desert, had now to be supplied entirely by air. After thirty months of intermittent and inconclusive battles it was clearly the royalists who had now seized the initiative.

XVI
Disintegration in the Republic

THE royalists' military successes in the eastern desert of Yemen vastly influenced Yemen's future. The Egyptians, whose failure at Haradh in August 1964 had prepared the ground for the Erkwit cease-fire three months later, were made ready by their defeat at Humaidat in May 1965 for the Jeddah agreement, which followed after four months. But military events alone could not bring about these political consequences. The decisive pressure towards coming to terms with the royalists was exerted by developments inside the republican régime.

In December 1964, the month following the Erkwit cease-fire, the republic was afflicted by various forms of political dissolution. This critical situation had been brewing for months. It came to a head in friction over efforts to organize a delegation to the national conference, which was intended to follow Erkwit on 23 November. Partly because the Egyptians began to realize the extent of disaffection in the country, a wave of arrests among sheikhs, ulema and republican officials followed the search for delegates. Hundreds of men were rounded up, hundreds of others escaped. One group of sixty, who said they belonged to a group called 'National Front', included a former leading security official in Sana, a former private secretary to President Sallal, a former mayor of Hodeidah, and Ibrahim Ali al Wazir, a member of the family which for generations opposed the Hamid Eddin. Al Wazir said that it had proved impossible to convene the conference because the Egyptians had insisted on selecting the delegates themselves. From Aden the National Front sent representatives to all Arab countries in an effort to inform the Arab world of the real situation in Yemen. They sent a delegation to King Faisal and telegrams to President Nasser.

On 11 December 1964 two deputy Prime Ministers, Abdurrahman Iryani, and Mohamed Mahmoud Zubairi, and the presi-

dent of the consultative council, Mohamed Nomaan, resigned from
the government of the Yemeni republic. A few days later Nomaan's
son, Mohamed, succeeded in travelling from Cairo to Beirut with
a manifesto, signed by the three men, denouncing 'corruption,
impotence and bankruptcy' of the Sana government, and proposing
a draft constitution to replace the one introduced by President Sallal
in May.

The manifesto opened with the remarkable admission that the
Imam still had the support of 'some factions'; others were seeking
a compromise, because the régime 'had failed to fulfil the people's
aspirations or to win support for the revolution'. Some of these
feelings, the manifesto indicated, had rubbed off on the people's
attitude towards the United Arab Republic. There were 'doubts
and suspicions' concerning the 'noble role of the U.A.R.'. 'Corruption, impotence and bankruptcy' had been brought about by
lack of ideological and psychological harmony, lack of confidence,
lack of economic, cultural, social and military planning, and lack
of discipline. The manifesto recalled that resolutions adopted by
the Amran tribal conference of November 1963 had demanded
the creation of a legislature, the introduction of civilian administration and the removal of troops wherever no military threat existed.
None of these resolutions had been put into effect. Without naming
President Sallal or Vice-President Hassan al Amri, the manifesto
also accused 'certain people who consider themselves presidents' of
violating the constitution. As a result of their action security and
order had been undermined, the government had been unable to
carry out its own orders, money had been squandered and the
country divided.

The point of the constitutional draft in the manifesto was that
it called for an elected legislature which would in turn elect a five-
man 'republican council', whose chairman would be president of
the republic. This was the liberals' prescription for getting rid of
President Sallal's arbitrary dictatorship. Its immediate effect was
to bring about the fall of the government of Prime Minister Hamoud
al Jaifi, who resigned on 6 January 1965. He was succeeded by
Hassan al Amri, who attempted to restore the authority of the
régime by a policy of iron-fisted repression. In his attempts to
impose this authority Major-General al Amri seems to have
encountered some resistance. Four ministers nominated in his
new government – the Ministers of Justice, the Interior, Local

Government and Presidential Affairs – declined their portfolios. In this situation General Amri's plans to establish tribunals to try others were clearly impractical. This was not the time for such methods.

Another factor which shortened the life of the Amri government was the conference of the Hashid and Bakil confederations which began in the Khawlan on 23 March, presided over by Naji al Gadr, paramount sheikh of the Bakil. (The Bakil are said to have a fighting strength of 85,000 men, and the Hashid 30,000. Most of the Bakil have supported the royalists from the beginning, while all but one of the Hashid tribes supported the government until the summer of 1965, when most of them shifted to the royalists.)

The tribal representatives began by expressing their disgust with the continued Egyptian presence. They demanded the withdrawal of the Egyptian army by 21 April. Then on 1 April, when the conference had been meeting for a week, word came that Mohamed Mahmoud al Zubairi had been assassinated. It happened at a place called Bort, while he was travelling in Dhu Hussein territory as a guest of the Dhu Mohamed tribe. He was forty-eight years old. For years he had supported President Nasser in his radio campaign against the Yemeni monarchy but had gradually grown more critical of the Egyptians. He had been not only deputy Prime Minister, but Minister of Information, National Guidance and Education. The republican authorities arrested two men as assassins, and it was widely rumoured that they had implicated the Egyptians in the murder – a rumour later reinforced by the fact that the two men were able to escape apparently with Egyptian complicity. Pointing out that Zubairi had fought against the monarchy all his life, the republicans charged the royalists with responsibility. But the royalists said he had been killed by the republicans, because he was campaigning in northern Yemen for his 'Party of Allah', which sought a middle way between the Imam and the Sallal régime; also because he was on his way to Mecca and had sent word to the Saudi Arabians that he hoped to discuss the problem of Yemen.

The Party of Allah's charter, as published in Aden, explained that the men who formed the party were 'frightened and appalled by the tragedy, bloodshed and war' in Yemen. They had decided to resort to 'Allah's book', the Koran, and devote themselves to seeking a settlement in Yemen in the light of its teachings. The charter declared that Allah's Party believes that 'Allah gave Yemen to the people of Yemen; the government must be freely chosen by Yemenis unhindered by the Mutawakilite myth [an allusion to the royal family] or by military force. The Party believes in Allah, and the people's honour, and does not believe in bombs, mines, bullets and killings. It wants peace, not war; security, not fear; brotherhood, not enmity; construction, not destruction; life, not death. It wants to enable the people to till the pure Yemeni land and plant it with grain, fruit, flowers, and with brotherhood and love, instead of with mines, bullets and hatred.'

Zubairi's violent death was exploited by the astute Naji al Gadr after the Khawlan conference. To fan tribal resentment of the Egyptians he persuaded the Bakil and the Hashid to threaten to invade Sana, unless Zubairi's friend and associate, Mohamed Ahmed Nomaan, was appointed Prime Minister to replace General Amri.

On 20 April, acting, of course, on Egyptian advice, Major-General Amri resigned and President Sallal asked Nomaan to form a new government. At the same time President Sallal's authority was curbed by the formation of a five-man presidency council along the lines somewhat similar to those proposed by Nomaan, Iryani and Zubairi in their draft constitution. It looked as though Nomaan had won his long struggle against Sallal. Certainly the Egyptians had realized that these were times when force alone was not enough to cope with the disintegration of an authoritarian régime they had themselves created.

Mohamed Ahmed Nomaan, the most prominent of the liberals and leader of the Shaffei Moslem religious community, was a sophisticated intellectual of western outlook, a wealthy landowner and a lifelong revolutionary – an unusual combination of qualities. While studying law at the Islamic university of al Azhar in Cairo, which he entered in 1937, the young Nomaan read and observed widely. He found the socialist and reformist ideas he acquired difficult to reconcile with conditions in Yemen. Upon his return to Yemen four years later he obtained an appointment as director of education in Taiz, Yemen's second largest town, and attempted through Crown Prince Ahmed, who had not yet ascended to the throne, to encourage some reforms. Herein he was unsuccessful, but he did obtain an appointment as tutor to Prince Ahmed's oldest son, al Badr, who was then fifteen years old.

Finding himself thoroughly at odds with the monarchy Nomaan, accompanied by his friends Iryani and Zubairi, fled in 1944 to Aden, where they founded a 'Free Yemeni Party' and a newspaper called *Voice of Yemen*. While they did not at this time challenge the imamate they demanded a constitution and an end to arbitrary rule. In this way Nomaan, Iryani and Zubairi became allied with the al Wazir family, the family which had, along with the Hamid Eddin, for many generations dominated the politics of Yemen; in 1948 the young liberals, rushing in from Aden, backed the al Wazirs in the assassination of the Imam Yahya, who was replaced by Abdullah al Wazir. Unfortunately for them, however, Abdullah al Wazir ruled for only twenty-six days. Crown Prince Ahmed succeeded in regaining the throne, executed al Wazir and sent to prison Nomaan, Iryani and al Shami, while Zubairi escaped to Aden and later to Pakistan.

From prison the indomitable Nomaan managed to carry on a correspondence with the Imam Ahmed, who released him and Iryani in 1954. Also released, in 1953, was al Shami, who remained loyal to the imamate and is the present royalist Foreign Minister.

In the next attempted rising, by the Imam's brother Abdullah in 1955, the liberals chose the right side. They again went to Hajjah, in rather different circumstances, with Crown Prince al Badr, who sent Nomaan and al Shami to Riyadh to get support from the Saudis. Once out of the country Nomaan showed his true colours and moved off to Cairo, where he started a new movement against the Imam. He was joined there by Zubairi, who had escaped after the failure of the 1948 *coup* and had been living in Pakistan. Al Shami, who in the meantime had been sent to Cairo as imamic chargé d'affaires, broke with them politically but remained their friend.

Nomaan and Zubairi remained in exile until the 1962 revolution, but Iryani remained in Taiz, where he became the Imam's Minister of Justice, keeping secretly in touch with his friends in Cairo.

Nomaan's efforts during the ten weeks following his appointment as Prime Minister created an entirely new atmosphere in the Yemen government, and it was he who helped to arrange a meeting between Nasser and Faisal, and brought Yemen to the brink of peace. His cabinet assembled the most capable group of ministers yet seen in Yemen. In a country reputed to have only about fifty university graduates, six of his fifteen ministers had degrees. He established a new relationship with the Egyptians. They no longer attended cabinet meetings or sat in the offices of ministers. In addition, without checking with the Egyptians, Nomaan sent off a delegation to Kuwait, Jordan, Syria and Lebanon to explore possible alternatives to Egyptian aid and influence and, more important, to make indirect contact with the Saudi government. Anxious to avoid trouble where he could, and suspicious of Egyptian exploitation of the campaign against the British in Aden, he dropped the post of Minister for the Occupied South from his cabinet. Finally, he acknowledged the tribal origins of his power by calling a tribal 'peace conference'. He issued the announcement through his Minister of Interior and Tribal Affairs, Abdullah bin Hussein al Ahmar. The conference, which met between the 3 and 5 May 1965, at Khmer, twenty-five miles north of Sana, attempted to lay the foundations for an eventual settlement of the war.

The Khmer conference was in a sense a substitute for a follow-up conference of the March meeting of the Bakil and the Hashid in the Khawlan. Through the 4,000 tribal and religious leaders who participated he was able to make a bid in tribal areas for popular support. Although tribes from both sides had participated in the Khawlan conference, the fact that Iryani was chairman and that Nomaan attended, both of them ministers of the republican government, made it difficult for royalist tribes to take part. Royalist policy was however not completely hostile; the line given the royalist tribes was that they might attend if they wanted to. None of the top royalist leaders did in fact take part.

At its final meeting on 5 May, the Khmer conference decided to establish a national peace organization, consisting of five tribal and four religious leaders, to make contacts with the tribes opposed to the republican régime. It welcomed a 'fraternal resolution', taken by a recent Islamic conference in Mecca, which called for peace in Yemen. In the same vein it offered peace to Saudi Arabia in these terms: 'We appreciate the rights of neighbourliness and are prepared to extend the hand of understanding to our brotherly neighbours for the sake of peace, for the sake of building our country.'

The conference resolutions urged Nomaan's government to find means to end the war, to 'regulate' relations with the United Arab Republic and to end the 'critical state' of relations with Yemen's neighbours. It formed a committee whose task was to work with the government, in general for the implementation of the resolutions, and specifically for the election within three months of a consultative council. The committee was to undertake the responsibilities of the proposed consultative council until its creation under a new interim constitution, which the conference also proposed. The conference's draft, which was intended to replace the constitution which had been imposed, somewhat arbitrarily, after the March 1964 visit of President Nasser, provided for an elected parliament, freedom of expression and an independent judiciary. It was in fact approved by President Sallal, four days after the conference. Another conference resolution called for the creation of a 'popular army' of 11,000 tribesmen to replace the Egyptians on the borders.

On 1 July 1965, the only independent-minded government Yemen had had since the 1962 revolution resigned. When Ahmed Mohamed Nomaan's resignation was announced on Sana radio, he had already flown to Cairo to protest to President Nasser against what his son and spokesman called a 'succession of acts and decisions by President Sallal, which were completely in contradiction to the Yemeni constitution'. In particular Nomaan had been incensed by President Sallal's decision, four days previously, to set up a supreme armed forces council without consulting the cabinet. Not only had he set up the council but he had sent armed guards to Sana radio station to make sure that his decree was announced.

President Sallal's council, headed by himself, would have assumed all authority for handling military affairs and matters related to the war. It would have restored much of the power the president lost by the formation of a presidential council when Nomaan first came to power. And it would have frustrated the efforts of the so-called follow-up committee of the Khmer conference to create a 'popular army' of 11,000 men provided by the tribes. The purpose of these efforts, to replace the Egyptians in frontier areas, was most unwelcome to the Egyptians because it was meant not as a reinforcement but as a device to prod the Egyptians into withdrawal. There had been signs a few days earlier that the Egyptians had 'taken' about all they were willing to 'take' from the Nomaan government. They had begun to put pressure on the Nomaan government to remove six of the fifteen Yemeni cabinet ministers on the grounds that they were members of the Baath Arab Socialist party. The Baath party, whose Syrian headquarters had been eloquent in its praise of Nomaan, was particularly disliked by President Nasser because it opposed his leadership of Arab socialism. In particular the Egyptians appeared to be anxious to get rid of Mohsin al Aini, the Yemeni Foreign Minister. But the real reason why Cairo could not tolerate the Nomaan government, which looked so hopeful to the rest of the world, was that it could not tolerate Nomaan's independent attitude and his demand for Egyptian withdrawal. Although the Cairo government may have been embarrassed by President Sallal's lack of popular support and may have had doubts about his ability, Nomaan's appeal against him to President Nasser was futile. Cairo was bound to support Sallal as a symbol of the Egyptian-sponsored revolution that had overthrown the Yemeni monarchy in 1962.

On 6 July, President Sallal formed a new government, with thirteen military officers in a fifteen-man cabinet – quite the opposite of Nomaan's predominantly civilian government. Sallal himself provisionally took the post of Prime Minister but handed it over to Amri a week later. Nomaan and a group of his friends headed by Iryani, including Mohsin al Aini, who had flown to Cairo to persuade him to withdraw his resignation, were prevented by Egyptian authorities from returning to Sana. In Sana forty or fifty followers of the former Prime Minister were arrested. Many were young intellectuals who had criticized republican Yemen's heavy dependence on Cairo. Questioned by the press, Nomaan said in Cairo: 'The question is not who receives power, but what to do with the power – to create peace in the country, or to go ahead with the war.'

At that time it looked very much as though the Egyptians had decided to continue the war. There were reports that the Egyptians, having switched their men in Sana, were continuing to build up the armed strength of the Egyptian army in Yemen. According to information gathered by western diplomats this army now amounted to 50,000 or 60,000 men. The Egyptians were building brick military barracks, as well as an all-weather road down the steamy plain along the coast.

Tension between Egypt and Saudi Arabia reached an all-time peak in July and the beginning of August. On 22 July President Nasser threatened in a speech to use force against Saudi Arabia if the Saudis continued to back the royalists. The phrase he often repeated was that he would 'bomb the bases of aggression'. The

Saudis were reported to have reinforced their border defences.

But then, after a flurry of diplomatic exchanges came a dramatic reversal. On 22 August President Nasser arrived at Jeddah to see King Faisal and attempt once again – for the third time – to seek ways of restoring peace to Yemen.

XVII

Nasser Comes to Terms

••

IT is to President Nasser's credit that he knows when he must
tack before the wind. The wind blowing against him in August
1965, when the President made his journey to Jeddah, was both
military and political. On the military side, the royalists were in
their glory that summer. The Saudis had been more generous with
military and civilian supplies than ever before. Some weapons had
also come from Iran. There were now seven so-called royalist
armies, each varying in strength between 3,000 and 10,000 men,
making a total somewhere between 40,000 and 60,000. In addition,
of course, there were five or six times as many armed men among
royalist tribesmen. Most important, perhaps, there was the small
hard core of well-trained regulars in the Jawf under the capable
command of Prince Mohamed bin Hussein. This force had seriously
hurt the Egyptians at Humaidat in May, and it was probably after
this that the Egyptians deliberately reduced the size of the area
they were committed to defend.

Whatever the reason, the royalists moved ahead from one
Egyptian strongpoint to another. At the beginning of June they
moved into Sirwah in eastern Yemen. On 14 June they entered
Qaflan, the historic capital of the Hashid tribal confederation, and
on 16 July they occupied Marib. There were no great battles, but
many small incidents took place which demonstrated arrogant and
aggressive spirits. Kassim Munassir, one of the royalist commanders
in the Khawlan mountains, became a Robin Hood legend among the
townsmen.

On the political side, too, the royalists were able to generate
pressure. While few of them talked any longer about outright
military victory, the most informed of the princes now believed
that they would be able to force the Egyptians into a political
compromise. Hatred of the Egyptians had become so general that

it offered a basis for collaboration between royalists, dissident republicans and various other elements who occupied the political ground between royalists and republicans.

At Taif, in Saudi Arabia, representatives of three groups met towards the end of July and worked out and signed the Taif Manifesto (see Appendix 2) as a basis for collaboration of all elements against the Egyptians. One of the groups at Taif called itself 'the Organization of Young Men of the Khmer conference'. A second was 'the Federation of Popular Forces', headed by Ibrahim Ali al Wazir. The third were the royalists, represented by Prince Abdurrahman bin Yahya, the Imam's uncle.

At such meetings the royalists assumed political posture meant to foster collaboration with non-royalists. Ever since February 1963 Ahmed al Shami, the Foreign Minister, had been talking about constitutional limitations on the powers of the Imam – in particular an imamate council to share his functions, and an elected assembly with power to override him. Finally in January 1965 the royalists had published in Aden a 'National Charter'. This took the form of a draft constitution which they proposed to submit to the people after the Egyptians had been driven out. It claimed to be based 'on the most modern international practices of advanced democratic countries within the framework of Islamic law'. Its article XI stated that the Imam could veto any law passed by the legislative assembly, but if the assembly overrode his veto three times by a three-fourths majority the measure would become the law of the land.

Besides the royalists' military and political initiative, the economic side of the war must have weighed heavily in President Nasser's determination to swallow his pride and go to Jeddah. According to official Egyptian army figures, obtained by a foreign intelligence service from Yemenis who had access to the records, the Egyptian expeditionary force in Yemen during the period between October 1962 and June 1964 lost 15,194 men killed. One may reasonably estimate four times that number in wounded and captured. The Egyptian killed included 456 officers and 1,029 N.C.O.s, and they amounted to an average of twenty-four men killed every day between the start of the fighting, in October 1962, and June 1964. The heaviest losses were in December 1962, when 1,741 officers and men died in one month. The highest figure for a single engagement was listed for the Sana-Hodeidah road in January-February 1964, when the royalists succeeded for a time in cutting the Egyptians' main communications artery to the coast. Nine hundred Egyptians were reported to have lost their lives in the fighting. In two other costly battles in November 1962, 280 parachutists were killed at Marib and 195 at Sirwah.

The casualty records for officers included two lieutenant-generals, four air vice-marshals, and three brigadiers. It was stated that General Anwar al Qadi had been seriously injured near Sana in December 1963, and that his fate was unknown. Caught in an ambush, he had been blinded, according to reports which I received in Beirut at the time, and had been flown to a hospital in Switzerland for treatment. Estimates of the cost of the war, ranging between half a million and a million dollars a day, were made by Western diplomats during the first year of the war. But it is hard to reduce to dollars the mixture of local costs and foreign exchange costs, let alone the Egyptians' long-term debts to the Soviet Union in arms, ammunition and jet fuel. The figures given were probably too high, even for the first year; since then the extent of fighting has declined and the costs have doubtless decreased proportionately. Nonetheless, the burden on Egypt has been very great. To the military cost should be added the price of economic aid, both in the form of loans, supplies and technicians, and in subsidies paid to the tribes and tribal forces to ensure their good behaviour and their active participation in the fighting. Bonuses paid to Egyptian soldiers serving in Yemen ranged from £2 or £3 a month for privates, to £20 or £30 for officers. Service in Yemen was popular among some men, who returned to Egypt at the end of their service with duffle bags full of goods, unavailable in Egypt, which they were able to buy in Sana or Taiz, in shops supplied from Aden – transistor radios, cameras, high-grade cloth and woollens, and even better quality television sets. Other men saved their money to buy a bit of land or a taxi, when they got home. According to one authority's estimate, in May 1965 the Egyptians had, in one way or another, spent $125 million on the war in the preceding two and a half years.

All these factors were in the backs of the minds of leading Egyptians and Saudi Arabians when President Nasser flew to Jeddah on 22 August. They must have had in mind also the larger political context of the meeting. It had been a lean year for the Egyptian President. He had had to back down on his threat to recognize East Germany when the West Germans opened diplomatic relations with Israel. He had had to advise the Arab states to postpone plans for diverting the Jordan river waters and attacking Israel. The Algerian *coup d'état*, which toppled Ahmed ben Bella, had sharpened the President's sense of isolation in the Arab world. The Egyptian régime was under pressure also inside Egypt, where discontent had showed itself in insolent demonstrations at the funeral of the former Premier, Mustafa Nahas Pasha. If Nasser could come to terms with King Faisal, at least temporarily, this pressure would be relieved.

In the damp furnace heat of Jeddah the political atmosphere was sombre. The Saudis saw President Nasser's willingness to come to them at this time as an admission of defeat. They made no fuss over their Egyptian visitor, though they extended to him the minimum courtesies due to a visiting head of state. King Faisal went down to the harbour to welcome President Nasser, who arrived aboard his yacht, *al Horriya*, having crossed the Red Sea from the southern Egyptian port of Ras Benas. The King escorted him to the palace, built by former King Saud, where, on the occasion of the signing of a mutual defence pact between Saudi Arabia, Egypt and Yemen, Nasser had stayed ten years before as a fellow guest of the late Imam Ahmed.

In a perfectly air-conditioned room, beneath thirty-one enormous chandeliers, some 600 lean Saudis in white and black Arab robes and about 100 fleshy Egyptians in western-style suits or uniforms were served a western-style meal of soup, entrée, turkey and two choices of meat, dessert and several kinds of fruit on gold-rimmed plates. They drank pineapple juice and water. Before dawn the King and the President were up for a quick trip to Mecca, less than fifty miles away, to pray for the success of their meetings. Many of the Egyptian party, dressed now in sandals and white robes worn off one shoulder, accompanied them on this short pilgrimage.

The agreement the two heads of state signed on 24 August was the culmination of long secret negotiations. It was the basic document around which all discussions, negotiations and political manoeuvres concerning the Yemeni problem were to circulate in the years to come. (See Appendix 3.)

Essentially the agreement reasserted the central principles of the Erkwit cease-fire concluded in November of the previous year, namely, that the two sides should stop fighting and hold a national conference to determine their political futures. But this agreement went further. Its main provisions were these:

1. The U.A.R. will withdraw all its military forces from Yemen within ten months, beginning on 23 November 1965.

2. Saudi Arabia will stop military aid of all kinds, and the use of Saudi Arabian territory for operations against Yemen.

3. 23 November 1966, a date two months after the departure of the last Egyptian soldiers, will be the latest date for holding a popular plebiscite 'to decide and affirm their view of the kind of government they want'.

4. The two countries will co-operate in forming 'a transitional conference of fifty members representing all the national forces and people of authority in Yemen', to meet at Haradh in Yemen on 23 November 1965.

5. The tasks of the conference shall be as follows: Determination of the system of government during the transitional period and until the popular plebiscite is held; formation of a provisional cabinet to be in charge of government during the transitional period; determination of the form and kind of the plebiscite, which will be held by 23 November 1966, at the latest.

6. To enforce the cease-fire and supervise the agreement a joint peace commission will be formed by both sides to supervise the frontier and ports and stop all kinds of military aid.

7. The commission will be backed up by a force formed by both countries.

Twelve days later an 'appendix' to the Jeddah agreement was announced. It stated that the peace commission would meet in Sana on 11 September to ensure that a national congress of Yemenis took place in Haradh on 23 November. The committee would see to the manning of border observation posts by a joint force, to be manned by 25 September, and to be commanded in alternate months by Saudi and Egyptian army officers with the rank of major-general. The peace force would consist of an infantry brigade from both sides and a fighter and bomber squadron.

A few weeks later, this decision was put into effect, and a battalion of about 400 Saudis entered Yemen to serve with an Egyptian battalion as a joint peace force.

The Jeddah agreement said nothing about whether President Sallal and the Imam al Badr were to withdraw while its provisions were carried out, nor did it determine whether members of the Hamid Eddin family were to be allowed to participate in the proposed national conference. There may, however, have been a secret agreement covering these points, for members of the royal family did not in fact participate in the conference and some months after the agreement went into effect both President Sallal and the Imam did withdraw at least temporarily from their countries, although ostensibly for other reasons. President Sallal withdrew to Cairo until 20 September 1966, when he returned to Sana more powerfully backed by the Egyptians than ever. The Imam meanwhile moved to Taif in Saudi Arabia, where he underwent medical treatment for kidney trouble, suffering something of a political eclipse. He remained a significant symbol in the Yemeni struggle but he was rarely consulted by the princes on the political and military questions of the day.

In addition to this, the agreement as published did not tackle the vexed question of what the transitional state of Yemen should be called. Hitherto the Egyptians and republicans had insisted that the word 'republic' be retained, while the Saudis and royalists had proposed that the term 'state of Yemen' should be used until the plebiscite had determined the form of government.

The commitment to withdraw was crucial: it was the royalists' central demand, it was stated unconditionally, and the Egyptians treated it as unconditional during the first months after the agreement. A despatch to *The Times* of London from Cairo on 30 October said the Egyptian forces would begin their withdrawal on 11 December and would complete it the following July, three months ahead of schedule provided in the Jeddah agreement. Later, however, the Egyptians were to argue that they had agreed to withdraw only on the assumption that the royalists and republicans would come to terms politically. In fact, no withdrawal took place.

During the period of preparation for the Haradh conference, both sides engaged in what might be called electioneering for their causes. The Imam emerged from his cave and made a triumphal tour of the north. New areas were said to have declared for the royalists in anticipation of Egyptian withdrawal. The royalists held a great rally of some 7,000 tribal leaders in the Razih mountains, where they heard speeches upholding the imamate as the only acceptable system. In private, however, royalist leaders took a flexible line. Holding that the Jeddah agreement had been a victory for them and that they could afford to be generous, they drew attention to their willingness, so long as the institution of the imamate itself was preserved, to limit the Imam's powers in a future constitution. Whereas the Erkwit conference of 1964 had called for a national conference composed of two-thirds republican, and only one-third royalist delegates, the Jeddah agreement had recognized the equality of both parties, each of whom was to have a half of the delegates at Haradh. They insisted on the right of members of the ruling Hamid Eddin family to participate in the Haradh conference and in any institutions that developed out of it. As one spokesman put it: 'All the Hamid Eddin have fought well for two years, and successfully. They are good citizens. They have a right to speak.' But in the end, so as not to give the republicans any excuse for not holding the conference, the royalists decided not to send any member of the Hamid Eddin to Haradh.

The republicans, on 21 October, conducted a somewhat similar rally at Janad, near Taiz. There President Sallal declared that the revolution had, in his own words, 'ended a historical tragedy when it destroyed the stinking imamic rule'. Shortly thereafter Sallal, accompanied by Prime Minister Amri and other leading members of his régime, went to Cairo to consult President Nasser. What they basically wanted was assurance that the republic would be preserved. But President Nasser took the line that it was up to them to argue it out with the royalists. At a youth camp near Cairo he said on 18 November: 'We did our duty towards Yemen. We shouldered the whole burden, spent a lot of money and sacrificed many of our boys. It is the Yemenis' duty now to shoulder the burden themselves, and preserve their own revolution. We will withdraw our troops at the time prescribed in the armistice agreement.'

As the date of the conference approached, the members of the republican group returned to Sana, with the exception of President Sallal who remained in Cairo, apparently as part of the secret agreement reached at Jeddah. Meanwhile a nine-man committee, chosen at the Janad rally, was at work in Taiz selecting the republican delegation.

The cease-fire was maintained by both sides. The Egyptian-Saudi peace commission, operating in eight areas, reported no incidents.

At Haradh, eighteen hours' drive, or forty-five minutes' flight,

from Sana, the delegates found a town of three hundred houses,
all but about eight of them built of mud. The town had thirty
shops and a primary school for sixty pupils, but no clinic or other
social institutions, and no electricity. The women here, in contrast
to those in larger towns, appeared unveiled. The conference was
to meet in a tent city of two hundred tents, surrounding a central
marquee, erected by the Egyptian army about two miles outside
the town. Adjoining the main conference tent was another desig-
nated as a mess hall. Another was to be a mosque. The military in
charge had established radio communications with Cairo, Riyadh
and Sana. An 'information office' was set up in the camp to inform
newsmen, who were told that they would not be allowed direct
contact with delegates during the conference.

The day before the conference, the heads of the joint Saudi-
U.A.R. peace-keeping mission, Prince Abdullah al Sudairi, a
younger member of the famous Saudi Arabian family, and
Mohamed Farid Salamah, an Egyptian politician, reviewed the
military force from both countries at the conference site, which
constituted the peace-keeping force provided by the Jeddah
agreement. In his speech Salamah told the troops: 'We and you
have come here on the most sacred of all missions – the spread of
peace. These conferences will bring the happiest and most prosperous days for the Yemeni people.'

The republican delegation of twenty-five included four members
of the republican council, Qadi Abdurrahman al Iryani, Ahmed
Mohamed Nomaan, Sheikh Mohamed Ali Uthman, a prominent
Shaffei tribal leader and Major-General Hamoud al Jaifi, who had
been serving as ambassador in Cairo. Among the tribal chieftains
was Sheikh Abdullah bin Hussein al Ahmar, paramount chief of
the Hashid tribe. Other members of the republican delegation
including eight members of the cabinet, three former ministers,
seven tribal leaders, two area governors, and one religious leader.
The royalist delegation was headed by the royalist Foreign Minister,
Ahmed al Shami, and the Defence Minister, Salah al Masri; it
included eight members of the cabinet, three former ministers,
Qaid bin Rajeh and Ibrahim bin Ali al Wazir. (See Appendix 4 for
list of participants.)

A joint observation team, intended to stand by in the case of
serious differences between the two sides, was present in addition
to the peace-keeping mission. In the case of a deadlock the delegates,

according to the agreements reached at Jeddah, were to refer back to King Faisal and President Nasser.

The opening meeting was addressed by Prince Abdullah Sudairi, the Saudi representative on the peace-keeping mission, by Abdurrahman al Iryani for the republicans, and by Ahmed Shami for the royalists. But news from the conference came almost exclusively from republicans and Egyptian sources. The royalists and Saudis simply lacked the necessary information media to present their own version.

The agenda confronting the conference was as follows:

1. To determine the type and form of the plebiscite to be held.

2. To determine the system of government to be in effect during the transitional period from the present until a plebiscite was held, not later than 23 November 1966.

3. To form a provisional cabinet to rule during the transitional period.

In addition to these central problems the conferees were supposed to find answers to such questions as how to unify the administrations of the republican and royalist régimes; how to ensure unification of republican and royalist armies; how to distribute senior posts between the two factions; and how to choose representatives in the Arab League, at the United Nations, and in countries with which Yemen had diplomatic relations. One proposal was that the projected interim government should be formed of seven members: two republicans, two royalists, two neutrals, and one member representing the third force and dissident republicans. The head of government, it was suggested, would be elected in rotation.

After thirteen days of talks the conference seemed to be revolving in circles. On one side the royalists were insisting that an interim government of the state of Yemen should be organized to hold an immediate referendum, and that Egyptian troops should withdraw within two or three months, that is, well ahead of the Jeddah agreement. Against this, the republicans argued that, while they had no objection to an early referendum, it would be difficult to arrange so swift a removal of 60,000 Egyptian troops. They suggested that, to precede the removal of the Egyptians, a neutral committee representing Saudi Arabia and Egypt, or possibly other Arab countries, supervise a referendum. They complained that under an agreement reached at Jeddah both sides were required to include in their delegation fifteen Zeidis (Shia Moslem) and ten

Shaffei leaders (Sunni Moslem). The royalists, they said, had chosen only six Shaffeis; and these, it seemed to them, were only representative of themselves, because the royalists controlled no Shaffei areas whatsoever. The republicans also complained that, although the agreement at Jeddah excluded members of the royal Hamid Eddin family from the conference, a nephew of the late Imam Ahmed, Mohamed Abdul Quddous al Wazir, was included in the royalist delegation. They claimed he had been freed by the republicans two months before on condition that he took no part in politics. On their side, the royalists complained that the Egyptian army had landed 6,000 troops on the beaches near Haradh during the conference, thereby running counter to their undertaking, under the Jeddah agreement, to withdraw troops, and unduly influencing the conference itself.

The confusion, perplexity and frustration of the delegates, especially on the republican side, was eloquently expressed in a telegram addressed to King Faisal and President Nasser by the head of the republican delegation, Abdurrahman al Iryani. 'We were hoping,' he wrote, 'to arrive at a solution with our brothers, although the distribution of representatives between the two sides is unjust and not correct.

Every one of us quarrelled in interpreting the Jeddah agreement and every one of us understood it as he liked. When we referred back to the supervision committee (the Saudi-Egyptian observation team) the committee informed us of the terrible reality of the situation, which is that the two régimes are supposed to be abolished – the republican régime, which exists, and the imamic régime, which does not exist – and that we are supposed to choose a régime which is neither republican, nor imamic, to be in charge until the date of the plebiscite to be held within ten months.

Unfortunately the agreement at Jeddah made no mention of the Hamid Eddin family, which has always divided our people, which has been the cause of our troubles in the past and the present, the cause of all our destruction and blood-letting.

If the Saudi and Egyptian governments have agreed on what the supervision committee has announced (that the Egyptians will withdraw), we, the representatives of the republicans, assert that you bear full responsibility, and that the fate of the Yemen is in your hands. For it is only you who can silence all the weapons that have been put into the hands of the two parties throughout the whole period of the past three years. You alone are in a position to solve the problem without involving your own peoples in war or without subjecting Yemen to more destruction and blood-letting.

The sons of Yemen were obliged to fight one another, disputes have been cultivated among them, and arms of all kinds were offered them by both your governments. You have offered great sums of money which benefited the merchants of war. If you had the power to make the Yemeni people fight one another we do believe that you have the power to establish peace and stability.

We would like to inform you that the republicans are the legal régime, which exists in fact and is recognized by the United Nations and the Arab League. This régime, supported by the people, has made enormous sacrifices and suffered great losses among their young men and among their leaders. To abolish such a régime, which enjoys recognition, in contrast to a régime which is not recognized by anyone, will certainly have grave consequences and will certainly lead to civil war, which is going to cause destruction in our land. This surely will serve only the enemies of the Arabs and Islam. In the name of Almighty God, may you extend a helping hand to your brothers in this country, who aspire to your help.

In any case we decline responsibility for the consequences of political actions which were beyond our control.

ABDURRAHMAN AL IRYANI

By 21 December, nearly a month after the conference had begun, the conferees had held only three formal sessions. Sixteen of the fifty delegates were reported to have departed in disgust. The conference was falling apart. Meanwhile King Faisal had sent a message to President Nasser, asking whether the projected evacuation of Egyptian troops from Yemen had begun or not. He received no answer. The central achievement of the Jeddah agreement was apparently void. A Yemeni royalist spokesman in Beirut said the Haradh conference was a complete failure, and that his side was ready to begin fighting again under the leadership of the Imam al Badr .

Commenting on this royalist statement in a speech at Port Said, President Nasser said that if the royalists resumed the war the republicans would hit back. As the Ramadan fast began, just before Christmas, and the Haradh conference delegates dispersed, the wheel of Arab politics began to turn again. President Nasser no longer felt the need to be conciliatory. His mood was not determined by events in Yemen or the Arab world alone. He was angered by a new development: King Faisal in his search for wider backing had agreed with the Shah of Iran to call a Moslem summit meeting. Nasser and the Shah had been at odds for years, the Shah fearful of Nasser's penetration of the Arabian peninsula and the Persian Gulf, Nasser resentful of the Shah's tolerance of the flow of oil from Iran to Israel.

Did Nasser never intend to withdraw his troops? Did he play as cynically with King Faisal as he had with Ambassador Bunker, General Von Horn and Pier Pasquali Spinelli? Was he just gaining time until his forces were ready for another round? Or had he never been cynical at all and was he the victim of circumstances beyond his control? Had ambitious generals forced his hand? Did the generals exploit republican Yemeni intransigence to gain a hearing? Had the Egyptians had second thoughts?

One may reasonably suspect that there is truth in each of these propositions. It is still too soon to know. But it would be hard to deny Egyptian responsibility for the collapse of the hopes that were successively centred on Erkwit, Jeddah and Haradh. King Faisal had everything to gain from a successful conference. It was to him the first fruit of victory. Some royalists who still dreamed of military victory may not have appreciated his willingness to come to terms. Perhaps he made a fundamental error in raising the spectre of an Islamic alliance – against Nasser – while the Haradh conference was still in progress. But then perhaps, being a canny old man, he realized from the start that there could be no compromise, that a further test of strength would be necessary, and that the war in Yemen was liable to drag on so long as there was Arab disunity.

XVIII

The International Red Cross

••

A TINY speck of Switzerland flourished amidst the sands of the
north-eastern Yemeni desert between November 1963 and the
beginning of 1966. This was the International Red Cross Field
Hospital. While its composition was entirely Swiss, it also represented the most advanced western technology and the best of
western humanitarianism.

This outpost of the western world provided the only medical
services to the royalist army in Yemen and the first twentieth-
century medicine ever experienced by the people of this region.
Nestled in the lee of a giant U-shape of black basaltic rocks, the
white tents of the Red Cross were intended to accommodate fifty
patients, but in fact the hospital rarely had fewer than seventy or
eighty beds filled, while one hundred to five hundred Yemenis,
bedouin and Saudis camped permanently on the outskirts, waiting
for treatment as out-patients. The hospital treated about one
hundred a day, sometimes more.

Dr Ulrich Middendorp, thirty-seven, an orthopaedist and head
of the university clinic in Basel, together with his wife Reni, a
psychiatrist, first established the clinic; they returned for a second
period of six months in the summer of 1965, which was the time of
my visit. They had a Swiss staff of four doctors, at least three
nurses, two laboratory technicians, a radio man and a car repair
man; the latter came from Switzerland for tours of duty of a
minimum of three months, usually renewable for a second period
of three months. One of the doctors was usually at one of the
royalist fighting fronts, another on the republican side, in Sana.
In addition, they trained several dozen Yemenis as first aid workers.

This was the first time the International Red Cross had established a field hospital on its own; usually it works only as representative of national Red Cross societies. (Although a Swiss organiza-

tion, it is quite separate from the Swiss Red Cross; nor should it be confused with the League of Red Cross Societies, which is an association of national Red Cross societies.) The I.R.C. took on the task after a survey of northern Yemen by two Red Cross delegates and two largely fruitless appeals to national Red Cross societies. The survey, a report on which was published in October 1963, included the following passages:

Malaria is rife. Food is lacking in calorific content. We treated about 30 men, for some of whom we had to extract rotten teeth. One warrior even brought us a transistor radio to repair, thinking that electricity was a branch of medicine.

We found several open cases of medical supplies in a cave: anti-scorpion serum, serum against burns by gas, plasma, tetanus, anti-toxin, phials of terramycin, fluoton, &c. The lot was covered with sand and dust and no one knew what it was for.

We found two soldiers lying in the back of a cave, seriously wounded by grenade splinters, who had been waiting for five days for someone to give them attention. They lay on sheepskins soaked in their own blood and pus.

At Kharia oasis we dealt with some 20 patients, several of them children. One 10-year-old girl had advanced pneumonia; a boy of 12 was dying.

We were authorized by a commanding officer to visit prisoners who had been held for five months. They sleep on the bare rock, as do their guards.

War continues in the Yemen as ruthlessly as when it began. Undernourishment and the chronic shortage of water is giving rise to an alarming increase in amoebic dysentery. Men and animals drink at the same sources of filthy water.

The first of the appeals in February asked for medical teams to be sent to northern Yemen and for medicines only to be sent to the republican side. But, while a good deal of medicine was received, the I.R.C. got no offers of medical teams. A second appeal in the autumn urgently pleading for medical teams or field hospitals also had disappointing results. However, some financial contributions came from Britain, West Germany and India; the British also offered a medical team and the Indians sent sheets.

'Apparently,' an I.R.C. official said to me sadly, as he reviewed the history of the mission, 'Europeans don't feel concerned about the people of this part of the world.' He said that since the Yemenis on the royalist side had no medical corps or other medical facilities of their own, and no national Red Cross society was willing to meet the need, the international committee of the Red Cross felt morally obligated to act on its own. 'It was impossible to let the victims die,' he said.

To carry out its project the I.R.C. borrowed money from the Swiss government and from the Swiss Red Cross to buy a field hospital, a sum amounting to between 6 and 7 million Swiss francs (about £496,000 or $1,384,000). The Red Cross men calculated that it would cost 150,000 Swiss francs (about £12,500 or $35,000) per year to maintain.

In addition to the main field hospital at Uqd, in the north-eastern desert of Yemen, the Red Cross decided to establish a smaller medical post, towards which the British Red Cross had contributed, at Qafl, in north-western Yemen, near the Imam's headquarters at Qara.

The man who directed all International Red Cross activities in Yemen, including the field hospital, the medical team, the distribution of medicines, vitamins and milk in Sana, the exchange of prisoners, and later the investigation of the use of gas by the Egyptians, was André Rochat. He was a young man who had risen to the rank of major in the Swiss army and to positions of responsibility in the Swiss hotel industy, and who craved more idealistic pursuits. In Yemen he revealed a talent also for diplomacy. Through his efforts the Red Cross got both sides to agree to free movement of Red Cross personnel between royalist and republican-controlled territories. Indefatigably enterprising, Rochat went beyond the usual humanitarian functions of the Red Cross by helping to arrange a secret meeting in the autumn of 1966 in Paris between Prince Mohamed bin Hussein and Marshal Abdul Hakim Amer. No immediate results ensued from the meeting, but it may have prepared the ground for agreements that were reached later.

In November 1963 the I.R.C. arranged with the American air force to send a C-124 transport to carry a field hospital from Geneva to Jeddah at a cost of 110,000 Swiss francs (about $9,100 or $25,000). In Jeddah it was reloaded aboard a DC-4 of a company called Balair, and flown to Najran, from where trucks transported the material to Uqd.

Dr Middendorp, who had a hand in selecting the site of the field hospital at a point four hours drive south of Najran, later defended the choice against critics who contended that it was too far from water and too far from the fighting. 'When the wadi is flooded,' he said, 'we stay dry. And we are protected from wind by the surrounding hill of rocks. Admittedly we have a water problem, but we get enough for all medical purposes by truck from a spring one hour's drive away.' He noted, incidentally, that there was probably once a spring or well at Uqd because traces of foundations of an ancient village had been found, and on the rocks above the camp were many prehistoric drawings of camels, ostriches (now extinct in the Middle East), snakes, unicorns and human figures, including phallic symbols, as well as inscriptions. It might have been possible to sink a new well on this site, but the Saudis discouraged the Red Cross from making the attempt because a well would prove an attraction to permanent habitation in a strategic area near the border which the Saudis preferred to leave uninhabited.

Patients were attracted to the hospital from as far away as Jeddah in Saudi Arabia, Aden and Bahrain. Some arrived in buses. Although they worked in tents, under the most austere conditions, the skill of the Swiss doctors and nurses acted like a magnet. Ten to fifteen per cent of all patients were bedouin (nomadic Arabs from all the surrounding countries), ten to fifteen per cent were Saudis, and most of the rest Yemenis. Dr Middendorp estimated that seventy per cent of the Yemenis suffered from complaints related to the war, battle, bomb, or mine injuries. The rest were just sick. They gathered outside the area of the hospital camping in the desert, waiting for treatment. One patient was a wealthy lady from Bahrain with gall-stones. Although the hospital was not intended for that sort of thing and offered none of the comforts the lady hoped for, the Swiss took her in. Other patients came from the Saudi hospital at Najran, which took to sending its most difficult cases to the Swiss.

Almost nightly, sometime after midnight, the camp would be awakened by the roar of four-wheel-drive supply trucks returning from battle areas with wounded. Lights would flash on and doctors and nurses turn out of their tents to man X-ray and operating units. A high proportion of the wounded were mine injuries, many beyond hope after having been driven five or ten hours across the desert. The nauseous stench of infected, gangrenous wounds filled the air. (Explaining the high proportion of mine injuries, one of the princes told me that in the preceding two years the tribesmen had been given a lot of mines to lay and in many cases had not reported or had forgotten where they had laid them. Thus the tribesmen were sometimes blown up by their own mines. If peace were restored it would take many years before they could all be cleared.)

The much smaller medical post at Qafl was first staffed in November 1963 by an American, Dr William George Bartlett of Johns Hopkins University, who had been studying at Edinburgh. He was accompanied by a British male nurse named Arnold Plumber, and a member of the I.R.C. named Laurent Vust. The post closed down about a year later when Dr Wilson-Pepper of the British Red Cross, who had succeeded Dr Bartlett, returned home for reasons of health, and the male nurse Arnold Plumber had to be withdrawn as a result of a curious error which exposed him to Nasserite pressure. Mr Plumber, for forty years a Red Cross male nurse in the field, held British army medical corps reserve status. A letter releasing him for medical work in Yemen and relieving him of any reserve duties or training, was inadvertently addressed to Sana instead of Qara and fell into the hands of the Egyptians. President Nasser's representatives at the United Nations exploited this as evidence of 'British imperialist interference in Yemen', and demanded his withdrawal.

Neither the Egyptians nor the republicans would recognize the inviolability of the International Red Cross medical post in the west and the post was actually bombed in April 1964. But the field hospital at Uqd was tacitly recognized by both the Egyptians and the republicans, and was never attacked.

Red Cross visits to prisoners were begun by Laurent Vust, who towards the end of 1963 found a royalist prison camp at Wassha with Egyptian prisoners as well as political detainees of the Imam, presumed traitors and hostages. Later he visited political detainees in Sana, including twenty-three members of the Imam's family. The royalists eventually established five different prisoner-of-war camps. On both sides of the line the Red Cross collected names, distributed clothes and medical supplies, and picked up and delivered letters. It used its influence to alleviate the prisoners' condition so far as was possible; often its representatives had to remind the Egyptian prisoners that their captors had no more and sometimes less than they in the way of food and clothing. To a complaint about prisoners whose legs had been shackled after they attempted to escape, a Red Cross man once responded: 'Well, I have also seen some Yemeni royalist soldiers in shackles.'

Some observations about the medical condition of the Yemeni people were made to me by Dr Felix von Tobel, a blond and youthful Swiss scouting enthusiast who had been trained as a doctor of paediatrics at the University of Basel. Von Tobel had also spent some time training at hospitals in New York and San Francisco, and he was a fellow in cardiology at Stanford University. He found the Yemeni people healthier than the people of Haiti whom he had recently visited, probably because the Yemenis get a lot of protein from camel and goat milk. He said their worst complaint was bilharzia (schistosomiasis), a debilitating disease that is carried by a microscopic snail common to the Nile river, from which it is spread by birds. 'The Yemenis are relatively clean people,' von Tobel observed. 'They wash in the stream beds and ponds when they can, and that is where they get bilharzia.' He said he had also seen much of a virulent form of tuberculosis but only a moderate amount of venereal disease. He was astonished to find so much anaemia and arthritis. Most common, he said, were intestinal complaints, blood in the urine and liver pains. For many of these the Swiss were able to offer very effective antibiotic treatment.

Other doctors remarked that they had done things in the Uqd field hospital that they had never dreamed they could do. One said, for instance, that he had to operate on infected bones because if he delayed to clear up the infection the patients would die. Surprisingly, only ten per cent developed infections of their wounds in spite of the omnipresence of flies and sand.

One of the doctors' most difficult problems was making themselves understood; they had only one official interpreter and one man in the kitchen who spoke English. They were also dogged by unexpected technical problems caused by their isolation. Their gasoline pressure cooker, for instance, was not brought into operation until May 1965 because no one could figure out how it worked. In the meantime the camp kitchen used wood as fuel.

Not many of the patients were children, possibly because in Yemeni society children are not valued as highly as among Europeans. Some of the children who were brought in could not urinate because of stones in the bladder, probably caused by prolonged insufficiency of drinking water. Some of the others were infants with terrible burns on their hands caused by crawling into open fires; some had healed up with hands clenched, so that the children could not open them. The Swiss surgeons cut the hands open and grafted skin on to them. With some pride the doctors told about a child born by caesarean section whom its parents named Hussein al Salib, meaning 'Hussein of the cross', in recognition of the role the Red Cross had played. Some of the Arab women took off their veils after they had been in the camp for about three weeks. The Swiss regarded this as a great compliment, for it meant that the women felt at home.

One of the doctors had amputated a hand of a tribesman who had fallen victim to an Egyptian booby trap, the detonator of which had been hidden inside a cigarette. The doctor observed sadly: 'It will save his life but it will also end it, because here if you are not a whole man you are a dead man. There is no sympathy for weakness. It begins with birth. If a child does not start breathing by itself they let it die. These mountains have one of the highest infant mortality rates in the world.' When some of the patients died there was no lamentation or weeping. Funerals were cheerful affairs. The Yemenis said of the dead: 'It is Allah's will. They are with Allah.'

The young Swiss volunteers were serious about their work. But during the burning hot afternoon, when their tents became almost unbearable, many of them liked to retire to caves among the surrounding rocks where it was cool and where, incidentally, they could examine the remarkable pre-historic drawings and inscriptions. If an emergency arose in the camp during this period someone blew a blast on an automobile horn. Sometimes the young Swiss even found time to do the twist or hully gully, to the music of a gramophone discreetly situated at the top of a hill on which was located the camp's radio station, which linked them by radio telephone with I.R.C. headquarters in Geneva. Up there they were safe from the eyes of the Yemenis, who could hardly imagine their nurses and doctors in bikinis and shorts.

In the evening the Swiss were sometimes invited for tea by neighbouring tribes. Sometimes they went to Najran, across the border, whose most recent claims to modernity were two garages and a telephone exchange with seven telephones. The Saudi authorities altered their local regulations to allow the Red Cross people to go into the town at a time when the American pilots of airliners were still not allowed to leave the airport. Mrs Middendorp may have been the first white woman to go into Najran.

Dr Middendorp pointed out that the Swiss were launched on this, their first desert experience, at four weeks' notice. 'But by and large we seem to have done the right thing,' he observed. 'For instance, when it gets very hot, we add two per cent salt to our water. We put a little lemon in the water to cut the taste of the disinfectant, and about the time one crew is worn out we are ready to send in another. One advantage of a changing staff is that the Yemenis become attached to their particular doctors and usually leave when their doctors leave, thereby making room for new patients.'

This, then, was the camp which Rigos and I visited on our way back from the royalists' positions in the Jawf in May 1965. After a long morning talking to the doctors and nurses we lunched with them in their mess hall tent and were invited in the afternoon to their 'rock and roll' session on the mountain top. We sang, and Rigos and I even danced, and we laughed a lot. It was quite a party.

At about four o'clock, when shadows began to lengthen and the heat abated, we made our way down among the rocks and tried to photograph some of the prehistoric rock paintings and inscriptions. Our jeep was waiting in the Red Cross camp to drive us on to Najran, across the border in Saudi Arabia, that evening. The back seat was occupied by three men who had been appointed as our guard when we set out from Amara some days before. John Rigos and I squeezed into the front next to the driver, and off we went.

Our driver was in good spirits. The difficult journey was nearly over and he had presumably spent the afternoon chewing *qat*. He sang a Yemeni song as he drove and we all relaxed in an aura of good feeling. This was the end of my last journalistic journey in more than four years in the Middle East. I had been reassigned to London, and as we jounced across the desert so merrily I was lost in reverie. We were moving across a vast expanse of semi-desert, broken only by the tyre marks of royalist supply trucks and occasional tufts of thorny bushes that could survive with almost no moisture. We had been driving for perhaps thirty minutes, and suddenly I became aware that the jeep was careering wildly in a long arc off to the right. Probably we had struck some soft sand which turned the front wheels and broke our speed in a manner beyond the control of the driver. I braced myself against the floor boards and the door of the jeep, for I was on the outside, with Rigos between me and the driver.

But the driver could not regain control. In retrospect, so acutely conscious had I become in those seconds, it seemed as though the jeep leaned slowly, inexorably, to the left, gradually lifting its wheels on one side. I clung to the sides of the jeep as I felt it going over, and then there was a crash.

I was unconscious only for a few moments. When I regained consciousness I became aware of the wreckage of the jeep all around me. There seemed to be absolute silence, and I recall a sense of relief at knowing that I was alive. I felt no pain at that moment, but realized that my head was twisted in a strange position over on to my left shoulder. Some parts of the jeep were lying on my legs, but with my right arm I was able to pull myself up and out of the wreckage. For a moment I was on my feet, and then realized that I could not straighten up my head nor move my left arm.

One of the guards who had been in the back seat was standing in front of me. He and his companions had been thrown clear and were uninjured. I put my right hand on this man's shoulder and tottered a few feet away from the wreckage. Then, clinging to his arm, I lowered myself on to the sand, face down. I realized almost immediately that I had probably broken my neck, and when I sensed that some of the Arabs were gathered around me I yelled at them: 'Don't touch me.' It came to me automatically, that a person with a broken neck must not be moved except by experts.

Then I could hear the driver groaning, and I heard John Rigos' voice. He was talking quite normally but was not making sense. He walked over to me and asked: 'Dana, where are we? What are we doing here?' I replied: 'John, we have been visiting the Yemeni royalists and we have had an accident. Tell the Arabs not to touch me because I think I have broken my neck. Tell them to try to stop a truck going back to the Red Cross camp. Tell them to go and tell Doctor Middendorp what has happened and ask him to come.' I had to repeat Dr Middendorp's name over and over again for Rigos, for although he knew me he did not understand what I was saying about the Red Cross. The immediate past seemed to have blotted out from his mind.

Sometimes one can drive for hours over this desert and never see another vehicle; but we were lucky. Almost immediately, it seemed, another truck, heading south, arrived and I heard Rigos talking to the Arabs. He had not forgotten the little Arabic he knew.

After that it was all a matter of waiting and putting up with the pain which began, when the shock subsided, to spread through my neck and shoulder. I cannot say that the pain was excruciating. It just hurt. The worst part was waiting and realizing that the sun was going down and that the Arabs might not have understood or might not have done as they were asked.

All at once, it seemed, it was dark and then I heard the engines of approaching vehicles and saw their lights reflected on the sand. The engines stopped and I heard the soft, low, confident, infinitely reassuring voices of Dr Middendorp and the men of the International Red Cross. Someone was bending over me, speaking softly and touching me with firm, gentle, understanding hands. Two or three of the young Swiss, I didn't know which ones, slid me on to a stretcher so gently that I felt no extra pain. I was so relieved that they had come that my spirits sang within me and I really experienced no fear from that moment on.

They lifted me into the back of a truck. A nurse sat next to me, and I grasped her ankle in a vice-like grip to still the pain in my neck and shoulder. She laughed when she felt me grip her ankle and that made me feel a lot better. The driver, who had suffered painful internal injuries, and Rigos, who had serious head injuries, must have been in other vehicles; at least I was not aware of them in the truck. The truck, which had dashed over the desert at maximum speed to reach us, now crept back slowly, slowly over the rocks and dunes so as not to jar the patients. Dr Middendorp gave me an injection which made the journey, which must have taken a couple of hours, more bearable.

At the Red Cross camp we drove up to the X-ray tent where the driver, whose condition seemed more critical than mine, was given first attention while I lay in the darkness outside. Then at last I was again in those strong confident hands, on an operating table. They made X-rays and then carefully straightened my head and neck, which up to that moment had remained grotesquely twisted.

Already I had sufficient reason to be eternally grateful to the International Red Cross; the ensuing week endeared them to me. No one could have provided more efficient or more considerate and good-humoured care under such difficult circumstances. In the middle of that first night the young doctor who worked under Middendorp devised a harness which fitted under my chin and was connected to weights hanging from the top of my bed. The device was meant to keep my neck straight and stretched, so that the fractured vertebrae would not injure the nerves in the spinal cord. Although improvised on the spot and quickly, it proved marvellously efficient.

Certain things stand out in my memory of that week. I remember the cool reassurance I derived from the frequent visits by Dr Middendorp and the other doctors. I remember the nurses, especially one whose efficiency exceeded her gentleness, whom I called 'the elephant'. And I remember the two very dark Yemeni brothers who were assigned to give us special attention. The younger of these was especially intelligent, and had learned a good deal of English while working for Americans in the oil-fields of north-eastern Saudi Arabia. He was given the task of spoon-feeding me, for I could not at this time raise my head enough to feed myself. Not satisfied with the insipid, lukewarm lemon drink which the Swiss apparently thought best for their patients, John Rigos and I carefully explained to our young servant how to prepare for us a good strong lemonade, with lots of lemon, lots of sugar and lots of the extremely precious ice cubes obtainable only by special favour of the cook. He did exactly as instructed and the results will be long remembered, I am sure, by both of us. Much later, in the summer of 1966 when I was in London, the older of the brothers turned up for a few weeks. He had got a job tending a fellow Yemeni whose hands had been blown off in a booby trap and whom the British Red Cross had undertaken to fit with artificial hands.

It immediately occurred to me, even on the first night of our arrival, that we would either have to remain in this camp for many weeks, until we were well enough to be transported over desert trails to Najran, or else we would have to devise some way of getting out of Uqd by air. I knew that the International Red Cross camp was near a landing strip originally prepared for the United Nations observer team which had departed from Yemen in the previous year. I therefore dictated to Dr Middendorp several telegrams which he undertook to send on the I.R.C. transmitter to his headquarters in Geneva, from where they would be relayed to their destinations. One telegram was addressed to King Faisal, whom I had interviewed in Jeddah just before I had undertaken this journey and whom I knew from many previous interviews. I asked him if he would send an aircraft to Uqd to pick us up and take us at least to Najran where we could be put aboard commercial aircraft.

Another telegram I sent to United States Ambassador Parker T. Hart, in Jeddah, telling him of our plight and asking him to follow up my request to King Faisal. Others still I sent to Tania, my wife, in Beirut, to my mother, in Los Angeles, and to Emanuel Freedman, who was then foreign editor of the *New York Times*.

As it turned out it was not the Saudis but the American air force that got us out of Uqd. Ambassador Hart, whom I knew well from many visits to Jeddah, moved like lightning. With André Rochat's help he obtained from the republican government of Yemen in Sana clearance for an American plane from Dahran to fly to Uqd. He also arranged with the American training mission at Dahran to send the plane. Plastered with a huge red cross (on which Rochat had insisted), and with Rochat in the cockpit to help find the obscure landing strip at Uqd, it arrived as soon as we were fit to be moved.

Meanwhile the *New York Times*, working through the American embassies in Beirut and Jeddah, had chartered an airplane to meet us in Jeddah. So we were flown to Jeddah and thence to Beirut. I must have been given some kind of sedative, for it all seems very hazy now except for our arrival in Beirut. Never will I forget the joyful moment when Tania climbed into the ambulance with me outside the airport, and put her arms around the dreadful plaster cast in which I had been specially encased for the trip, and we were alone together for a moment.

XIX

Gas Warfare

THE most characteristic and appalling aspect of the Yemen war has been the use of gas by the Egyptians. When I first heard, in Beirut, the report that the Egyptians had gassed Yemen villages, I did not believe it. It seemed to me quite implausible that the Egyptians would risk the obloquy which such a crime would bring upon them. In particular, I felt they would not do such a thing to fellow Arabs. I was inclined to believe an explanation that came to me second-hand from French mercenaries who had been affected by vapours that blinded and attacked the lungs. They were sent to a hospital in Saudi Arabia and recovered in a week. In their opinion what the Egyptians had dropped was not gas but napalm, that had ignited imperfectly and formed a kind of gas. And it is possible that this happened on some occasions.

But there can be no doubt that the Egyptians did use gas. The first attack I considered confirmed took place on 8 June 1963, against the village of al Kawma, a village of about 100 inhabitants in northern Yemen, where gas killed seven people and inflicted serious damage to the eyes and lungs of twenty-five others; many others developed open wounds on their bodies as a result of the gas. The villagers appealed to the Imam, who sent to the village an investigating group accompanied by Lieutenant-Colonel Neil McLean. They reached al Kawma twenty-five days after the gas bombs had been dropped. Although it had in the meantime rained three times, they found 'a peculiar odour of putrefaction hanging over the area'. Neil McLean told me that in the ensuing weeks he also saw the results of gas attacks at the villages of al Darb, al Jaraishi, Hasan, Bini, Awair and al Ashash, south of Sadah.

The first news that the Egyptians were using gas in Yemen reached the world in the form of a despatch by Richard Beeston in the *Daily Telegraph* of 8 July 1963. He had been to al Kawma:

I reached al Kawma after a three-day journey in a lorry, on donkey and on foot from the Saudi Arabian border. The village is perched on top of a high rugged mountain in the unmapped part of northern Yemen. I approached the village late at night. From more than a hundred yards away I could hear the coughing of the gassed villagers, which went on ceaselessly.

In the morning villagers crowded me, pleading with me to send medicines and doctors to cure their coughs and blisters. The face of one woman had turned a vivid yellow.

Another woman was blinded by rubbing her eyes with contaminated fingers. One of the worst-affected villagers I saw was Mohamed Nassr, 12, who had a perpetual cough and deep open wounds on his body, the size of a half-crown, from gas blisters.

The gas bomb was dropped on the village during the evening early last month and six people, including a five-year-old girl, Hadia Rashid, died in agony within four days. Last Monday the seventh death took place. It was of a boy of 13.

The population of the village of al Kawma is about 100, a third of whom have been gassed. The village headman told me that when the bomb fell it gave off a cloud of brown smoke and had a 'dirty smell'.

'We thought it was just smoke, because nobody had ever heard of poison gas,' he said. 'Soon after, people began coughing up blood. Some bled from the nose.'

I was shown the remains of what the villagers stated had been the gas bomb. It consisted of two circular bands of metal about two feet across. Into each were screwed fifteen canisters about the size of a car's carburettor.

It was obviously a complicated piece of machinery, probably beyond the engineering capabilities of the Egyptians. Since the Russian bloc supplies all military equipment for Egypt, it is likely that the bomb was manufactured in Russia or Czechoslovakia.

The *Daily Telegraph's* scoop had widespread repercussions. United Nations Secretary-General U Thant was reported to have ordered two of the United Nations observer team then newly arrived in Yemen to make an investigation. State Department officials said they took 'a serious view' of the matter but suggested that the reported gas might have been caused by white phosphorous, an incendiary substance which causes terrible wounds but is not forbidden by the conventions which outlaw gas. The Saudi Arabian government passed the report about the use of gas to the International Red Cross. In Jeddah, a representative of the International Red Cross, Doctor Beretta, said on 9 July that he had been receiving reports of gas warfare for more than a month but had no means of checking.

In the House of Commons, Edward Heath, then Lord Privy Seal in a Conservative government, said in reply to a question that both the United Nations and the International Red Cross had promised to make investigations. He added that the British ambassador in Cairo had told the Egyptian government of 'the extreme seriousness' with which the British government would view the use of gas, should it be confirmed, and noted that Egyptian authorities had suggested that the reported incidents were probably caused by napalm, not gas. The Israeli Foreign Minister, Golda Meir, suggested in an interview that President Nasser, having used gas against other Arabs, would not hesitate to do so against Israel.

David Smiley, a retired British officer who had served for three years as commander of the army of the Sultan of Muscat and Oman, and was now acting as an occasional correspondent for the *Daily Telegraph*, wrote a letter to *The Times* on 29 July 1963 which, in addition to its repetition of the gas charge, served as a reminder that the Egyptian terror at this time was not exclusively a matter of the use of gas. During four weeks he had spent with the royalists – months after a period of disengagement between combatants was supposed to have begun under an agreement reached in April through the mediation of the United States ambassador in Jeddah, Ellsworth Bunker – there had been only one day when he had not seen a bombing attack. He said he had seen no United Nations observer in the bombed areas of Yemen.

The Egyptian use of gas in 1963 appears to have been experimental. In the opinion of Neil McLean, who maintained his interest throughout the Yemen war, these early Egyptian gas bombs were 'home-made, amateurish and relatively ineffective'. There were no more reports of gas during 1964. In 1965 McLean reported only one in the summer of 1965. Also, the royalists circulated copies of a letter allegedly signed by an Egyptian Lieutenant-Colonel Saad Hassan al Shami, military commander of the Hajjah area, dated 26 March 1965, and addressed to a Sheikh Mohamed bin Qaid al Gudmy. The letter said that the Egyptians had been reluctant to use gas but had resorted to it when faced with 'the aggression upon us and the peaceful population'. The letter went on: 'We singled out for that purpose the village of al Dhanoob, with the object of reducing casualties to a minimum. This strike was designed to be a warning to all other aggressors.' It continued that the Egyptians could have wiped out larger villages, 'but our aim was to give a warning only'. In particular it warned the Beni Hajar tribe that they would be 'struck and exterminated by means of gas if they did not within two days withdraw from Qurb al Rab'. The letter ended with an Arab proverb: 'He who has given warning is never to blame.'

While this letter may have been a forgery, it does fit into the pattern of what I believe to have been the pattern of Egyptian use of gas in the early part of the war. Much worse was to come.

Egyptian gas bombing was resumed in much more deadly fashion in a raid on Halbal, a village of 150 inhabitants thirty miles north of Sana, on 11 December 1966. A month later, when he reached Aden, the attack was described in detail by Mohamed al Yazali, the former republican director of press and publications, who had fled from Sana after a dispute with his superiors. He said he had observed the bombing from a neighbouring mountain, where he was hiding. 'I saw two Ilyushin bombers drop fifteen gas bombs,' he said. 'Yellowish smoke rose after the bombing, and then I went down to the village. Two people had been killed, three blinded, and thirty-five were suffering from the effects of the gas. I saw one woman bleeding from the nose and mouth. Some suffered burns and some had difficulty in breathing. There was an unexploded bomb about five feet long embedded in a patch of green near the village.'

Then, on 5 January 1967, came the biggest and most devastating of the Egyptian gas attacks, against the village of Kitaf. Its objective was probably the headquarters which the royalist Prime Minister, Prince Hassan bin Yahya, had installed in caves near the village.

A careful report on this raid, compiled from all available sources, has been written by Neil McLean, who has spent many months of the war in the mountains with the royalist forces. The text of the report which he supplied me is as follows:

At 0730 (GMT) on 5th January '67 gas bombs were dropped on Kitaf. The raid started with two MiGs each dropping one smoke bomb. Nine Il-28s then dropped the gas, three aircraft at a time, three bombs per aircraft, upwind of the village of Kitaf. The bombs made a crater three feet deep and six feet wide and released the gas in a grey-green cloud which drifted with the wind over the village of Kitaf. All but 5% of the people within two kilometres downwind of the bombs' impact point have died or, in the opinion of the International Red Cross mission sent to the spot, are likely to die. Deaths now total well over 200. All animals in the area also perished, and crops and vegetation turned brown. Until the following morning a grey-green cloud of gas hung low over the village. Those unfortunate enough to breathe it compared its smell to yeast or fresh fruit. Most of the victims were dead within 10 to 50 minutes of the attack. They died with blood emerging from mouth and nose, but without any mark on their skin. Affected survivors have no blisters or skin injury, but have difficulty breathing and cough continuously

He added that in the period immediately preceding and following the raid on Kitaf the Egyptians had also carried out similar, though less lethal, air attacks against royalist villages in the region of Jabal Ayal Yazid, to the north of Sana, on the al Ans tribal area to the south of Sana, and on the Bani Matar and al Haymatain tribal areas to the west of Sana.

McLean wrote that he believed the Egyptians were using a new and more effective type of gas bomb received from the Russians. By its use, he believed, the Egyptians hoped to break the spirit of the royalist tribes and at the same time intimidate the Saudi Arabians, by showing them that they could suffer a similar fate if King Faisal continued to oppose them in Yemen and the Arabian peninsula generally. The Saudis undoubtedly feared that similar gas attacks might some day be directed against them, and they at first said nothing. Perhaps they felt that these were remote areas, and that if you said nothing about the terrible things that took place in them it would be as though they had never happened.

But the Saudis had not reckoned with Bushrod Howard, the young American former oil company employee who had embraced the royalist cause. As told in Chapter Thirteen, Howard headed for Kitaf as soon as he heard about the attack, and not only collected reports from survivors but persuaded them to dig up some of the animals who had died from the gas. These he loaded into the back of a truck and rushed back to Saudi Arabia where they could be examined by Saudi doctors. Howard then began organizing press coverage of the Kitaf disaster. As a result of his efforts twenty newspapermen gathered in Jeddah on 21 January, sixteen days after the gas bombing of Kitaf, and were flown to Najran the next day. The American press was represented by Robert Conley and Rushan Arikan of NBC, John Cooley of the *Christian Science Monitor*, John Lawton of UPI, David Lancashire of AP and Andrew Borowiec of the *Washington Star*. The British correspondents included Richard Beeston of the *Daily Telegraph* and Nicholas Herbert of *The Times*.

In a report to the overseas press bulletin of the Overseas Press Club of America, Mr Borowiec wrote that 'some brought sleeping bags and mountain boots, water-purifying tablets and first aid kits; others came in city suits'. His account of the expedition, which began on 23 January, continued:

> The unwieldy caravan set out from Najran on donkeys with a guard of some sixty Yemeni warriors who fired their rifles signalling our approach to lookouts perching on mountainsides. Camels carried the baggage, including television equipment. One collapsed under his burden and the convoy halted until a replacement was found.
>
> Tripping on rocks, falling from their animals, quarrelling, swearing, complaining, threatening to go back, the caravan of exhausted newsmen reached Kitaf after a twenty-seven-hour march.
>
> All correspondents participating in the trip agreed that evidence strongly pointed to the use of poison gas.
>
> Terrified survivors were still telling of a brown, wind-whipped, 'sweet-smelling' cloud that caused foaming at the mouth, vomiting, nose-bleeding and death from one to twenty-four hours after the attack. Bodies of killed animals were strewn through Kitaf's dusty alleys without any visible trace of wounds. In Najran, local doctors who treated 118 patients said all symptoms pointed to gas.

The journalists got back to Najran and set up camp in the customs house on 27 January, the day before an Egyptian air raid.

At dawn eight Soviet-made Ilyushin bombers and two MiG escorts swooped down and came in low over the town. Saudi anti-aircraft guns on both sides of the oasis town opened fire at 6.37 a.m., just as the sun appeared over the hills to the east of the town. Many of the bombs fell in the densely populated town, sending clouds of smoke billowing towards the sky. There were numerous casualties. Three bombs which fell within 100 yards of the journalists' encampment failed to explode.

Meanwhile, on 26 January, the Jordan government had informed Sana that, should it be proved that gas had been used against the inhabitants of royalist Yemen, Jordan would feel obliged to withdraw the recognition it had accorded the republic. Since the Jordanians had not followed up their recognition by sending a diplomat to Sana it remained obscure whether the Jordanian government ever carried out the threat.

Immediately after the gas bombing of Kitaf, some personnel of the International Red Cross withdrew from Yemen into Saudi Arabia, demanding that they be supplied with gas masks. However, André Rochat, the head of the I.R.C. in Yemen, soon persuaded them that it did not make sense for the Red Cross to be equipped in this fashion when no one else had gas masks. If they alone had such equipment, he pointed out, they would be exposing themselves to the possibilities of theft, if not of outright attack. Within a few days, and well before the arrival of the journalists, two representatives of the I.R.C. arrived at Kitaf, where they were reported to have removed part of the lungs of dead animals and taken samples of contaminated soil and clothing. On 1 February, while still discreetly refraining from publishing the results of this investigation or accusing anybody, the I.R.C. expressed 'great concern' over reports that poison gas had been used. It appealed to all parties concerned 'to respect the universally recognized humanitarian rules of international morality and law'.

The Egyptian government, which had repeatedly issued flat denials that it had used poison gas in Yemen, and had alleged that Britain and the United States were using the reports as a form of psychological warfare against Egypt, said on 12 February that it would accept a United Nations investigation of the allegations. But on 1 March Secretary-General U Thant, in a reply to a Saudi Arabian complaint that the Egyptians had used poison gas, said that he was 'powerless' to deal with the matter. Although he must have seen the journalistic evidence and the International Red Cross must have put its evidence at his disposal, he added that 'the facts are in sharp dispute and I have no means of ascertaining the truth'.

Meanwhile gas attacks in Yemen continued. On 10 May the twin villages of Gahar and Gadafa in Wadi Hirran, where Prince Mohamed bin Mohsin was then in command, were gas-bombed and at least seventy-five persons killed. On 13 May André Rochat set out at the head of a medical mission to investigate the bombing and bring help to its victims. He was accompanied by I.R.C. delegate Jacques Ruff, Dr Willy Brutschin and Dr Raymond Janin, as well as the male nurse René Vuille. Also in the party was Yahya bin Saleh, the Yemeni male nurse, who had then been working for the Red Cross for four years. Claudio Cesaretti, an Italian journalist who travelled with the group, wrote in the German illustrated magazine *Sie und Er* that at three o'clock in the morning the convoy got stuck in the mud of a small stream. He reported that Rochat ordered the medical supplies to be unloaded and stacked up 150 yards from the truck. He had an enormous Red Cross flag, twelve yards long, spread out on the ground. Then, while Yahya bin Saleh remained on guard, the party bedded down on a nearby hillside and waited for the dawn.

At 7.45 a.m., well after the sun had risen, three Egyptian Ilyushins appeared and wheeled away behind a mountain. 'But they came back and this time they flew lower. As we rushed to cover, the first bomb fell. In seconds the area was transformed into a landscape of craters. We sought shelter in a grotto. But already the bombs were there again. Three enormous explosions shook the air.' As the bombers departed, he said, two MiGs appeared, presumably to observe the extent of the damage. At the same moment the bedouin escorting the Red Cross mission raised a cry that Yahya bin Saleh had been hurt. André Rochat, one of the doctors and a male nurse rushed from their shelter on the hill to his side. The Ilyushins returned once more and three more bombs fell, but without causing further casualties. The injured man was lying under a bush. A bomb splinter had penetrated near his kidneys and lodged in his lungs and he had an open wound in his left leg. His left arm was broken.

Although many of their supplies had been destroyed in the bombing the Red Cross party pushed on to the gas-stricken villages. They examined the casing of three bombs at the foot of a hill on which the villages are situated. The gas, under pressure inside the bombs, had apparently been released slowly and had crept up the hill where it surprised the population of the village in their sleep. Seventy-five persons died on the spot, and most of the rest of the villagers were affected. Their eyes burned, they spat blood and breathed with difficulty. Many would die unless they received medical care. But except for this visiting group of Swiss doctors, the nearest physician was 500 kilometres away in Najran.

While the Red Cross men did what little they could for the gas victims Prince Mohamed bin Mohsin's men succeeded in pulling the Red Cross truck out of the mud. They drove back over the desert trails to Najran, with Yahya bin Saleh screaming all the way in spite of morphine injections. He was flown to a hospital in Jeddah, where he later recovered.

The incident may have induced the International Red Cross to speak up more boldly about what was happening. On 2 June the I.R.C. issued a statement in Geneva saying 'that it was extremely disturbed and concerned by the incidents in which gas had been used against Yemeni villages'. Still it did not mention Egypt, but it was pretty obvious that only the Egyptians could be responsible. Reporting the Red Cross mission to Gahar and Gadafa the Red Cross said: 'Delayed by an air raid, doctors at arrival on the site immediately treated some of the wounded and collected various indications pointing to the use of poison gas.'

A few weeks later, on 3 July 1967, the American weekly magazine *U.S. News and World Report* published two International Red Cross documents which it had obtained from private sources, which finally provided official evidence, if such were really still needed, that gas was being used in Yemen. Although they did not mention Egypt no one could doubt that this was the International Red Cross's way of condemning the Egyptians.

The first document was a statement by two doctors who accompanied the Red Cross party to Gahar. It read as follows:

At Geneva

The undersigned doctors, members of the International Committee of the Red Cross medical mission to the Yemen, arrived at Gahar (North Yemen) in the Wadi Hirran, on May 15, 1967, following an appeal for assistance from the inhabitants who claimed to have been under gas attack by airplanes on the morning of May 10, 1967.

265

The following statements were made by the inhabitants who witnessed the incident:

1. Seventy-five persons died of poison gas shortly after the raid.

They showed the following symptoms: shortness of breath, coughing, pink foam at the mouth, general edema, especially the face; no physical injuries.

2. The undersigned doctors examined the four surviving victims and observed the following:

— Subjective symptoms: burning eyes and trachea, internal thorax pain, extreme fatigue, anorexia.

— Objective symptoms: dry cough, negative auscultation in two patients, signs of bronchitis in the other two, conjunctivitis, facial edema, no traumatic lesions, tympanum intact.

3. The undersigned doctors examined a corpse, four days after death and 12 hours after burial.

Immediately, the common grave was opened, and, well before the corpses – which were only wrapped in shrouds, without coffins – were visible, there was a sweet penetrating smell not unlike garlic. The bodies showed no traumatic lesions. The skin was pink. Advanced and general edema all over the body.

Examination of lungs: reddish-brown throughout, enlargement, consistence and fragility greatly increased, crepitation considerably reduced.

The undersigned doctors draw the following logical conclusions from their findings:

I. None of the victims examined, whether survivors or corpses exhumed from the common grave, showed any traumatic lesions.

II. The statements made by witnesses who escaped from the raid unharmed, in respect of the circumstances in which 75 inhabitants were killed, are consistent with the International Committee of the Red Cross medical mission's own findings by examination of the four survivors and the corpse exhumed from one of the common graves.

III. The cause of death in the case of the corpse examined was pulmonary edema. The over-all consistency of the ICRC medical mission's findings shows that in all probability this pulmonary edema was caused by inhalation of toxic gas.

(Signed) Raymond Janin, ICRC Doctor-Delegate

Willy Brutschin, ICRC Doctor-Delegate

Signed at town of Najran, May 18, 1967.

The second document was a statement by the director of the Institute of Forensic Medicine at the University of Berne on conclusions to be drawn from the Red Cross report:

Dear Sirs—

In accordance with your instructions of May 21, 1967, we have duly examined the report drawn up by two doctors of the International Committee of the Red Cross on observations made by them after the bombing of a village in the Yemen. Their investigations can be summarized in the following manner:

1. Information collected from the survivors in that village regarding the death of 75 persons.

2. Medical examination of four survivors.

3. Examination of a corpse four days after death and 12 hours after burial.

The phenomena observed are the effects of skin irritation, conjunctivitis and of mucus in the respiratory tract and lungs. General edema had been noted, especially facial and also hae-morrhagic pulmonary edema. On autopsy, red hepatization and a liquid of reddish scrapings were observed in the lungs.

The observations collected are gradually diversified and unspecific, but form a definite entity as a whole.

We know of no epidemical disease presenting a similar symp-tomatology or clinical development. The conclusion according to which the death of the deceased persons as a result of bombing is ascribed to a toxic gas, seems to us to be perfectly justified. This conclusion is supported by the total absence of traumatic lesions caused by the effects of pressure-explosion.

Amongst the various poison gases which can produce the effects observed, phosphonic esters-nervine gas would not, in our opinion, be involved, in view of the local irritations observed. Their effects would, moreover, have been characterized by copious salivation, myosis and muscular cramp.

On the other hand, the employment of halogenous derivatives – phosgene, mustard gas, lewisite, chloride or cyanogen bromide, or Clark I and II etc. – would appear to us the most likely. However, neither bromide nor cyanogen chloride causes an edemic irritation of the skin. This also applies to phosgene.

As against this, all the symptoms observed are explainable by the hypothesis of the use of mustard gas, lewisite or similar substances. The odour resembling garlic, smelled on opening the common grave, would indicate the employment rather of mustard gas. These toxic substances are pulverized when the bomb explodes in the form of aerosol.

(Signed) Yours sincerely,
Professor D. E. Lauppi,
Director of the Institute.

The Red Cross statements notwithstanding, the Egyptians went right on using gas. During the month of May a series of gas attacks were reported to have killed about 360 persons. In addition to the raid on Gahar and Gadafa there were two raids on the Bani Hushaysh district, twenty miles north-east of Sana. In a statement made in Rome on 7 June, Prince Abdurrahman bin Yahya said that the Egyptian air force had made more than twenty gas attacks since the first attack against al Kawma on 8 June 1963. He said that more than 400 persons had been killed by gas in 1967 alone.

This was the time of the June war between Israel and the Arabs. After their defeat by the Israelis the Egyptians withdrew most of their aircraft from Yemen, and the Yemenis enjoyed a respite of about three weeks up to the end of June. In July, however, the bombers returned, carrying out their raids with high explosives and gas with redoubled ferocity. There were reports of gas raids in all parts of royalist Yemen, in the Khawlan, in Arhab, in Wadi Hirran, and in the vicinity of Hajjah. One report spoke of 375 casualties at Mabian, outside Hajjah, which had been occupied by royalists after the withdrawal of the Egyptians from Hajjah. Fifty persons were said to have died immediately and many others in the days that followed the attack.

Militarily the Egyptians undoubtedly used gas as a supplement to the general bombing, in an attempt to break the spirit of royalist resistance and, particularly during the last phase, to exert control where there were no Egyptian troops.

In these objectives I believe the Egyptians failed. Yemen is uncommonly well equipped with caves in which its mountain-dwellers can shelter from bombing in general. Except in the immediate vicinity of Egyptians positions, where the fear of bombing was supplemented by the fear of occupation, the Yemenis' reaction was not to submit but to resist. In their relatively primitive state the tribesmen could exist even though their villages were in ruins, but under these circumstances the venality which so often determined their loyalty was overlaid with a genuine hatred.

The fact remains that the Egyptians did use gas; experimentally, it seems, in 1963, systematically in 1966. The parallel between the two periods is that in both cases the Egyptian use of gas was accompanied by an extension of general bombing across the border to the two Saudi frontier towns, Jizan and Najran, through which, the Egyptians allege, flows the Saudi support for the royalists.

The United States intervened to contain the Egyptian offensive in 1963 by pledging support for the integrity of Saudi Arabia and insisting on an Egyptian-Saudi agreement for disengagement from Yemen. At that time the United States had some influence, for the Egyptians depended heavily on American food. But in 1966 the United States, while saying much the same things through diplomatic channels carried much less weight. The Egyptians had by that stage despaired of United States aid and reconciled themselves to dependence on the Soviet Union. Furthermore, the United States was profoundly preoccupied in Vietnam. Its moral position was complicated by its own heavy bombing of the Vietnamese and the fact that it had used certain forms of non-toxic gases and also chemical weapons in Vietnam. While the United States was more or less on the side-line, the possibility of British influence on the course of events in Yemen emerged. The British were, it is true, deeply involved in Saudi Arabia constructing a system of defence against air attack; but the Foreign Secretary, George Brown, was at the same time exchanging messages with President Nasser in an attempt to restore diplomatic relations and gain a foothold in the Egyptian camp.

Although the British government found it undesirable to take any overt action on the gas issue, the House of Commons, as in many other situations, proved to be a voice of conscience. In reply to a question in the House on 4 July, George Thomson, the former Minister of State, said that there had been 'well-substantiated reports' on the use of gas in Yemen. 'Both a mustard gas type and a choking gas have been used on different occasions,' he said. However, in response to a motion introduced by Duncan Sandys, the former Conservative Minister of Colonial Affairs, deploring the 'continued use of poison gas by Egyptian forces in Yemen' and calling on the government to raise the matter urgently at the United Nations, Mr George Brown said that he considered it was not for Britain but for an Arab country to raise this matter.

In a continuing exchange of letters between Duncan Sandys and George Brown, the Foreign Secretary said that he could find no government prepared to censure Egypt. He did not say what governments he had approached at the United Nations regarding the use of gas in the Yemen. Mr Sandys replied asking why Britain had not taken the lead. 'Should Britain be afraid to speak alone for humanity?' he asked.

Mr Brown's letter of reply, dated 15 September, said: 'While all the governments we have approached deplore the United Arab Republic's use of gas, they all seem to feel they have compelling reasons of national interest for not publicly taking the lead in censuring the U.A.R.' Mr Brown went on to point out that the situation in the Middle East and in Yemen had been 'very greatly altered' by decisions taken at the Arab 'summit conference' in Khartoum at the end of August. There, King Faisal and President Nasser had agreed that Egyptian forces would be withdrawn from Yemen and Saudi aid would cease. 'The chances of this agreement being carried out seem to be high,' Mr Brown wrote. 'In the light of this I think the chances of getting any government to attack the U.A.R. in the United Nations for its use of poison gas in the Yemen are nil. Indeed, to raise the matter now would almost certainly be counter-productive.'

The House of Commons debate, stretching over several months, was accompanied by publication of some authoritative letters in *The Times*. The most important of these, published on 14 July, was written by David Smiley. It ran as follows:

Sir, – In July, 1963, I wrote you a letter,[1] which you published, drawing attention to the fact that the Egyptians were dropping poison gas bombs in the Yemen. It was not until May this year, nearly four years later, that the International Red Cross issued a statement that their delegates had evidence that poison gas was being used in the Yemen.

During May this year there were 13 bombing attacks with poison gas bombs and on June 5 and 6, the same days on which Egypt has complained to the United Nations of Israeli air attacks on herself, Egyptian Ilyushin bombers were dropping poison gas bombs on the Yemen villages of Immed and Boa. I have seen

[1] See page 259.

the most harrowing and gruesome photographs of the victims of one of these attacks taken by a British journalist who was present.

After their defeat by Israel, Egypt transferred most of her aircraft from the Yemen to Egypt, the Yemenis securing a respite of three weeks from bombing attacks. Now, however, the bombers have returned, and since July 1 bombing raids have been almost a daily occurrence, including a raid on July 2 on the village of Bani Saham when poison gas bombs were dropped killing 45 people, including women, children, and a great number of animals.

Last week Mr Brown, the Foreign Secretary, stated in the House of Commons that he considered it was not for the United Kingdom to raise this matter at the United Nations, but that it should be raised by one of the Arab countries.

Saudi Arabia has, on more than one occasion, informed the United Nations of Egyptian poison gas attacks in the Yemen, but no action has resulted. It is most unlikely that any Arab country would now raise a subject to embarrass Egypt at a time when they are all demonstrating solidarity with Egypt against Israel.

I returned from the Yemen a few days ago, where I have seen the surviving victims of poison gas bombs. There I have been continually asked by Yemenis why the United Nations choose to ignore these attacks, while Israel and the United States are criticized for their attacks with conventional weapons.

The use of poison gas is forbidden under the Geneva Convention. One would have thought that the more voices raised at the United Nations in condemnation of this type of warfare, the more chance there would be of world opinion forcing Egypt to abandon this inhumane method of killing innocent Yemeni civilians.

Yours truly, David Smiley.

Smiley's letter was followed by a letter from Lord Dalkeith. He wrote in *The Times* on 17 July: 'That such an atrocity can be perpetrated against innocent Arab civilians by a nation with a supposedly enlightened régime seems almost incredible. That no one should raise a protest at the U.N. save Saudi Arabia, whose muted whispers were ignored, seems still more incredible. Yet this is not for lack of evidence from the International Red Cross and

YEMEN: THE UNKNOWN WAR

other sources.' Observing that he understood why no Arab state wished to rock the boat of Arab unity, he asked why Mr Wilson did not 'send a gritty, purposeful message of protest to President Nasser, even if only to show that the British sense of justice is not yet dead'.

In an editorial comment on 22 July *The Times* condemned the Egyptian use of gas in Yemen as 'disgusting' and 'full of menace'. It noted that although Egypt had not used gas against Israel the Israelis had recognized the possibility by ordering gas masks from Germany. The value of gas as a weapon for Egypt, *The Times* observed, was that it could be 'economically and effectively employed against remote centres of royalist opposition where troops and civilians have no means to counter it, and little to record it'.

While one must acknowledge the voices that were briefly raised in protest against the use of gas in Yemen, I believe that in general there is validity in the complaint which I heard from Neil McLean about 'the conspiracy of silence' in the world on this subject. Indeed, the issue has been quickly forgotten in the world's press and the United Nations. It may be that Europeans do not really care very much what happens to non-Europeans when their own interests are unaffected, and that among non-Europeans it is unfashionable to condemn the inhuman acts committed by Africans and Asians against one another. In the particular case of Yemen I have found that the world does not easily heed the voice of the royalists; against the background of centuries of fearsome imamic cruelty the royalists have even less moral credit in the world than their Nasserite tormentors.

But in addition to morality there is also a question of law. The use of gas has been outlawed by a long series of treaties, beginning with the Treaty of Versailles of 1918 which prohibited the use of 'asphyxiating, poisonous and other gases'. This provision was reaffirmed by the treaties of St Germain of 1919, Trianon of 1920, Washington, 1922, and finally by the Geneva Protocol of 1925, which was signed by forty nations. Egypt ratified the Geneva Protocol in 1928.

But in the final analysis perhaps neither the world's opinion, nor morality, nor law can determine the course of a conflict such as the one in Yemen. This is fundamentally an Arab war, a quarrel between two incompatible Arab systems. They are ideological systems and power systems. One need only point to the contrast between King Faisal's policy of gradual reform of the traditional system and the relatively revolutionary character of President Nasser's system; the contrast, also, between the Egyptian longing for access to the oil wealth of the Middle East and Saudi Arabia's abhorrence of the Egyptian presence on the Arabian peninsula. The Yemen war has been fought – and the Yemenis have been gassed – only partly because of Yemen. More of the struggle has been due to the rivalry between Egypt and Saudi Arabia. The fact that the Egyptians used gas is the measure of that rivalry.

XX

From Jeddah to Khartoum

BETWEEN the time of the Jeddah agreement in August 1965 and the Khartoum agreement of August 1967, Nasser lost the war for Yemen. But Nasser's enemies did not necessarily win it. The Jeddah agreement called for Egyptian withdrawal; the Egyptian president signed it under very real pressure, militarily from the royalists in Yemen, politically from the increasingly disaffected republicans. But Nasser appears to have signed that agreement tongue in cheek. He still believed he could achieve his aims on the Arabian peninsula.

The Khartoum agreement was quite another story; it followed the disaster of the June war with Israel. Nasser could no longer afford the dispersion of his energies in Yemen. But there was more to it than that: a variety of pressures had been building up against him which, as we shall see, might well have forced him out of Yemen even if there had been no war with Israel. These pressures were exerted by events in Britain and South Arabia, in Saudi Arabia and among the Yemeni royalists, and inside the Yemeni republic.

Between Jeddah, 1965, and Khartoum, 1967, two distinct periods emerge. The first is a period of Egyptian equivocation characterized by Egypt's 'long breath policy' (a phrase invented by the Egyptians themselves). Although frustrated, the Egyptians still had hopes, but they could not decide what line to follow. They had allowed the liberal Ahmed Mohamed Nomaan free rein as Prime Minister for ten weeks up to 10 July, but then had replaced him with General Hassan Amri, a reliable, tough pro-Egyptian who was no friend of reconciliation. Amri showed his colours by helping to break up the Haradh conference, the great meeting of sheikhs and notables which strove between late November and the end of the year to implement the Jeddah agreement. He flew down to the conference in person, although he was not a delegate. Immaculately tailored, and, as always, twirling his military baton, he strode into the tent where the sheikhs were arguing and declared contemptuously: 'Nothing is happening, why don't you go home?'

In October 1965 Amri became acting President as well as Prime Minister upon the departure of President Sallal, who went into a political eclipse in Cairo which lasted until August 1967. Certainly the Egyptians had reason to be dissatisfied with their man in Sana; Sallal was dull, lacking in popularity and not very competent, and they had already agreed, just before Nomaan took over, to the dilution of his powers by a seven-man presidential council. There was also, I believe, a personal, unwritten agreement between King Faisal and President Nasser at the Alexandria meeting which preceded Jeddah, to seek a convenient moment on each side to withdraw both President Sallal and the Imam al Badr, whose joint presence had come to symbolize irreconcilability. The availability of Amri as acting President enabled President Nasser to evade the intent of the deal.

The counterpart of Sallal's eclipse was the withdrawal of Imam al Badr to Taif, the summer resort in the mountains near Jeddah, in April 1966. Al Badr had shown himself in quite vigorous health, touring the royalist areas during the period preceding the Haradh conference; he even moved to a new headquarters at Adh-Dhahr, south-east of Jabal Razih, in the province of Khawlan ibn Amr. Now he was declared to be ill. He went into the hospital at Taif for treatment of the chronic nephritis which had in fact troubled him for years.

As he withdrew, the Imam declared his youthful cousin Prince Hassan bin Hassan 'deputy general of the Imam'. The prince, who was not yet thirty years old, boldly shifted his headquarters back to the Jabal Qara caves which Imam al Badr had abandoned during the Egyptian offensive of August 1964. He began to busy himself not only with military but with civil matters, reorganizing administration, opening schools and resuming the collection of taxes.

The reorganization of leadership on the royalist side was carried a step further in August 1966 when the Imam al Badr and a council of princes and notables, meeting at Taif with King Faisal as their guest, established an imamic council, making the imamate a limited monarchy, as provided by the royalist draft constitution of 1964. Prince Hassan bin Hassan gave up his title as deputy general of the

Imam, but remained military commander of the western region of Yemen.

The Prime Minister, Prince Hassan bin Yahya, assumed the title of deputy general, as seemed appropriate in recognition of his age and the fact that he had already held the title of Imam during the first days of the revolution when al Badr was believed dead. But the new arrangements also recognized the fact that the real power was now in the hands of Prince Mohamed bin Hussein, Commander-in-Chief of the eastern region, who became deputy President of the new Council of Ten, over which he was to preside in the absence of the Imam. From this time many of the royalists thought of the irrepressible young Prince Mohamed as Imam, because he was certain to succeed al Badr if the royalists should succeed. Sometimes he himself was called 'deputy Imam' although the title had been given to his uncle, Prince Hassan.

If the withdrawal of Imam al Badr to Taif had indeed been the counterpart of the withdrawal of Sallal, the royalists had also evaded the intent of the deal. Now it was Prince Mohamed bin Hussein, firmly based with his semi-regulars in the Jawf, against acting President and Prime Minister Hassan al Amri, in Sana.

Under the impulsive leadership of Prince Mohamed, the royalist conference also took a step of a different nature, which deeply antagonized cautious King Faisal. It decided, and so informed the Saudi government, to open a general offensive. In Beirut thereafter, Prince Abdurrahman bin Yahya told correspondents that the offensive would begin in mid-November.

King Faisal was angry. He and the prince quarrelled. Apart from the general unwisdom of telegraphing military intentions in advance, the King had very substantial reasons for not wanting the royalists to resume fighting or do anything that might provoke the Egyptians.

The first of his reasons was that he did not feel he needed the royalists as much as he had in the first years of the war for Yemen, when Egyptian threats against Saudi Arabia seemed to carry more weight. Now Saudi Arabia was in all respects better equipped to cope with the Egyptian threat. Internally there had been reforms to ease the pressure of Islamic law and Wahabi custom on the lives of ordinary people; internationally, in his extensive travels, the King had cemented relations with the Shah of Iran, King Hassan of Morocco, King Hussein of Jordan, President Bourguiba of Tunisia, and President Johnson of the United States.

Above all, he was, or would soon be, strengthened militarily. In December 1965 Saudi Arabia had already negotiated a package deal with Britain and the United States for the purchase of about $400 million-worth of British aircraft and United States Hawk missiles. When, on 22 February 1966, the British government issued its White Paper announcing Britain's intention to withdraw from Aden by 1968, King Faisal decided that his whole programme needed to be stepped up. Withdrawal of the British, though much to be desired from an ideal Arab point of view, would upset the balance of power in the Arabian peninsula. The King would be coping with the Egyptians on the peninsula almost by himself. He first asked the United States government if it could speed up the installation of Hawk missiles. The answer was 'No'. He then turned to the British, who agreed to a 'crash' programme to install thirty-seven mobile Thunderbird ground-to-air missiles and to put into operation ten jet fighters at a base near the Yemen frontier. The installation was nearly completed by the end of September. In the absence of trained Saudis, British pilots were on hand to fly the jets—whether they would fly in combat against raiding Egyptian aircraft was a point on which Saudi and British authorities preferred to remain vague. My information was that they would: they were mercenaries like any others, and their activities would not necessarily involve the British government.

A second and even more persuasive reason for King Faisal's opposition to a royalist offensive was that the Egyptians had in fact been withdrawing their troops from eastern and northern Yemen since the beginning of the year; as long as they were moving back, it seemed unwise to interfere. This was the 'long breath policy'—as already mentioned, the salient characteristic of the period following the Jeddah conference. It had developed throughout the spring and summer and was about to be replaced by a more aggressive policy; but King Faisal could not have known that at the time of the royalists' conference in Taif.

In March the Egyptians had withdrawn from al Hazm, their last stronghold in the Jawf, after persuading Prince Mohamed, somewhat against his better judgment, to give them safe conduct. In the same month they had given up Sirwah, with its two forts, in eastern Yemen, which the royalists had been harassing from time to time ever since December 1962. In April they left Sadah, and in May 1966 the royalists could reasonably say that the entire north and east of Yemen was in their hands. Only at Sadah a republican garrison remained; the royalists refrained from forcing their way into the town for fear of provoking Egyptian bombing.

The reasoning behind the Egyptians' 'long breath' strategy was that, by concentrating in a smaller, more defensible area they would be able to cut their losses and costs and in the end achieve their aims more effectively. I believe that the British government's White Paper of 22 February 1966, announcing final withdrawal from Aden 'by 1968', brought a new dimension into President Nasser's calculations. The British intention, largely brought about by Britain's domestic economic problems, was made to his order. He had long opposed the British in Aden and South Arabia and was already using Taiz, in southern Yemen, as a base for nationalists fighting the British. Now Aden and South Arabia became the principal objective; under cover of the 'long breath' strategy he would shift his sights from north to south. If he could get out of the troublesome royalist area and isolate it, he might yet hold the parts of republican Yemen contiguous to South Arabia, take credit for the British withdrawal, and gain a foothold in Aden for further adventures on the periphery, if not the heart of the Arabian peninsula.

To cover his change of strategy, the Egyptian President blustered a day after the British White Paper that he was willing to stay in Yemen for twenty years if that were necessary for the preservation of the republic. On 22 March he added that if any foreign troops were to invade Yemen (presumably the Saudis) his armed forces would 'destroy the bases of aggression' (Jizan and Najran?). On 1 May he declared that Jizan and Najran were really part of Yemen, and that Egypt was prepared to march with the Yemeni republic to liberate them.

All this King Faisal knew, and some of it he said to the royalist leaders gathered in Taif in August 1966. It was, he concluded emphatically, not the time for a royalist offensive or for talking about one. The King proceeded to give his impulsive Yemeni friends a practical demonstration of the power of the man who holds the purse strings. A few days after his extraordinary row with Prince Mohamed, he departed on another of his international tours without signing the order for monthly payments to the royalists. Suddenly the royalists were without money. Worse, word reached them that Saudi agents were busy making contact in Yemen with the sheikhs of the tribes in the areas the Egyptians were evacuating, and were liberally dispensing the gifts and promises of future munificence which are the stock in trade of the Saudi government's tribal relations.

The war for Yemen might have ended at that point. But Prince Mohamed bin Hussein was sure of himself and his cause. He had a sense of his own tribesmen's psychology which was necessarily more intimate than Faisal's. It was expressed by one of the princes in the phrase: 'If we don't fight, we will die.' He knew that a tribal force and even his own relatively disciplined semi-regulars could not be held together indefinitely without action. Even money would not be enough. There must be excitement and the prospect of loot. It would never do to let the Egyptians simply withdraw without harassment from the parts of Yemen they no longer wanted; if the royalists were to regain power they must crowd the Egyptians every inch of the way, snapping at their heels. Prince Mohamed also had a personal sense of the Egyptians' intentions and weaknesses derived from a meeting about which King Faisal may, just possibly, not have been informed, for it was very secret.

During the period between the Jeddah and Haradh conferences, late in 1965, the Egyptians had, through intermediaries, approached Prince Mohamed and asked him if he would meet Marshal Abdul Hakim Amer in Paris to discuss the peaceful withdrawal of the Egyptians. The Egyptians wanted to get their men out of the deserts and mountains of the north and east without losses and embarrassment. Beyond that, the Egyptians were interested in finding out what kind of a general settlement they might be able to make with the royalists behind the Saudis' backs; and Prince Mohamed was understandably curious to know what they might offer.

In due course in a Paris hotel, Marshal Amer asked Prince Mohamed if he could 'become a republican'; he implied that, if the prince could see his way clear to such a metamorphosis, there would be a place for him as president of a Yemeni republic. Prince Mohamed replied by asking whether the Egyptians would agree to the preservation of the imamate; he implied that he would be a candidate, in due course, for Imam. The conversation got nowhere, and the question of peaceful withdrawal of Egyptian troops remained unsettled. Although Prince Mohamed did later agree, in talks with local Egyptian commanders, to an unmolested withdrawal of the last Egyptians from the Jawf, he was in general convinced that the Egyptians would never voluntarily withdraw from Yemen, and that the royalists must for their own good maintain maximum pressure at all times.

Therefore, without asking King Faisal's leave, Prince Mohamed proceeded on his own international tour, in pursuit of funds for the offensive which he deemed essential. He flew to Shah Pahlevi of Persia and then to King Hussein of Jordan, both of whom had no small differences with President Nasser. From both he received promises of help. The Shah later sent a quantity of arms, and King Hussein discussed sending a training mission to Amara, the royalist base camp in the Jawf. The prince flew on to Europe, to Rome, Paris, Bonn and London, and sent word back to Saudi Arabia that he did not intend to return until Saudi aid had been restored. He could not believe, he said, that the King really meant to humiliate the Hamid Eddin family before the tribesmen of their country; that he really meant to cut off supplies to the royalist territories at a time when Yemen had suffered two years of drought and many villagers faced starvation.

In the end King Faisal, although still furious, relented, and Prince Mohamed returned to Riyadh, the Saudi capital, in October. Ahmed al Shami, the royalist Foreign Minister and Rashad Pharaon, one of the King's most trusted advisers, were the peace-makers. But the King insisted that if Saudi aid was to continue there must be united action by all concerned. The royalists must co-operate with the 'third force' of dissident republicans and of tribesmen who were anti-Egyptian but not royalist.

Reasonable as this policy would seem, King Faisal's insistence may have reflected a personal distaste for the Hamid Eddin family. The Hamid Eddin were under no illusion about the King's feelings; but they were convinced that, the Saudis' new armaments programme and intrigues with the third force notwithstanding, the royalists would remain essential to Saudi interests in Yemen, that the King could never wholly drop them.

Negotiations with the third force, whose spokesman was Ibrahim al Wazir, dragged on in Riyadh through December, January and February 1967 and culminated in an agreement which went into effect on 12 March 1967. It was little more than a re-statement of the 'all for one, one for all' principle of the Taif agreement of 10 August 1965, and probably had little effect on the course of events. The third force was an interesting political idea but it lacked organized following and carried no weight militarily.

No more was there any practical consequence of negotiations in October 1966 between the Saudis and representatives both of royalists and of the federal government of South Arabia. Ahmed al Shami proposed a council composed of two Saudis, two royalists and two representatives of the South Arabian federation. This council would form a single front against the Egyptians and their creatures, the Yemeni republicans and the terrorist organizations of South Arabia, the NLF (National Liberation Front) and FLOSY (Front for the Liberation of Occupied South Yemen). It was a plausible idea, which might have had far-reaching consequences had the South Arabian federal government lasted. No one could imagine then that less than a year later all the sixteen sheikhdoms and sultanates which formed Aden's hinterland in the federation would have disappeared like dust before the wind of a revolutionary onslaught by the National Liberation Front.

As the Egyptians receded under cover of their 'long breath', the royalists moved forward into a sadly ruined land. As the fighting had shifted back and forth across the landscape since the *coup* of September 1962, Egyptian bombers had done their work all too well. Wilfred Thesiger, who has been called the last of the great British Arabists, was a witness of this during long months of travel that spring and summer. By camel and on foot he went from the Imam's cave deep into the western mountains, then north of Sada across to the east, to the desert fringe, and up into the mountains of Khawlan, where he could look down on the lights of Sana. 'Most of the towns and villages which I visited,' he wrote in *The Times*, 'had been bombed, and many were in ruins. At Mabian not a single house was undamaged and most were utterly destroyed; several other towns, such as Sudah and Saqain, had suffered nearly as badly.' In the town of Mahabishah he learned that more than seventy people had been killed when the mosque was bombed at prayer time. 'The Egyptians have used mustard gas and a blinding gas extensively,' he reported, 'and I saw a number of people who had been permanently blinded by them.'

These people asked only to be allowed to rebuild their villages and heal their wounds. But it was not to be. The most ferocious Egyptian onslaught of all was yet to come. It was the second of the two distinct periods between Jeddah and Khartoum, and might be called 'the wave of anger'. The wave began with the return of President Sallal to Yemen in August 1966, and ended at last with the overthrow of Sallal on 5 November 1967. It involved some of the most vicious bombing of the war, including the most widespread gas bombing. It involved an angry purge of the republican government, civil service and army, mass dismissals, arrests, trials and executions. It also involved an anti-American campaign directed especially at the aid mission. It was as though the Egyptians had sensed in the 'long breath' not just a change of strategic concepts, but the breath of defeat. They were angered by the need to abandon the rocks and sands of northern and eastern Yemen where they had expended so much blood and treasure; angered also by the Yemeni republicans' increasing claims to independence. Their anger welled up in a paroxysm of violence on every front.

It was the increasing claims to independence by the acting President and Prime Minister, General Hassan al Amri, that sparked the change in Egyptian mood. Once so pro-Egyptian, the general had fallen more and more into league with the liberals, among whom the three most outstanding were Ahmed Mohamed Nomaan (the former Premier), Qadi Abdurrahman al Iryani and Mohamed Ali Uthman. Allied with them were Ali Seif al Khawlani, the Chief of Staff, and Hussein al Dafai, the Minister of the Interior.

Handsome in his tailored uniforms, General al Amri had a well-developed sense of his own importance. Egyptian authorities in Cairo had deeply offended him in the spring of 1966 by preventing him from making a call on the visiting Soviet Premier Kosygin. Clearly the Egyptians did not want any independent deals between the Russians and the Yemenis. Then there was the affair of the armoured cars which General al Amri had ordered directly from East Germany. The Egyptian command coolly informed him that they would take charge of the cars and make them available as they were needed. Disgusted, the general cancelled the deal.

When General al Amri heard of the plan to send Sallal back to his post as Prime Minister he protested to Cairo. But in vain; President Sallal returned on 12 August. Desperately, General al Amri sent a military force to Sana airport to prevent his landing, but it was headed off by the Egyptian army. During the next ten days al Amri came close to insurrection. He withdrew with some of his supporters to al Urdi barracks and attempted from there, unsuccessfully, to send out parties to seize control of the radio station and to enlist the support of the Bani Matar tribe west of Sana. He sent a message to

Aden to be broadcast from radio Aden calling for a meeting of the consultative council.

Finally the Prime Minister, whose powers were quickly pre-empted by President Sallal, attempted to leave the country. He flew to Taiz, apparently in an attempt to get aboard the Ethiopian Airlines plane to Asmara and to fly from there to put his case before the United Nations in New York; but the Egyptians did not let him get beyond Taiz. As a last resort Premier al Amri, who was now little more than a prisoner of the Egyptians, asked to go to Cairo to put his case to President Nasser. His request was granted and he departed with a large retinue of liberals who had become his associates by virtue of their common opposition to President Sallal's return. These were headed by former Premier Nomaan and Qadi al Iryani. But in Cairo neither President Nasser nor any other top-ranking official would see them. After a few days they found themselves under house arrest, doomed to remain in Cairo indefinitely.

In Sana President Sallal set about consolidating his position by bringing to the top men who had shown him constant and un-questioning loyalty, and by ruthlessly purging the combination of al Amri's men and liberals who had opposed his return. As his deputy Premier and deputy commander of the armed forces he named Abdullah Juzailan, a man who had played a big role in the first days of the revolution by rallying tribal support. Juzailan's rank went up from brigadier to major-general. Mohamed Ahnoumi, possibly the most ruthless man in the new government, was promoted from colonel to brigadier and became Minister of the Interior. Abdul Latif Dayfallah, another stalwart, was also boosted from colonel to brigadier and got the post of Minister of Public Works.

After General al Amri had, finally, telegraphed his resignation from Cairo on 17 September, the new régime maintained civilities until after the anniversary of the revolution on 26 September. Then it began to wield the axe. Fifty high-ranking individuals in army and government were arrested immediately; by 14 October the number had risen to 200. A people's court headed by Brigadier Ahnoumi himself conducted a secret trial of fifteen individuals including Colonel Mohamed al Ruwainy, a former Minister of Tribal Affairs who had served as acting President during the absences of Sallal and al Amri, and Colonel Hadi Issa, deputy Chief of the General Staff. They were accused of high treason involving contacts in particular with American intelligence, which had allegedly paid Ruwainy

$20,000 as a first instalment on a $100,000 bribe for which he was to overthrow President Sallal. According to the prosecution, the whole group were related, in one way or another, to a series of incidents which had included a bazooka raid on President Sallal's house on 1 October. Other incidents were bazooka attacks on the Egyptian headquarters, the radio station and the Soviet embassy, and two explosions outside the capital's principal cinema. (It seems probable that some of these incidents were in fact the work of Kassim Munassir, a Robin Hood-type royalist raider who was apparently based in the territory of the Bani Hushaysh tribe to the east of the capital.) The people's court sentenced eight of the accused to death and the other seven to long prison terms. Those condemned to death were loaded into a truck and driven to Shararah square on the morning of 25 October. They were told to kneel on the ground— beneath the flags, as it happened, of the United Nations — and they were executed, one by one, by spurts of fire from a sub-machine-gun.

Scores of lesser trials followed a similar course. Hundreds of people in all walks of life were arrested and held without trial. They included a former Chief of Staff, a former Minister of the Interior and a former chief of propaganda. The lucky merely lost their jobs. The purge continued into the first months of 1967. It produced a surge of fugitives, some of whom actually joined the royalists, some of whom found safe havens in Aden or Beirut, and a great many of whom disappeared among the uncommitted tribes in the parts of Yemen from which the Egyptians had withdrawn.

Some who escaped through tribal territory told horrifying tales of a mounting Egyptian campaign of bombing, including the use of gas, which began during the last quarter of 1966. The bombing was probably formally intended to maintain Egyptian control over the territories from which Egyptian ground forces had withdrawn. The Egyptians may have told themselves that they were using the same methods that the British had employed for decades against the remote tribes of South Arabia and the Hadhramaut. But I think the raids more than anything reflected the Egyptians' growing sense of frustration, as they felt their grip on this primitive country slipping away.

On 14 and 15 October 1966, Najran and Jizan were bombed once again. On 19 October the night bombing of the Jawf (reminiscent of 1962-63) was resumed with flares as the Egyptians sought to destroy supply convoys. On 20 October the town of Mahabishah was also again heavily bombed, with 100 persons reported killed. On 26 and 28 October the al Haymatain tribe in the mountains north of the Sana-Hodeidah road suffered especially heavy raids. And so it went on through the autumn, winter and spring of 1967.

A by-product of the purge was an angry anti-American campaign. One did not have to look far for the reasons. Apart from their pro-Soviet, pro-Egyptian, socialistic orientation, which would have inclined them against free-enterprise America in any case, the Yemeni republicans resented the United States' support of Saudi Arabia. It was easy for them to convince themselves that American recognition of the republic had been nothing but a sham, and that the United States was attempting through Saudi Arabia to destroy the republic. The point was illustrated by a collection of American weapons captured from the royalists on display in Sana.

Then there was the unpopularity of the dusty American road, to which we will come later. Yemeni officials also resented the refusal of the United States to move its economic aid through Egyptian channels. The United States, having obtained the right to use the port of Mocha from the Imam in 1961, stuck to this route and refused to submit to Egyptian control. In consequence the Egyptian-trained or -inspired officials of the republic subjected the Americans to every possible harassment. They were obliged to submit every scrap of equipment to three checks, security, customs, and finally the economics ministry. When the American embassy was moved to Sana at the beginning of 1967, every piece of furniture had to be inspected even though it had been in Yemen for years. The American diplomatic pouch was held at one time for six weeks while Yemeni officials argued about the maximum permissible size of pouches.

After President Sallal's return in August Yemeni security began picking up local employees of the American aid mission and of the American embassy, questioning and in some cases imprisoning them. One of the victims was an American of Lebanese origin named Michel Harriz, who had lived in Yemen since 1958 and had built up a small contracting business frequently used by Americans and the American aid mission. Without explanation he was expelled from the country on seventy-two hours' notice.

In another case a young man who worked in a ward of a Taiz hospital, who had taken some American-sponsored English lessons, was brought to court apparently on suspicion of having perpetrated a bazooka attack on the new Russian school at Taiz. He accused his English teacher, Mrs Dorothy Stewart, wife of an American water engineer who had been in Yemen for eight years, of recruiting spies at the American language centre. But the accusation was so ridiculous in the eyes of the large number of Yemenis who knew this shy and gentle lady that the authorities dropped this particular charge and sent the young man back to work in his hospital.

While I was in Sana Yemeni authorities began to put a guard in front of the American library; attendance dropped from 200 per day to zero.

When I went to see President Sallal in March 1967, he said that he would welcome a great deal of American aid but that unfortunately he had had to arrest some aid mission employees as spies. He was replying to a question about a statement he had made in the preceding month that 'there is no value in Point Four[1]; we can do without their aid and say goodbye to them'. Now he repeated a line I had heard from General al Amri when he was serving his first term as Premier in 1963, namely, that the American road was a gift to the Imam, and that he was still eager to know what the Americans proposed to give the republic.

After I had spent an hour interviewing Minister of the Interior Mohamed Ahnoumi, I felt I had better understood the psychology behind the anti-American campaign. Here was a man who was reputed to have a wide range of complexes. Son of a poor, non-tribal family in the Tihama coastal strip, he was said to hate rich men, including those among his fellows who boasted of the tribal or aristocratic background esteemed by Yemenis; a dark, swarthy man, he was said to resent those who were fair-skinned. While much of this may be unjust, when I met him I found him crouched behind his desk like a leopard about to spring, unsmiling and fingering a small string of beads. His demeanour was menacing. Asked about the number of executions, he replied there had been seventeen, but fifty cases remained to be investigated. 'Don't be afraid,' he said, 'we don't kill except in the service of our country.'

My visit to Sana in March 1967 gave me an opportunity to observe the republic during the final period before President Sallal's overthrow and the final withdrawal of the Egyptians. I formed the opinion that the régime had been gravely compromised

[1] This refers to Point Four of President Truman's 1947 inaugural address, in which he proposed a programme of foreign technical assistance.

by its association with the Egyptians and by the purge, but that nonetheless the republic had gained in substance since I visited it for the first time in 1963. The vested interest in preservation of the republic now extended to a considerable bureaucracy and to an army of some 7,000 men. Beyond that, the revolution had affected a wide range of people both socially and economically. The old sayed class of those who claimed descent from the prophet and who monopolized the government services under the imamate was now broken. This was a social revolution of a kind; few indeed except the sayeds would want to undo it.

On the economic front the régime had done little that was revolutionary or remarkable; but a good deal had been done for the régime in the way of foreign aid. Outstanding in this respect were the new roads driven through the mountain wilderness thanks to Chinese, Russian and American enterprise. While these had been begun in the time of the Imam Ahmed, with whom the Chinese agreed to build the road from Hodeidah to Sana and the Americans the road from Mocha through Taiz to Sana, it was the republic that felt their economic and social impact. Leaving aside the military significance of the Chinese road—it was this which enabled the Egyptians to wage their campaign for five long years—it was the roads which began to open up this land, lost for centuries in medieval isolation. Where the roads went, went vehicles, people, goods, new ideas. Tribesmen who had never been outside their own valleys now hitched rides to Sana and gawked at the important luxuries from Aden in the shops, went to the movies, relaxed under the bright lights of the cafés and resolved to become city-dwellers. The sheikhs in the village could never make the old virtues competitive with the lure of what seemed like modern life in the town. There were young people who saw in the towns an opportunity to escape the restrictive life of their village, to get an education and to make themselves modern men. This, indeed, was the trump card played by the republic, by the Egyptians who backed the republic and by the Russians who backed Egypt. It was also my own strongest impression of its achievement.

One afternoon, the Minister of Education received me at his house just after his afternoon sleep. Although he seemed an implausible figure, shuffling out from his bedroom in bare feet, red nightcap and heavy woollen sweater, he recited some impressive statistics, perhaps the most important ones in the republic. He said there were now 225 Egyptian teachers in the country, 25 Iraqis and 3 Syrians. In addition to launching general primary education in hundreds of villages (he offered no exact figures), 3 vocational schools had been opened and 4 more planned, divided between Sana, Taiz and Hodeidah. About 2,000 students had been sent abroad, more than 1,000 to Egypt, 900 to the Soviet Union, 6 to the United States, 1 to Britain. To the credit of the United States there were also 50 in Lebanon, mostly financed by the United States.

Later I visited one of the new girls' schools, where a young Egyptian woman marvelled at the quickness with which her charges were learning. Some of the girls hastily drew on their veils as I entered; others wore starchy school uniforms and smiled eagerly, and one of them got up and declaimed: It is an honour for us that you visit us. In the time of the Imam women lived in darkness. They stayed behind four walls and never saw the light.'

An American embassy official estimated that, with 90,000 out of 700,000 children of primary school age now at school Yemen was expanding as fast as was possible. The biggest contributor to primary education was Kuwait. Hungary and Bulgaria had each contributed model schools. The three secondary schools contributed thus far by the Soviet Union looked impressive with large expanses of plate glass, laboratories and hard wooden floors for basketball.

Hand-in-hand with expanding education went economic developments. Here it may be interesting to take the countries one by one.

The West Germans, formerly active commercially and in an agricultural project in the Tihama, had been thrown out during the general Arab dispute with West Germany over German aid to Israel in 1964. The Italians were there but kept to themselves.

United States aid played an exceptionally important role because the United States was the principal representative of the West in Yemen. The American road, completed late in 1965 at a total cost of $22 million, was a remarkable engineering achievement. Linking the capital, Sana, to the old diplomatic capital at Taiz and the port of Mocha, with a spur to the South Arabian border, it is profoundly affecting the life of the country. But it is sadly unappreciated. Because they calculated, quite rightly, that Yemen could not afford to maintain a hard-topped tarmac road, the Americans, in contrast to the Chinese, gave Yemen a stabilized earth gravel-topped highway. Although it became possible on the American road to travel from Taiz to Sana in four or five hours, a trip which used to take as many days, motorists inevitably arrived at either end covered from head to foot in thick clinging dust. The Yemenis hated it. Furthermore, the thick dust clouds, obscuring visibility on difficult curves in the mountains, made the road dangerous. The Yemenis called it 'the road of death'! They remained unimpressed by American observations that the Chinese Hodeidah-Sana road had, by American standards, ditches that were too shallow, grades that were too high and curves that were too sharp and unbanked; what impressed the Yemenis was the smooth, clean black tarmac.

An American water project for the city of Taiz, known as the John F. Kennedy Memorial water system, proved a greater propaganda success. Completed in 1966 at a cost of nearly $9 million, it made Taiz the first Yemeni town to have plentiful pure piped water. Other towns eagerly clamoured for similar projects: some, such as Yarim, entered into schemes under which they raised half the cost locally as a counterpart to American financial and technical help.

Communist bloc aid agreements in March 1967 added up to between $110 and $118 million. In contrast to American aid, which was strictly a gift, Communist bloc aid, with the exception of certain schools and hospitals, was all to be paid for by the Yemenis. It included an East German loan of $10 million, and a Chinese loan of $28 million for a textile mill and the first stage of a road from Sana to Sadah. In 1966 the Chinese also sent in a team, reportedly as a gift, to repair the severe damage to the Hodeidah-Sana road caused largely by Egyptian tanks. When I visited the Chinese textile mill I found 698 workers, of whom 225 were girls. Opened in December 1966, it was to expand to 1,500 workers and supply all Yemen's internal needs in textiles; it was also providing the first opportunity for women to work in factories in Yemen.

Soviet economic aid to Yemen in March 1967 was in a 'maximum phase', in the words of an American embassy economist. Based on a $72-million, fifteen-year loan agreement, it included the following projects: a road from Hodeidah to Taiz, which was completed towards the end of 1967; a cement plant for which equipment began arriving in April 1967; a cotton project where they were raising a variety of cotton similar to American short staple; a fish freezing plant and cannery at Hodeidah; and a small fishing port. All this was in addition to an active military training programme based at Taiz.

At Hodeidah the Soviet impact could readily be felt. Many Yemenis were learning Russian, Russian and East European goods were in the shops, and Russians and East Europeans walked in the streets. Everywhere new buildings were going up. There were probably about 700 Russians in the country in March 1967, more than half of them military, and the figure increased greatly later. As royalist pressure put an end to economic aid projects, the Russians stepped up military aid.

When the Arab-Israeli war broke out on 5 June 1967, the Egyptians in Yemen were at the end of their tether, under economic strain at home and military pressure in Yemen, frustrated by Saudi military defences, unable to concentrate the contentious South Arabian nationalists, and weary of the whole enterprise. Defeat at the hands of the Israelis gave them the excuse for withdrawal which some among them, including Marshal Abdul Hakim Amer (who committed suicide soon after the June war), had been seeking for several years.

For a few more weeks after the war the air-raids, even the gas raids, went on. Then, on 29 August, began the Khartoum summit conference. Mohamed Riad, Foreign Minister of the United Arab Republic, indicated that his government was willing to revive the Jeddah agreement of August 1965. But the Saudis would have none of it. They saw now an opportunity to force the Egyptians to take the only step that really mattered, namely to withdraw from Yemen, and to leave everything else to the Yemenis to work out their own way. They agreed to halt their own support of the royalists, not when the Egyptians began withdrawing, but when they finished. King Faisal was taking no chances this time. He joined with Kuwait in pledging a subsidy to Egypt to compensate her in part for the loss of Suez canal revenues; but he made his payments payable not monthly but quarterly. An Egyptian delegation which sought, immediately after Khartoum, to obtain monthly instalments, got no sympathy from the Saudis. They made it clear they were waiting until the end of the quarter to see whether the Egyptians really withdrew this time or not. The quarterly subsidy in effect put the Saudis in the position of buying the Egyptians out of Yemen.

To work out the problems that might in other circumstances have been regulated by the Jeddah agreement, the summit conference established a tripartite commission headed by Mohamed Ahmed Mahgoub, Premier of Sudan and moderating member of the group. The others were Ismail Khairallah, acting Foreign Minister of

Iraq, the nominee of Egypt, and Ahmed Laraki, Foreign Minister of Morocco, nominee of Saudi Arabia.

Beginning its work on 17 September, the peace commission flew to Beirut and held two days of conversations with Ahmed al Shami, the royalist Foreign Minister. Al Shami proposed that the first move towards peace must be to convene a conference of 150 to 200 Yemeni leaders of all shades of opinion, from inside or outside Yemen, to choose a sovereignty council of eight men who would head the country as soon as Egyptian troops had withdrawn. In addition, the conference would set up a cabinet of eighteen to twenty-four members and a parliament or deliberative council of about eighty members. This government would, according to al Shami's plan, prepare for democratic 'consultations,' in the form of a plebiscite or elections, to determine the permanent form the government would take.

At its next stop, in Cairo, the commission consulted the Egyptian government which, while raising no objection to al Shami's scheme, took the proper view that details of the transitional régime should be worked out by the Yemenis themselves. The Egyptians also agreed to release a number of Yemenis whom they had kept under house arrest, or, in some cases, in prison, since al Amri's ill-fated attempt to resist the return of President Sallal. General al Amri himself was not immediately released, but Qadi Abdurrahman al Iryani and Ahmed Mohamed Nomaan were set free, and the former, with a large group of his former associates, returned to Sana. But Nomaan, who had been much more roughly treated than his colleagues, perhaps because he was more defiant, went to Beirut for medical treatment.

Meanwhile President Sallal was bursting with indignation. At last he had an issue on which he was prepared to resist the Egyptians, namely, the Egyptians' decision, as it seemed to him, to abandon him, Sallal. He declared his opposition to the whole Khartoum agreement and announced that he would not permit the tripartite commission to visit Sana. Nonetheless, the mission, travelling in the aircraft of the Commander-in-Chief of the Egyptian armed forces, General Mohamed Fawzi, managed to arrive in Sana. As the word got around that they had arrived, a menacing crowd, encouraged, no doubt, by the highest republican officials in the land, gathered at the Egyptian headquarters and began throwing rocks. The Egyptians guarding the building opened fire, killing two Yemenis and wounding others. At the sound of gunfire the crowd went mad. It rampaged through the streets, grabbing any Egyptian it could find: according to some accounts, nearly thirty Egyptians were killed.

Horrified, the tripartite mission fled from Yemen after only eighteen hours. Travelling via Cairo, it flew to Saudi Arabia to see King Faisal, and from him it heard a general endorsement of the royalist proposals. The King also suggested that the mission take advantage of its presence in Saudi Arabia to meet Imam Mohamed al Badr at Taif. Having consulted President Sallal, the King argued, they should consult his opposite number, the Imam. In view of the Imam's semi-retirement the King also suggested they might like to go to royalist Yemen to see the deputy Imam, Prince Mohamed bin Hussein. But the mission refused point-blank. They had already heard royalist views in Beirut, they said. After their experience in Sana they were disinclined to return to Yemen at all, let alone the wilds of the Jawf under the aegis of an unrecognized and indubitably violent prince. The mission's reluctance suggested a certain bias, which seemed ironical in the light of the republic's fierce opposition to the commission and all its works.

In Sana certain army officers had submitted an ultimatum in fifteen points to the government on 3 October, the day of the mission's arrival. It excoriated the government's corruption, inefficiency and dictatorial practices, and demanded the formation of a new and representative cabinet. The President accepted all these demands, but it was no use. His fate had been sealed from the day that Egyptian withdrawal became a certainty, and President Sallal was not slow to realize it. The Egyptians had announced that they would finally and irrevocably withdraw between 1 and 15 December.

On 3 November President Sallal departed from Sana, ostensibly to attend the fiftieth anniversary of the Russian revolution in Moscow. Before he left, he sent to Qadi Abdurrahman al Iryani a letter which read as follows:

Dear Brother,
I am writing this message for two reasons. Firstly because I do not want to leave my good country except in the knowledge that I will be leaving it in good hands. Secondly because I want to explain a few things which may help to verify to you the truth about my position and feelings.

I am not unaware of what is going on in Sana. I am aware of all the tribal, military and political contacts that are being made to get rid of the régime that I lead. I have learned that the exiled officers and officers of all the services, together with tribesmen, will raid the republican palace and my house and will seize the broadcasting service and stage a *coup d'état* against the régime.

Because I have learned that the force that will move against me is not a small one, and because I am convinced that staying here will lead to bloody fighting between our supporters and our opponents, I have decided to leave Yemen in order to ensure the unity of the people and safeguard their achievements, which have been realized by blood, iron and fire.

I am aware that the military and the tribesmen have chosen you to replace me. I would like to bless their choice so long as you safeguard the republican system and work for the stability, security and peace of the country.

I am aware of sharp criticism aimed at the nature of the relationship between me and our comrades-in-arms, the Egyptians, and I am aware that many mistakes have been made at the expense of a number of men. But any man in my position, who received such a bankrupt legacy from the imamate, and lived under such compelling circumstances, would inevitably have done what I have done.

I would like to inform you that I will not go to Moscow and that I have chosen Baghdad as my new home, for there I spent part of my youth and there I shall spend the rest of my life, wishing our noble people progress, and you success, and our Arab nation happiness.

In fact Sallal broke his journey in Baghdad and there heard news of the *coup d'état* on 5 November. The Iraqi government offered him a home and a monthly grant of 500 dinars.

XXI
The Siege of Sana

FOR one fleeting moment the overthrow of President Sallal and the return of the liberals offered Yemen a chance to grasp at peace. But the new government threw it away.

This new government was headed by a Presidential Council composed of three men: Qadi al Iryani, Ahmed Mohamed Nomaan, and Mohamed Ali Uthman. The Prime Minister was Mohsin al Aini. But Nomaan, ostensibly ill but actually doubtful of the wisdom of the régime of which he was to be part, remained in Beirut.

Nomaan's doubts centred on the refusal of his colleagues (like Sallal before them!) to co-operate with the tripartite commission or to enter into negotiations, direct or indirect, with the Hamid Eddin family. The government took the dogmatic and unrealistic stand that the integrity of the republic required the permanent expulsion of the Hamid Eddin from Yemen. Ignoring the fact that the princes had waged a successful war over a period of five years and simply could not now be dismissed from the scene, it presumed to negotiate only with the leaders of individual tribes from the royalist side. But in Jeddah on 12 November the royalist Foreign Minister gave me this comment on the republican government's attitude: 'If they won't talk to us, we will have to fight them.'

In Beirut, Ahmed Mohamed Nomaan understood the position. He warned on 23 November that the Sana government was 'pushing the country into a new war', and he resigned. His place was immediately taken by Lieutenant-General Hassan al Amri, who had at last been released in Cairo. Returning to Sana he assumed the additional function of Commander-in-Chief.

Prince Mohamed bin Hussein was at the same time mobilizing his forces. While the Egyptian army was leaving Sana and clogging the road to Hodeidah to keep their Khartoum pledge to have all men out by 15 December (and the British in South Arabia were preparing to keep their commitment to withdraw by 30 November), Prince Mohamed was beginning the royalist march on Sana.

For five years the royalists had been talking about marching on Sana. In fact the royalist radio station had announced the encirclement and imminent assault of the capital so often that the world hardly took it seriously any more. But now the admonition Qadi al Sayaghi had uttered in Harib in the first days of that war, to 'crush the head of the snake', was at last being heeded.

Prince Mohamed knew his time was limited. The Saudis had undertaken at Khartoum to cut off financial support of the royalists as soon as the Egyptians had withdrawn; and King Faisal was a man of honour and did not in any case care much for the Hamid Eddin family. The royalists had other sources of financial support though these would not suffice in the long run.

Prince Mohamed was reported to have had the equivalent of $4\frac{1}{2}$ million in hand as he rallied the tribes; the story was that he told the tribal sheikhs: 'You will get your share—in Sana.' The story rang true. It sounded like Prince Mohamed, with a mischievous but very meaningful twinkle in his eye.

The beginning of December 1967 was also the beginning of Ramadan—a poor time for ordinary work, but a great time for Zeidi mountain warriors to gather in the mountains around Sana, roasting their sheep at their camp fires all night, and dreaming all day of the fight to come and the prospect of loot.

Prince Mohamed had taken personal command. He was reported at al Arush, he was reported in Khawlan, he was everywhere, directing the emplacement of guns, organizing a growing force around the hard core of the semi-regulars he had been training since 1964. Town after town around Sana fell to the royalists. They took Amran, fifteen miles north of the capital and occupied mountains fifteen miles to the south-west of the city. They brought sporadic gunfire to bear on Rahabah, the main airfield outside Sana. They cut the road from Sana to Hodeidah on the coast. They sent commando groups up to the walls of the city and even into its streets at night to harass the republicans with bazooka shots at government buildings.

Although Prince Mohamed was reported at one time to have issued a forty-hour ultimatum to the republicans to 'surrender or be annihilated' it looked, as the days of December passed, as though the royalists had decided against or had indefinitely postponed an attempt to rush the capital. They did not wish, perhaps, to risk all in an assault which might be broken by concentrated defensive fire on the plain immediately surrounding the town. An unsuccessful assault could be disastrous to the whole royalist cause. Rather, it seemed, they were following the strategy of the slow squeeze—an old-fashioned siege that might last for many months.

In Sana arms were issued to civilians during the first week of December. Radio Sana issued appeals to the citizens to unite against the 'bloodthirsty mercenaries'. A band of royalist commandos was caught, shot, dragged through the streets and hung at the gates of the city.

The Egyptian, Soviet and other east European embassies withdrew to Hodeidah; so did the personnel of United Nations agencies such as W.H.O. and U.N.I.C.E.F. Foreign Minister Hassan Maaki flew off to Moscow with an urgent plea for help. All signs suggested that the Russians, having made a considerable investment in Yemen, were attempting to protect their investment with last-minute deliveries of aircraft. The republicans boasted that they were putting a new air force into the sky, and the royalists claimed in early December to have shot down a red-haired MiG-17 fighter pilot who had a Russian watch on his wrist and instructions from the Soviet Ministry of Defence in his pocket. Commenting on this claim and reports that twenty-four MiGs and forty Soviet technicians and pilots had arrived in Yemen, the American State Department said they appeared to be 'substantially correct'. The Department deplored this new foreign military intervention which was 'only likely to increase tension in the region'.

In January 1968, when the siege of Sana was more than a month old, the republicans were defending Sana with about 2,000 regulars and tribesmen, plus some armed townsmen, equipped with plentiful artillery and about ten tanks (three had defected to the royalists, half a dozen had been knocked out in combat and another dozen had become mechanically inoperable). They were backed by a score or more fighter aircraft piloted by Russians and by Yemenis who had received hasty one-year courses of instruction in the Soviet Union. Their commander and the absolute ruler of the town was General Hassan al Amri, who had in effect ousted the previous government and established himself as sole authority at the head of a 'war cabinet'. Although the roads to Hodeidah, Taiz and Sadah had been closed by the royalists, the town could still feed itself, meagrely, from the immediately surrounding countryside.

The royalists, pressing in from the surrounding mountains, had 4,000 to 5,000 tribesmen with some military training among a large gathering of purely tribal warriors. While they suffered heavily from republican air power, they enjoyed the advantage of high ground, from which their mortars and recoil-less rifles commanded the town and its airfields. Their problem was logistical. They could, for instance, lay down fire on Rahabah international airport to the north of Sana, but they did not have enough ammunition, and in any case lacked the transport to supply their guns with enough shells to maintain full control.

It was not true, as alleged by radio Sana, that the royalists were at this stage of the war using mercenaries. The last of them had been dismissed at the end of November. The only foreigners among the royalists were two old friends, Lieutenant-Colonel Neil McLean and Wilfred Thesiger. In the matter of mercenaries and foreign aid, the shoe was now on the other republican foot. The Saudis, observing the Khartoum agreement, had halted arms deliveries to the royalists at the end of November and had cut off financial subsidies after the December payment. However, on 4 January, radio Mecca, undoubtedly speaking for King Faisal, threatened to resume military aid to the royalists if the Soviet Union did not halt its support of the republic.

If the royalists were to win in Yemen, it would be victory indeed for all the traditional forces in the Arab world, headed by Saudi Arabia. The oil companies in the Arabian peninsula and the British in their remaining bases at Bahrein and Sharjah in the Persian Gulf would feel more secure. United States and British interest had already been served by removal of the Egyptians from Yemen, which eliminated them as a military threat to Saudi Arabia and South Arabia. A royalist victory would eliminate the further danger of the republic becoming in the Middle East something like Cuba in Latin America—a Soviet political and military base for the political penetration of the Arabian peninsula, or as a staging post on the way to Africa. But the State Department and Foreign Office studiously refrained from acknowledging this argument from their side.

Although the Americans recognized the republic and the British did not, both remained equally embarrassed by any suggestion of association with the supposedly reactionary royalists. In fact, Prince Mohamed bin Hussein does not seek restoration of an autocratic, oppressive imamate; he is a liberal, committed to a limited, constitutional monarchy with an elected legislature according to a draft constitution published by the royalists three years ago.

Examining possibilities from the opposite point of view, it was difficult at the end of 1967 to conceive of a republican victory. After the Egyptian withdrawal from Yemen and the rout of FLOSY, that other creature of the Egyptians, from South Arabia, the Sana government, emasculated by its own purges, did not seem capable of imposing its will in Yemen. The republican army, on the other hand, had shown by the end of the year that it was capable of fighting; it did not, as the royalists had hoped, disintegrate as soon as the Egyptians were gone.

The ideal solution was still, as it was at the moment of President Sallal's overthrow, a compromise between royalists and republicans. A neutral transitional government, in the guise of a 'State of Yemen', might lead to one in which the imamate would be a figure-head. Ahmed Mohamed Nomaan was still available in Beirut to lead the way; there were moderate royalists like Ahmed al Shami and tribal leaders like Naji al Gadr who could appropriately participate in a compromise régime.

Unfortunately reason and moderation seemed too much to hope for. To me it seemed more likely that the royalists would eventually take Sana without achieving victory and that the republicans would make a fighting withdrawal to the southern Shaffei-populated districts and the western coastal plain, where the Zeidi mountaineers would be hard put to follow. I can imagine then an amalgamation of the rump republic and the government of South Arabia (renamed South Yemen). South Yemen's militant National Liberation Front, its first independent government, could be counted on to spread into Yemeni republican territory. Yemen would be divided. The royalists would find themselves confronting a combination of the British-trained South Arabian army and the remains of the Egyptian-trained Yemeni republican army. Prince Mohamed Hussein and President Qahtan al Shaabi, the two strong personalities who have emerged from the struggles of their respective countries, would confront one another.

The prospect necessitates some additional remarks about South Arabia. Whereas in Yemen the traditional element represented by the royalists has exhibited great vigour, in South Arabia the traditional régimes of sultans and sheikhs collapsed at the first challenge by NLF and FLOSY after the withdrawal of British protection.

One explanation was that the traditional régime in Yemen was Zeidi, hence firmly identified with the religious life of the country; the South Arabian rulers had no comparable identification. Another was that the Yemeni monarchists were more or less continuously backed by Saudi Arabian money; the South Arabian régimes collapsed when they knew they could no longer count on the British. A third was that the royalists in Yemen were cast as true nationalists fighting the Egyptian invader. Except among the minority of tribesmen, who thought in terms of progressives and reactionaries, the royalists' association with the Saudis was much less compromising; there is a certain kinship among inhabitants of the Arabian peninsula from which Egyptians are for ever excluded. By contrast, the South Arabian rulers were unequivocally compromised by their association with the British.

After the climactic battle of Sheikh Othman in early November, the NLF imposed its absolute supremacy. The British were not able to leave governmental authority in the hands of a régime of their own choice, but they were at least able to leave behind a stable régime. Moderately socialist and Pan-Arabist, the NLF might be lacking in democracy, and alarmingly militant in its intentions towards the Yemen republic, Muscat and Oman, and the rest of the Persian Gulf; but it was absolutely disciplined. Except for the sad case of a German television correspondent who was assassinated while walking to the post office, terrorism ended the moment the NLF made the decision to end it.

This assertion of authority was a dynamic move, and it could not fail to interest the Russians, whom the Egyptians and FLOSY had perhaps disappointed as vehicles of Soviet political penetration. The NLF might serve as an alternative, the more promising because of the opportunities for exploitation presented by the desperate need for financial aid of the new State and its expensive 10,000-man army.

Only a little while ago the Egyptians saw Yemen as a most desirable foothold on the Arabian peninsula. The British defended Aden because it had the best harbour in the Arabian peninsula, because it was a staging post half-way between Britain and the Far East, because a garrison there could be used to defend British interests both in the Persian Gulf and on the eastern coast of Africa. But when the Egyptians and British, for largely extraneous reasons, had to withdraw from these places they decried the strategic importance of the whole area. Even the Americans took the attitude that Yemen and South Arabia 'don't matter any more'.

I disagree with this view. The Soviet interest in the area has certainly never flagged. The Russians were interested enough in the time of Imam Ahmed to build him a new port at Hodeidah; they continued with a 'maximum phase' aid programme for the Republic; they have tried strenuously to save the republic militarily. They will undoubtedly involve themselves deeply in the People's Republic of Southern Yemen as well.

The Western great powers have abdicated in the region; British aid to South Yemen is now a transitional matter which carries with it neither future nor influence. The way lies open for the Soviet Union—except as it may find itself opposed by strong-minded, independent men like Qahtan al Shaabi, by the royalists in Yemen and by Saudi Arabia.

In this book I have examined, as it were through a microscope, a small segment of history, the war for Yemen. I have followed it from the time of the *coup* and the arrival of the Egyptians to the time of President Sallal's overthrow, the departure of the Egyptians and the siege of Sana. I have regarded it in the context of the history of Yemen from earliest times and of possible future developments. I hope that, with the help of this book, the war for Yemen may no longer be an unknown war.

U.S. Recognition of the Yemen Republic

++

American Embassy
Beirut, Lebanon.
December 19, 1962

WASHINGTON, December 19 —— The United States today announced its recognition of the Yemen Arab Republic in a statement which expressed U.S. pleasure at the new régime's plans to honor that country's international obligations. Following is the text of the U.S. announcement:

'In view of a number of confusing and contradictory statements which have cast doubt upon the intentions of the new régime in Yemen, the United States Government welcomes the reaffirmation by the Yemen Arab Republic Government of its intention to honor its international obligations, of its desire for normalization and establishment of friendly relations with its neighbors, and of its intention to concentrate on internal affairs to raise the living standards of the Yemeni people.

'The United States Government also is gratified by the statesman-like appeal of the Yemen Arab Republic to Yemenis in adjacent areas to be law-abiding citizens and notes its undertaking to honor all treaties concluded by previous Yemeni governments. This, of course, includes the Treaty of Sana concluded with the British Government in 1934 which provided for reciprocal guarantees that neither party should intervene in the affairs of the other across the existing international frontier dividing the Yemen from territory under British protection.

'Further the United States Government welcomes the declaration of the United Arab Republic signifying its willingness to undertake reciprocal disengagement and expeditious phased removal of troops from Yemen as external forces engaged in support of the Yemen royalists are removed from the frontier and as external support of the royalists is stopped.

'In believing that these declarations provide a basis for terminating the conflict over Yemen and in expressing the hope that all of the parties involved in the conflict will cooperate to the end that the Yemeni peoples themselves be permitted to decide their own future, the United States has today decided to recognize the government of the Yemen Arab Republic and to extend to that government its best wishes for success and prosperity. The United States has instructed its Chargé d'Affaires in Yemen to confirm this decision in writing to the Ministry of Foreign Affairs of the Yemen Arab Republic.'

The Washington announcement followed the broadcasting by Sana radio of a statement by the Yemen Arab Republic. The text of the latter statement was as follows:

'From the first day of the revolution in our country the Yemen Arab Republic has declared its determination to dedicate its efforts to raising the standards of the Yemeni people and to see cordial relations with all countries.

'During past weeks we have been forced to defend the territory of our republic against foreign invasion and against elements in contact with foreigners and receiving encouragement and support from them. These unfortunate events may have obscured in some quarters the basic principles and aims of Yemenis people's revolution.

'We therefore declare once again that it remains the firm policy of the YAR to honor its international obligations, including all treaties concluded by previous governments, and abide by the charters of the United Nations and the Arab League. We desire to live in peace and harmony with all our neighbors to the extent to which they share this desire, and we call upon our brothers, Yemenis living in adjacent areas, to be law-abiding citizens. We shall concentrate our efforts on our internal affairs, in order to ensure the equality of all citizens before law, raise social and economic standards of Yemen people and develop the country's heretofore neglected resources for the benefit of all the people. With good will and the assistance of friendly countries we shall advance toward these sacred objectives. May God crown our efforts with success.'

The Taif Manifesto

•••

In the name of Allah the compassionate & the merciful.

FOR Yemen's sake, for her people's happiness, according to Islam's spirit, to avoid the continuation of the tragedy that brought disasters to Yemen, and for our belief in the right of the Yemeni people to self-determination and the system of government that it chooses for itself without any external influence, the signatories of this manifesto (who represent all walks of life, tribal and non-tribal) have decided the following and have agreed to act according to these principles:

I. To advance the cause of Islam and act according to Islamic teachings.

II. To place Yemen's interests and the unity of its territories above all considerations.

III. To co-operate in a truthful and sincere manner to put an end to the tragedy of events in Yemen to find ways to unite the Yemeni people in their search for peace and security.

IV. All the participants at the meeting undertake on behalf of themselves and their fighting forces to carry on military operations in a unified manner.

V. To put aside the jealousies and feuds of the past and the present and to work for Yemen's progress and advancement.

VI. To seek for the Yemeni people the opportunity to practise its right of self-determination so that it may choose its own system of government without any external influence, after the withdrawal of the Egyptian forces and the cessation of Saudi assistance. The participants believe that to carry out these objectives a transitional period based along the following lines is necessary:

1. Establish a Yemeni state called 'The Islamic State of Yemen' based on the teachings of Islam. The affairs of this state are to be conducted provisionally by the following bodies:

A. A Council of State: to have the powers and characteristics of a president of a state, to consist of seven or eight members who should be representatives of all the groups in Yemen.
B. A Council of Ministers: to have the power and duties of an executive body in a state, to consist of eighteen to twenty-four ministers, to be comprised of educated and enlightened representatives of all groups in Yemen.
C. A Consultative Council: to supervise, direct and help the Council of Ministers in its functions, to consist of eight members (representatives of all Yemeni groups).

2. The duties of these provisional governmental bodies are to be:

A. Secure internal peace and order, observe the withdrawal of Egyptian forces and the cessation of Saudi assistance.
B. Prepare for a referendum to decide the permanent system of government.

The participants call upon their brethren of all ideological trends and tendencies in Yemen to join them to end the Yemeni tragedy on the basis of this manifesto.

To achieve these principles the participants will divide and co-ordinate work among themselves until they are joined by further groups and individuals. The participants hope for Saudi and Egyptian assistance in developing the Yemeni State during the transitional period and thereafter.

[Signed by 541 members
Republicans, royalists and the
intermediate group]
10 August 1965

APPENDIX 3

The Jeddah Agreement

....

24 August 1965

THE following is a partial text of the agreement on Yemen signed today by President Nasser and King Faisal, as broadcast by Cairo and Mecca Radios.

The aim of President Gamal Abdul Nasser and King Faisal in their talks in Jeddah was to make it possible for the Yemeni people to exercise their free will so that it could provide an atmosphere of peace, in addition to the removal of every cause of the transient disagreement between the United Arab Republic and Saudi Arabia, and to consolidate the historic ties between their two peoples.

As regards the relation of the United Arab Republic and Saudi Arabia to the present situation in Yemen, King Faisal and President Abdul Nasser, having got in touch with all the representatives of the Yemeni people and their national forces, and having been acquainted with their wishes, consider that the just and safest means of facing responsibility towards the Yemeni people is through:—

1. Giving the Yemeni people the right to decide and affirm their view to the kind of government they want in a popular plebiscite at a date not later than 23 November, 1966.

2. The remaining period up to the date of the plebiscite shall be considered a transitional period to prepare for the plebiscite.

3. Saudi Arabia and the United Arab Republic will co-operate in forming a transitional conference of 50 members representing all the national forces and people of authority in Yemen, after consultation with the various Yemeni groups in accordance with the agreement to be reached. The conference will meet at

Haradh (in Yemen) on November 23, 1965, and will undertake: determination of the system of government during the transitional period and until the popular plebiscite is held; formation of a provisional cabinet to be in charge of the government during the transitional period; determination of the form and kind of plebiscite which will be held by November 23, 1966, at the latest.

4. The two governments adopt the resolutions of the above-mentioned transitional Yemeni conference, support them, and co-operate to ensure their successful implementation. They declare from now their acceptance of a joint neutral follow-up committee of both to be in charge of the plebiscite should the conference decide the need for the presence of such a neutral committee.

5. Saudi Arabia will immediately stop military aid of all kinds and the use of Saudi Arabian territory for operations against Yemen.

6. The United Arab Republic will withdraw all its military forces from Yemen within ten months, beginning on November 23, 1965.

7. Armed fighting in Yemen will be stopped immediately and a joint peace commission from both sides will be formed to: supervise the cease-fire through a special supervisory commission; supervise the frontier and ports and stop all kinds of military aid. Food aid will continue under the supervision of the peace commission. The said supervisory commissions will be entitled to use all the necessary travel facilities within Yemeni territory as well as use Saudi Arabian territory, if necessary.

8. Saudi Arabia and the United Arab Republic will co-operate and act positively to ensure the carrying out of this agreement and impose stability in Yemen until the proclamation of the result of the plebiscite, by forming a force of the two countries to be used by the commission when necessary to prevent any departure from this agreement or any action to obstruct it or provoke disorder against its success.

9. In order to promote co-operation between the United Arab Republic and Saudi Arabia and enable this co-operation to continue beyond the present phase to the normal phase which should prevail over relations between the two countries, there will be direct contact between President Abdul Nasser and King Faisal to avoid any difficulties in the way of carrying out this agreement.

List of the Delegates to the Haradh Conference, November 1965

Republicans:

Lieutenant-Colonel Ahmar Rohoumy; one of the Free Officers who participated in the revolution; also Minister of Finance and Economy

Major-General Hamoud al Jaifi; former Premier; now member of Republican Council

Qadi Abdurrahman al Iryani; former Premier; member of Republican Council

Sheikh Abdullah al Ahmar; leader of Hashid tribe; father and brother beheaded by Imam Ahmed

Qadi Abdul Qarim al Ansi; former Minister of Justice and Education

Sheikh Abdurrahman Dhamran; Mayor of Dhamar

Sheikh Mutti Damaj; leader of Badani tribe

Qadi Mohamed al Haji; Minister of Justice

Colonel Abdullah Juzailan; leader of the Free Officers

Qadi Abdul Salaam Sabra; Minister of Commerce

Qadi Mohamed Ali al Akwaa; Minister of Information

Sheikh Abdullah Mohsein al Thawabi; leader of Dhu Mohamed tribe

Sheikh Mohamed Ali al Roaishan; a chief of Khawlan tribe

Ahmed Mohamed Nomaan; former Premier; member of Republican Council

Qadi Yahyia Mansur; religious leader of the Shaffei

Sheikh Mohamed Ali Osman; deputy Premier

Sheikh Ali Nasser Turaiq; chief of Murad tribe

Sheikh Ahmed Abdu Rabbouh al Awadi; leader of Awadi tribe

Brigadier Mohamed al Ahnoumi; Minister of State and former Minister of Defence

Abdul Ghani Muttahar; merchant who helped finance revolutionary movement

Republicans:

Hassan Makki; former Foreign Minister; adviser to Prime Minister on economy and finance

Brigadier Mohamed Ruwainy
Qadi Mohamed al Khalidi
Abdullah Mossein al Doaiss
Colonel Ali Saghi al Asham

Royalists:

Ahmed Mohamed al Shami; Foreign Minister

Ahmed Mohamed Basha; Imam Ahmed's minister in Bonn; joined the revolution, but later returned to the royalists

Mohamed Abdul Quddous al Wazir; member of the Wazir family who led the 1948 revolution

Hussein Murfiq; minister at Jeddah, al Badr's former Minister of Information

Salah al Masri; tribal chief; Defence Minister

Majduddin al Moayyadi; mufti of the royalists

Ali Naji al Shaiff; leader of Dhu Hussein tribe

Ali al Faidh; director of the royalist broadcasts

Naji bin Ali al Gadr; chief of Khawlan tribe

Hamiss al Awjari; chief of Dahmar tribe

Ghaleb al Ajdaa; a tribal chief

Ahmed Hamid al Habari; a tribal chief

Hassan bin Hadi; a tribal chief in the Tihama

Abdullah Yahyia al Saadi; a religious chief

Hadi Aittan; a tribal chief

Ali Shaiff

Ahmed al Hakkami

Ahmed Hassan al Houthy

Hussein Ismail al Madani

Yahya Turaiq

Abdul Qadr Mohamed Abdul Qadr; former army major
Ibrahim Ali al Wazir; uncle beheaded by Imam Ahmed
Sinan Bou al Lohoum; a tribal chief
Nomaan Kaid Rajih; a chief of Khawlan
Abdul Ali Hassan

The last five are 'third force'; two of them, Hassan and Qadr, deserted the republic before formation of the third force. These two fought with the royalists; the other three did not and objected to having them in their third force group. Three third force advisers attending but not voting were Ali Naji al Kawsi, Ahmed al Mattari and Nasser al Bukhaiti.

Index

························

INDEX

Bani Abd (tribe) 156
Bani Bahlal (tribe) 160
Bani Garuyi (tribe) 156
Bani Hajur (tribe) 260
Bani al Harith (tribe) 66, 154
Bani Hushaysh (tribe) 66, 154, 159,
    268, 284
Bani Ismail (tribe) 93
Bani Matar (tribe) 66, 93, 154, 155,
    173, 174, 282
Bartlett, Dr William George 249
Barzani, Mullah Mustafa 52, 125
Beeston, Richard 257, 262
Beihan, Sharif of 150, 161, 162, 165,
    214
Beit Kathir (tribe) 96
Ben Bella, Ahmed 236
Ben Zvi, President Itzhak 104
Beretta, Dr 259
Bigart, Homer 46
al Bohaiti, Sheikh of al Haddah 154
Borowiec, Andrew 262
Bourguiba, President 276
Boyle, Anthony Alexander 181
Boyle, Marshal of the R.A.F. Sir
    Dermot 181
Brown, George 269–71
Brutschin, Dr Willy 264, 266
Bunche, Dr Ralph 192–4
Bundy, McGeorge 193
Bunker, Ellsworth 166, 192–4, 199,
    244, 259
Burckholtzer, Frank 203

Camenada, Jerome 49
Carter, William 83
di Carvalho, George 66
Cesaretti, Claudio 264
Champion, Sir Reginald 109
Chosroes I, King of Persia 101–2
Chuwab, Hasseb 201
Condé, Bruce 127–31, 140–44, 152,
    158–61
Conley, Robert 262

Constantine, Emperor 101
Cooley, John 202
Coon, Carleton S. 91
Cooper, Major John 181

al Dafai, Hussein 210, 282
Dahm (tribe) 136, 158, 176
Dalkeith, Lord 271
Dayfallah, Abdul Latif 283
Dhamar (tribe) 154
Dhu Hussein (tribe) 136, 226
Dhu Mohamed (tribe) 136, 156, 176,
    226
Dhu Nuwas 62, 101, 104
Dionysius the Greek 142
Doughty, Charles H. 148
Downton, Eric 49
Dulles, John Foster 185

Effet, Colonel Hassan 218
Eilts, Herman 46
Eisenhower, Dwight D. 41
Ezra the Scribe 104

Faisal of Saudi Arabia:
    as Prince 34, 49, 51–5, 62, 176, 182,
        186, 193–4, 200, 213;
    as King 34, 114, 164–66, 178, 184,
        192, 224, 228, 243, 244, 256, 261,
        273, 276, 280, 292, 295, 297;
    at Alexandria 164, 205–7, 275;
    at Jeddah 205, 232, 236–7, 241–2,
        275, 304–5;
    at Khartoum 270, 290;
    at Taif 277, 278
Fatimah, Sitt 37
Fawzi, General Mohamed 291
Fountain, L. G. 202
Fraser, Hugh 190
Freedman, Emanuel 256
Fuje (tribe) 174–5
Fulbright, Senator 201

al Gadr, Naji bin Ali 131, 170–71, 226,
    227, 298